CHOSEN FAMILY
MEN'S & WOMEN'S
SUPPORT GROUPS
AN INSIDE LOOK

Tom Weiner

1

PRAISES for
CHOSEN FAMILY

"Be the change you wish to see in the world" and "Lead by example". It is easy to agree with these sentiments, but anyone who has tried to fully live up to them knows that it is not simple. This is especially true for how we are socialized to be 'male' and 'female.' Tom Weiner's book offers us many powerful lessons for those of us interested in 'untying the gender knot' that has resulted in our feeling limited and constrained by societal gender expectations. The book provides powerful testimonies from men and women who have participated in all-male or all-female gender consciousness raising groups and who have sought to do the necessary work to "be the change". The process of transformation, the essential role of empathic others in supporting our efforts, and the stages, processes, benefits and challenges of men's and women's support groups are amply demonstrated. This collection of powerful testimonies – expertly organized and commented upon by the author – will help us to walk our own gender transformation journeys as well as to assist those who are already in support groups, or thinking of joining or forming one, to learn from the lessons and valuable experiences of the others in this book who have done so.

Alan Berkowitz is a gender justice activist and scholar who developed one of the first all-male rape prevention programs. His deep and loving relationships with other men serve to confirm the insights and lessons offered in this book.

Tom Weiner offers a deep look from two generations of men and women at the social contribution of support groups. This work is essential for helping generations interlace so that we are making common cause together. I led a consciousness-raising group in the early 1970's and *CHOSEN FAMILY MEN'S & WOMEN'S SUPPORT GROUPS AN INSIDE LOOK* provides a way for others to learn how they are life-changing. The depth of sharing each participant offers in their interviews creates a living document that taken together shows how we can experience solidarity and stand by each other in a way that makes all the difference.

Sarah Pirtle, author of five social justice books including **An Outbreak of Peace** *about undoing racism.*

Long before the #MeToo movement jumpstarted an urgent campaign demanding men unflinchingly look at how we behaved in relationships, some men had already begun examining their inner lives. Recognizing the power of women's consciousness-raising groups, they formed men's groups where they could learn the benefits of not struggling in isolation but receiving (and giving) support in the company of other men. In a world torn apart by gender inequality, Tom Weiner's book provides both practical information and life-enhancing insights for all genders to become better supports for one another as we cross uncharted landscapes leading from uncertainty to understanding; from distrust to connection.

Rob Okun, editor of Voice Male magazine and the anthology, **Voice Male: The Untold Story of the Profeminist Men's Movement.**

My own group has been so deeply supportive and life-changing and I was inspired to see how true that was for all the other contributors to Tom Weiner's important book. I think it takes a village to heal and support a person...no one should have to do it alone. While for some, family is the ultimate refuge from the difficulties in life, it is important for people to know that we can create alternative families, powerful groups of friends who love and challenge us to be the best we can be. This book shows us the possibilities for creating deep and powerful bonds in a circle of friends.

Sara Elinoff Acker, women's group member and author of **Unclenching Our Fists: Abusive Men on the Journey to Nonviolence.**

Tom Weiner's latest book captures the ways in which men in particular have struggled with forging intimate connections with one another in order to be able to express a wider range of emotions. He lays out a model for the ways in which men can gain skills in being open, honest and supportive with themselves and one another as well as demonstrating that there are no age or gender limitations since he has included both women and younger and older examples of thriving groups. As a Swedish therapist who has seen my share of shut down men, this book encourages me to think of the ways men can assist one another in reaching their potential.

Henry Wising, Clinical Psychologist, Psychotherapist, Göteborg, Sweden.

To the memory of Michael S. Sample, beloved friend, wilderness brother and gifted photographer of the outdoors of Montana, which he so loved and shared so generously with my family and me.

To the memory of Stephen A. Trudel, men's group member, whose passing leaves an enormous hole in both my life and the group he cherished.

To my men's group of 40 years, a brotherhood that has provided abundant gifts of support, challenge and love.

To the men and women engaged with one another in the enormously demanding and rewarding task of seeking to fulfill one's potential.

Published by Human Error Publishing
Paul Richmond
www.humanerrorpublishing.com
paul@humanerrorpublishing.com

ISBN: 97809991985-9-9

Cover:
Photo taken by Tom Weiner
Cover design by HEP & Tom Weiner

TABLE OF CONTENTS

PREFACE

It is safe to say that we live in challenging times. It is also safe to say that our current president would not be a participant in the kind of men's group you will encounter here. In fact, with the election of Donald Trump, the men's movement with which I identify has felt both deeply disappointed and disillusioned. That white men are largely responsible for his election only adds to the anguish.

For this reason, it feels important to declare where this book is coming from. We are at a decisive period in the evolution of our definition of masculinity, which is part of what I am referring to when I describe these times as very challenging.

When I refer to the men's movement, I am conscious of its varied branches and elements over time. Here is a list of the understandings and positions that inform this book:

> • Men need to have access to a wide range of emotions and expressive skills in order to be able to articulate themselves respectfully and compassionately.

> • It is incumbent upon men to treat all women as equals.

> • Men need to nurture their mental, emotional, physical and psychological needs through healthy relationships with other men, women and children.

> • In order to ensure that healthy masculinity includes the nurturance of children, men need to take an active role in raising (or mentoring/coaching) children.

> • It is essential that men be allies in the various struggles waged by women, LGBTQ+ people, people of color and other groups fighting for their rights.

> • Men need to recognize their privilege in this society and actively work to support women seeking equality

from reproductive rights to equal pay for equal work, from affordable childcare to family leave policies, since these rights will accrue to the benefit of our society.

• Men need to speak out and organize actively against men's violence and abuse of women and children.

Each of the groups included in this project had different origins and different paths to the type of group they have evolved into over time. I offer this book to show the ways in which men's and women's groups can be vehicles for personal growth, group cohesion and social change. There is no one model that captures the essence of what such a group can offer. It is my hope that the four examples offered here provide encouragement and guidance for anyone interested in starting such a group or enhancing an existing one.

A few words about the title. I shared the final one with my son, Stefan, who told me that "chosen family" was an expression used frequently in the LGBTQ community. I discovered an article from *Psychology Today's* June 14, 2019 issue entitled, *Finding Connection Through "Chosen Families"*. The article is written by Jeremy Nobel, MD, MPH. He uses the definition of "chosen family" from the **SAGE Encyclopedia of Marriage, Family and Couples Counseling**: "Chosen families are nonbiological kinship bonds, whether legally recognized or not, deliberately chosen for the purpose of mutual support and love. The term originated within the LGBTQ community and was used to describe early queer gatherings like the Harlem Drag Balls of the late nineteenth century." He concludes that, "Friends who become your family of choice may provide you with a healthier family environment than the one in which you were raised, or their proximity may allow you to rely on them when your biological family isn't located nearby. A chosen family can be part of a person's growing network, and can help construct a wide foundation of support that continues to grow with time." You will soon see how this description fits the groups in this book.

One last enticement to read on, and it comes by way of Japan. "Moai – This Tradition is Why Okinawan People Live Longer, Better," an article on Blue Zones, a website that is "inspired by the world's longest-lived cultures" (bluezones. com), describes a tradition called moai (pronounced mo-eye). A moai is an informal group created by people who commit to offer emotional, social or even financial assistance to one another. When researchers sought reasons for why these people lived extraordinarily healthy and happy lives, they discovered the role the moais play:

> The term originated hundreds of years ago as a means of a village's financial support system. Originally, moais were formed to pool the resources of an entire village for projects or public works. If an individual needed capital to buy land or take care of an emergency, the only way was to pool money locally. Today the idea has expanded to become more of a social support network, a cultural tradition for built-in companionship. Traditionally, groups of about five young children were paired together and it's then that they made a commitment to each other for life. As their second family, they would meet regularly with their moai for both work and play and to pool resources. Some moais have lasted over 90 years!

> Members of these social cooperatives meet one another's practical needs – problem-solving, planning, pooling resources and collaborating. They also serve as extended family where social and emotional needs are met – managing a crisis, reducing stress, connecting emotionally and, at times, assuaging grief. Essentially, a moai is a group of people who "have your back" and commit to all aspects of your well-being.

Read on and discover the American version of a moai – though we'll have to wait to see the impact of support groups on longevity!

INTRODUCTION

I recently had the pleasure of teaching a Smith College pre-practicum to a diverse group of education students – some of whom had journeyed from as far away as Capetown, South Africa – about the importance of developing lesson-plan objectives when preparing to instruct a class. My forty years as a teacher have led me to the firm belief that if you can't clearly and concisely state what it is you want to teach, your teaching will invariably be hit-or-miss, with considerably more misses than hits.

So what better time to sit down at my laptop and put into words why I am writing this book and why I feel such a book is worthwhile reading? One reason was evident in that class. Of the 15 students I was speaking to, only one was a man. This is a disappointment personally as well as societally. I had once believed, some 45 years ago, that I was at the vanguard of what would become a significant sea change – men becoming teachers in general and teachers of young children in particular. I'm still waiting.

I've never had more than two male colleagues out of the 14 teachers at my elementary school, and I know it is similar almost everywhere else. The profession continues to lack the recognition it deserves, in terms of respect and financial compensation. That's the personal part, but societally I have always agreed with Dorothy Dinnerstein, who wrote some 40 years ago in her classic The *Mermaid and the Minotaur* that "until men nurture children, there will always be war." Given our current world, including the undeclared wars that have been waged against poor people, people of color, immigrants and refugees, gay, lesbian and transgendered people, and the environment, her words ring truer than ever.

I believe deeply that who I didn't see in that classroom and why this book is worth reading are directly connected. In the following chapters, I will present an up-close and personal view into the coming together, the being together and the staying together of a group of men who have made a deep

13

and lasting commitment to one another for almost 40 years. Meeting on the third Sunday of every month, we have committed ourselves to sharing values and goals, sharing from the heart, and sharing one another's lives on the most intimate of levels. Through this dedication, we've participated in the nurturing process I believe Dinnerstein was conceptualizing in her unforgettable and undeniable words. We have also been men who have taken an active role as parents ever since our babies were in utero, which serves to further underline our investment in raising young men and women. When you are so invested in children, seeking ways to prevent wars and to stop the ones we as a society seem unable to resist, comes naturally.

But there is another reason why such a book is critical for men as well as for the women who love them. This one starts with the personal as well. Four years ago, I lost a treasured friend who was part of my life for over 46 years. Michael was a renowned and remarkably skillful outdoor photographer with whom I shared over 20 adventures in Montana and Utah. In the time since his death, I have been utterly heartbroken. He was a beloved friend to me and an incredible friend to my family. When I heard the news of his untimely death, I wrote to my men's group to let them know what had happened and to let them know what they already instinctively knew – that I would want a block of time set aside at our July gathering. Much as I have done in the past – when experiencing the trauma of parenting a child with a serious birth defect who required numerous brain surgeries, or during the 12 years of my father's suffering from Alzheimer's disease – I sought the support, comfort and love of my men.

Of course, this has not been just my singular response to losses and traumas. Everyone in the group has made use of it as a place to grieve, to cry and to heal with the good attention, the words of consolation and solace, and the affection we offer one another.

If we're not already beyond help as a society, it is boys and men having access to a full range of emotions in the loving embrace of other men that will help to preserve us and the other species over whom we have so much influence on this planet. It is why I am dedicating this book not only to my men's group and to my dear, departed friend, Michael, but to all those men engaged in the monumental challenge of becoming fully human. This requires being vulnerable, supportive and expressive of a wide range of feelings as well as the nurturing of children, our partners and one another.

Since I first began this project, back in 2012, I have chosen to broaden my focus. The change began one day when I rode my bike to the local supermarket and encountered Ellen Augarten, the parent of a former student, who asked me what book I would be writing next, following the publication of *Called to Serve: Stories of Men and Women Confronted by the Vietnam War Draft* (2011). Ellen had recently co-authored a book with Andrea Ayvazian, *Psalms in Ordinary Voices*, which featured her photographs side-by-side with re-writings of the Psalms by a wide variety of contributors of all ages. When I told Ellen that I was about to set forth on a writing project about my men's group, which at that point had been together for 34 years, she told me that she had been in a women's group for almost that long.

As I was pedaling home, it suddenly occurred to me that it would be eminently sensible for me to include women in the project. I had already been wondering about the similarities and differences between men's and women's groups, in terms of both content and expression. I could compare and contrast their responses and perhaps bring in more readers. I immediately contacted Ellen, who was quite enthusiastic about asking her group to participate.

Ultimately, there were several reasons why it ended up not being Ellen's group whose voices you will be reading. One of the biggest factors was the unwritten agreement her group had not to talk about their marriages. On the one hand, discovering that all five of the marriages were still very much intact was quite fascinating, especially when Ellen shared with me that the reason the group chose not to deeply discuss their most intimate relationships was to avoid "trashing" their husbands. She told me that the group had feared that delving too deeply into marital issues could put a marriage in jeopardy, and that she knew a group where several marriages had fallen apart.

This was a problem. To include a group in this project that didn't look into what was happening in their marriages, for the purpose of better understanding the dynamics, the sexual politics and the nature of one another's relationships, felt like too big a contrast with our men's group. We've spent considerable time examining our primary relationships on every imaginable level. In any case, when one of the women's group members decided not to be part of the project, the others felt they could not continue, so our connection ended.

I did, however, very much want to include a women's group. I was aware of another group, co-founded by Sara Elinoff Acker, the ex-wife of one of the members of my group. When I told Sara about my book project she immediately offered her group – pending, of course, their agreement. I put together a proposal for them to consider and was invited to present my vision of the book at one of their monthly gatherings – a most satisfying experience, since I had always wanted to have a sense of what it is like to be in a women's group. They welcomed the project and the idea of being part of it. Having the opportunity to attend that session felt very privileged and confirmed my desire to know more about how women approach intimacy with one another in a group setting.

Now I had two groups of men and women, all of us 55-plus. What happened next was a gift from my son, Stefan, who connected me with a considerably younger men's group. At a party in Brooklyn, he and a fellow party-goer, Ben, were speaking of their respective fathers. When Stefan told Ben about my first book and then my support-group project, Ben told him that he's in a men's group. Within the month I had a most fruitful meeting with Ben and Kevin, another member of the group. Following that meeting we succeeded in organizing a Double Men's Group Weekend that occurred in April 2017, about which I wrote an article for *Voice Male* magazine that is in the Appendix.*

It was obvious that if I was going to include a young men's group in the book, along with the two older groups, I needed to find a young women's group. To my great relief, this also happened quite organically. Ruth, co-founder of the older women's group with Sara, put me in touch with her daughter, Amelia, who is in a younger women's group. The ensuing conversation grabbed her interest and she got an endorsement from her group for me to be part of one of their video phone meetings. I presented the project and they have joined as well.

So that's how the voices you are about to hear came together, much to my great satisfaction and appreciation. The interviews I conducted with the 27 participants gave me invaluable insights into many aspects of the group experiences described here. I have sought to provide some of the excitement and enjoyment of my process by reproducing the precise words of the participants.

This book is intended for two kinds of readers – those who are already in support groups, and those who are not, but are interested in their structure, process and outcomes. For the former, I hope that what you are about to experience will encourage you to think about whether your group is providing all it can, and if not, how to fix that; and for those of you who are not now in a group, perhaps what you find here will encourage you to join an existing group or create one yourself. The rewards are many and varied, and in this day and age of isolation and separateness that result from so many sources, support groups can provide much of what we all need in terms of intimacy, connection and meaningful ties that bind and last.

Voice Male has been chronicling the pro-feminist men's movement for more than three decades. voicemalemagazine.org.

The first two chapters in this book set the stage for my explorations of support groups. Chapter 1 explores the history of consciousness-raising groups created by women in the 1960s and '70s, and Chapter 2 focuses on the impact of the women's movement on men, leading to the formation of men's support groups. The subsequent chapter titles derive from the interview questions I asked the project participants. Their stories address a range of topics including the creation of groups, the establishment of ground rules, what members give and receive from membership, how groups handle conflict, the changes that groups and individual members go through, and their impact on the surrounding community.

A note on methodology. Most of the 27 interviews were conducted face to face and, with one exception, one on one. The younger women's group members live in a variety of places, but they meet regularly via video conferencing. I got to participate in one of their group calls to introduce myself and the project, and subsequently interviewed each of them via speaker phone and digital recorder.

For the most part, I asked all the participants the same questions, with variations and departures in response to their responses. (The list of questions is in the Appendix.) Not all of the questions and responses found their way into the book, which meant that the most challenging part of the writing process was choosing what not to include. That's why the last chapter is entitled "Miscellaneous Gems," because there were some responses that I simply could not leave out.

I also wanted to have the opportunity to add my voice, so I answered the interview questions myself and have included my responses in a few of the chapters. They reflect my experience of being a member of three different men's groups over a 45-year period and, as the most recent member of the older men's group, the perspective of a relative newcomer entering midstream.

In most of the chapters, the interview excerpts you'll be reading are presented in the same order. This project was originally going to be a celebration of our men's group's 40 years of thriving and enduring. It has grown over the six years since its inception to include three other groups, whom I contacted in this order – older women, younger men and younger women. Hence, that is the order in which the excerpts usually appear.

Confidentiality is not only a hallmark of all four of the groups – the dictum "What's said here stays here" is a centerpiece of their practice – but the participants also asked for and received assurances that they would have "right of refusal." I sent everyone the unedited transcripts of their interviews, and then the extracts that are quoted in the book, for approval and, if necessary, revision.

I hope you enjoy this ride through the world of support groups, and that you will see how they can lift you up.

THE PARTICIPANTS

What follows are brief biographical sketches of the interview subjects whose words are the centerpiece of this work.

Older Men's Group (age range 59–68)

Alan Surprenant is an organic apple orchardist living on Brook Farm in Apple Valley in Ashfield, MA. He is the father of Micah and Willow and married to Abby Straus.

Dick McLeester is owner and director of VisionWorks, which creates and distributes "Images & Ideas for a Changing World." He lives in Conway, MA, with his wife Malycha. He believes there is an underappreciated magic in dreaming and dancing.

Gary Phillips is the current poet laureate of Carrboro, NC. He is also a writer, a conservationist, an entrepreneur, a naturalist, and was once chair of Chatham County Commissioners and a pastor. His business, Weaver Street Realty, is a B-Corp-style enterprise (doing business to do good) and an environmental real estate company, dedicated not only to realty but also to do well for others and the local community, such as providing equitable salaries and sharing profits with the town. (Note: Since Gary moved to North Carolina, he has remained a member of the group, joining us at our annual retreat on one of the 1000 Islands in the St. Lawrence River, where I was able to interview him for this book.)

Paul Richmond is a poet, a publisher, and creator of Human Error Publishing, which organizes poetry festivals and monthly events. He was named the Beat Poet Laureate of Massachusetts for 2017-2019. His latest endeavor is being in a spoken-word musical group called, DO IT NOW, which performed in 'the 2018 Fringe Festival in Edinburgh, Scotland. He lives in Wendell with his partner, Eva Schachtl.

Robbie Leppzer is an award-winning independent filmmaker who has directed over 30 documentaries chronicling grassroots social-change movements, from the environmental protests of the 1970s to the growing global peace, social justice and environmental movements in the new millennium. His documentaries and television news magazine segments about contemporary social issues and multicultural themes have been broadcast by CNN International, NHK (Japan Broadcasting Corporation), the Canadian Broadcasting Corporation, HBO/Cinemax, PBS, CNN, Sundance Channel, HDNet, Link TV, Free Speech TV, National Public Radio, and Pacifica Radio. He lives in Wendell, MA. www. TurningTide.com

Stephen Bannasch wears a t-shirt that says, "Learn Make Teach Share" and he means it. He was the Director of Technology for 20 years at the Concord Consortium, an educational research and development organization dedicated to creating large-scale improvements in K-12 science and math education, and he has continued helping folks create powerful interactive collaborative websites. He plays saxophone, clarinet and harmonicas every week with his friends and makes all kinds of beautiful curved objects in wood that people enjoy touching and playing with, from guitars and bowls to hair picks and spoons.

Stephen Trudel has worked as a counselor in different ways for almost 40 years, predominantly intervening in domestic violence. He has a passion for singing with his a capella group, photography and his extensive garden.

Tom Weiner is the "new kid on the block" in his men's group, being the last to join, in 1989. He retired after 40 years of teaching 3rd–6th grade and supervising student teachers during the academic year and teaching middle and high school students for 34 summers. He is in the process of starting a mediation and trauma informed school reform consulting business. This is his third book. He is the father of four and the grandfather of four, who, along with his wife, Susan, contribute immeasurably to his life.

Tony Clarke is a furniture maker and co-owner of VCA,

a custom furniture and architectural millwork company in Northampton, MA. He is in the process of gradually retiring from the work he has been doing for well over 30 years and spending more time with his wife, Margot Menkel.

Older Women's Group (age range 57–67)

Annette Cycon is a clinical social worker, Tall Ships sailor and mom of two awesome adult daughters. Over 20 years she founded two organizations (MotherWoman and GPS – Group Peer Support) to give women and others the experience of support, healing and transformation that she received from her women's group. She has recently trained community health workers in Guatemala to incorporate GPS in their work with rural mothers. Annette believes that every person, young and old, deserves loving arms of support in order to thrive.

Diane Norman, having retired as a family nurse practitioner caring for Amherst College students for 28 years, has immersed herself in the world of photography. As a fine arts photographer she creates images that uncover the spirit of the people, places and objects she observes at home and in her travels. She has received numerous awards and recognitions and has recently had her work featured in two special editions of Black and White magazine. She lives with her partner in Hadley, MA, and her daughter, Morgan, was recently married.

Morning Star Chenven is a singer/songwriter, poet, choral director, mother and grandmother. Her spoken-word pieces and songs center around respect for all life and inner and outer freedom. Her poems have been published in local newspapers and journals, *Silkworm 7*, and in her book *Multiple Realities*. Morning Star is part of the duo Moonlight and Morning Star, who perform widely in New England. They create spoken-word/musical collaborative works, using voice, keyboards and percussion. www.moonlightandmorningstar.wordpress.com

Nancy Knudsen has been a marriage and family therapist since 1984. In addition to her private practice specializing in working with couples, she co-directs the Couples and Family Institute of New England with her husband, Jack LaForte, teaching workshops to other professionals and relationship enhancement workshops to the public. Privately, Nancy is committed to her role as wife, mother, daughter, sister, and friend to many. In her limited spare time, she practices the cello.

Ruth Olsen is a licensed psychotherapist with 33 years of experience providing clinical mental health counseling. She has worked as a social worker across all life stages, from childbirth to hospice and everything in between. As a certified music-thanatologist she does work in therapeutic harp music for palliative support in pediatric intensive care environments and for end of life care. She lives with her husband and is a proud mother and grandmother.

Sara Elinoff Acker is a proud feminist and has been a domestic violence activist since 1985, working with both survivors and perpetrators. In 2013, she published the book *Unclenching Our Fists*, profiling the mostly unknown stories of abusers who became nonviolent. Sara is a potter and singer and lives with her husband and teenage daughter, two dogs and a cat in Pelham, MA. She works as a psychotherapist in private practice and hopes to retire when she's 75. At that point, she plans to wear purple every day, drive a moped and still meet with her women's group!

Sara Schley is the mother of twins who are sophomores in high school. She is a sustainability consultant who has been doing the work for 25 years. She also is a facilitator of deep personal transformation "shadow" work. Her theory of practice is the inner and outer work of sustainability, integrating sustainability from the inside out – personal, professional and planetary.

Susan Loring-Wells is the mother of three daughters all three born at home, and with her husband, has been parenting her nephew since 2006. She loves participating and building community, and spent years growing a small non-profit in Amherst to promote contemporary textile arts and creating a gathering place for fiber activists, aficionados and artists. She has worked in law offices, arts organizations, camps and local schools. She currently maintains a studio at the Leverett Arts & Crafts Center. She has a passion for introducing weaving and fiber arts to all ages.

Younger Men's Group (age range 28–47)

Ben Blackshear is from Florida and has lived in New York City for the past six years. He works making maps for the city government and is a volunteer with several groups in the solidarity economy movement. He lives with three lovely roommates in central Brooklyn.

Ben Fuller-Googins works for a community-based organization in Brooklyn that organizes around housing issues and worker issues. He started a domestic worker program and a worker cooperative development program. He believes that being able to be amidst people's transformations and then, collectively in groups, transformation is absolutely life-giving. It looks towards re-imagining and building power for immigrant women and low income tenants and also how we can come into our own power.

Dave Ratzlow grew up in Chicago and has lived in New York since 1989. He came to the city for film school and worked in and out of the film business for a while. He's currently a secretary at a law firm using that stability to work on some writing projects. He lives in Brooklyn at the southeast corner of Prospect Park.

Joshua LaTour is a 41-year-old yoga teacher who, when he was interviewed, had recently finished a teaching 12-day yoga intensive that included a lecture on trauma-informed yoga. He is also doing the "New York hustle" – painting apartments and "trying to make money because funds are low and I need that cake."

Kevin Quirolo is a researcher at a healthcare workers' union, trying to bring data skills to movement organizing. When he's not in a cubicle with a spreadsheet, or on the picket line with a sign, he's probably on his couch with a book related to his latest pet topic (cyber security, Colette, psychology).

Younger Women's Group (age range 35–39)

Amelia Olsen is a small-town girl with a big-city spirit. After spending ten years in New York City, she now lives in North Carolina with her husband and two young children. She has worked in advertising for over a decade at some of the biggest and most well-known agencies in the world.

Charlie Evans lives in Western Massachusetts and is married with no children. She has a very small homestead and "lives as close to the earth as possible. We grow most of our own food."

Heather Price lives and works at a financial services company in New York City and is enjoying life as a new mom.

Liz Sharp moved to upstate New York to start her own catering business, after years of cooking professionally in New York City. Prior to that she had a decade-long career in theater, but she always loved food and is thrilled to have made it her life's work.

Michelle Chanson is the co-founder of a New York City-based media relations agency. She also serves on a number of non-profit boards.

Naomi Lutra works for a professional non-profit theater and occasionally teaches and advises at the university level. She lives with her husband and is expecting her first child.

CHAPTER 1
FEMINISM'S INFLUENCE:
CONSCIOUSNESS-RAISING GROUPS *

* The quotations in this chapter are drawn from the following in-
valuable works: *"Consciousness Raising: A Radical Weapon,"* by
Kathie Sarachild, 1973 (https://womenwhatistobedone.files.word-
press.com/2013/09/1973-consciousness-raising-radical-weapon-k-
sarachild-redstockings.pdf).
"Feminist Consciousness-Raising Groups: Collective Action Through
Discussion," by Linda Napikoski (https://www.thoughtco.com/feminist-
consciousness-raising-groups-3528954, updated 2017).
In Our Time: Memoirs of a Revolution, by Susan Brownmiller (Dial
Press, 2000).
Toward a Female Liberation Movement, by Beverly Jones and Judith
Brown (New England Free Press, 1968).

The challenges to authority during the 1960s brought on a surge in radicalism, but the oppressive treatment of women in the radical groups forced women to confront the patriarchy and caused the burgeoning women's movement to gain strength and influence. This chapter discusses the major changes in American feminism that resulted in what were known as consciousness-raising groups – a movement that has encouraged the creation of many different kinds of support groups over the years, including pro-feminist men's groups.

Women's consciousness-raising (CR) groups had their origin in 1968. Leaders at the time called the groups "the backbone of the movement and a chief organizing tool." The group known as New York Radical Women (NYRW) originated the concept and began the first groups. Anne Forer, one of the founders of NYRW, recognized that she needed to raise her own consciousness about women's lives and the ways in which they were oppressed. She asked the other women in the organization, largely middle class and white, to give her examples from their own lives, recalling that the "Old Left" labor movements "which fought for workers' rights had spoken of raising the consciousness of workers who did not know they were oppressed."

There were many traditions from which women's support groups emerged, seeking ways to end segregation and discrimination based on sex. The labor movement had been working for well over a century, ever since the New England "mill girls," daughters and wives of Yankee farmers, conducted their first turn-out in 1834 to protest wage cuts in an industry that dehumanized them. The civil rights movement, with its origins in abolitionism prior to the Civil War, was filled with inspiring stories of people, white and African American, fighting tirelessly for their rights against the forces of oppression.

Then came the '60s, when the fight for rights and social justice expanded exponentially to include the anti-Vietnam War movement, the gay/lesbian rights movement, the free speech movement, and a general atmosphere of questioning authority in all its guises. It is no accident that the women's movement, seeing the ways in which there was ongoing, unspoken patriarchy within the anti-war movement and other social-justice efforts, sought its own identity and power. Let us not forget that Stokely Carmichael, for all the ways in which he deserves to be credited for advancing the civil rights movement, responded in 1964 to a question regarding women's role in the Student Nonviolent Coordinating Committee (SNCC) by saying, "The only position for women in SNCC is prone." He was not alone.

This is the context in which Anne Forer and another trailblazing woman, Kathie Sarachild, helped bring to bear CR as a key component of the women's movement. Sarachild, born Kathie Amatniek, changed her surname to Sarachild after her mother Sara. It was she who coined the phrase *Sisterhood Is Powerful*. Like Forer, she had been thinking extensively about the many ways in which women were oppressed, historically and in the late '60s. She, too, realized that individual women's personal experiences could be instructive for many women.

Including the word "radical" in the NYRW's name was wholly intentional. The word means "root" in Latin and it was this group's purpose to get to the roots of this entrenched problem. The ultimate goal of the group was to lead a mass movement of women to end discrimination and segregation based on sex. Consciousness-raising groups had played a role throughout the labor movement, enabling workers to see their experience mirrored in the words of others, empowering the group to consider collective actions to secure better treatment and rights. This was the goal of the women, so not surprisingly they applied a similar analysis to their situation.

From the outset there was a strong belief that men would be excluded from these groups. The work of these women was to explore "the situation of women," and as Kathie Sarachild recalled Anne Forer stating, "I think we have a lot more to do just in the area of raising our consciousness. I've only begun thinking about women as an oppressed group and each day, I'm still learning more about it – my consciousness gets higher."

Residing somewhere above this notion that women needed to band together to explore their condition was another key element – the perception that "people don't find the real self of a woman attractive." Anne Forer took this idea to its logical conclusion as it manifested itself in society: "Playing dumb, always being agreeable, always being nice, what we had to do to our bodies, what clothes and shoes we wore, the diets we had to go through, going blind not wearing glasses, all because men did not find our real selves – our human freedom, our basic humanity – 'attractive.'" At the very moment that Forer was clarifying these conditions, the idea occurred that a very effective way to raise one's consciousness would be to meet together to discuss how it felt to be experiencing such oppression.

At the next gathering of the New York group there was considerable discussion as to whether the approach they would take should include reading literature on biological differences between men and women. In a 1973 address to a women's rights conference in New York, Sarachild argued against that approach: "The question is what we want to be, what we think we are, not what some authorities in the name of science are arguing over what we are. It is scientifically impossible to tell what the biological differences are between men and women – if there are any besides the obvious physical ones – until all the social and political factors applying to men and women are equal. Everything we have to know, have to prove, we can get from the realities of our own lives."

The group decided that reading could occur individually, and certainly could be brought back to the group, but the starting point for discussion would be the lived experience of the women in the group – topics such as childhood, jobs, motherhood, etc. Anne Forer brought a critical question to bear for every session: "Who and what has an interest in maintaining the oppression in our lives?"

With this as the stated purpose, the next question that arose was the kind of "actions" the group could initiate. Taking an example from SNCC, it was decided to undertake "consciousness-raising actions" – as group member Carol Hanisch, author of the influential essay "The Personal is Political" framed it, "actions brought to the public for the specific purpose of challenging old ideas and raising new ones, the very same issues of feminism we were studying ourselves."

This was a significant departure from the women's movement of the past, in which women often fought for their rights by organizing and protesting for single issues like the right to vote or workplace equality. As Sarachild said, "It would be a way of carrying theory about women further than it had ever been carried before, as the groundwork for achieving a radical solution for women as yet attained nowhere."

Such an approach meant really looking at one's own life and the lives of the women with whom one was involved. This substantiated the notion that all women would have to see the fight for women's equality as their own fight, not as something to assist other women. As Beverly Jones put it in *Toward a Female Liberation Movement,* "They had to see this truth about their own lives before they would fight in a radical way for anyone." To Stokely Carmichael's instruction to white civil rights workers, "Go fight your own oppressors," Jones added, "You don't get radicalized fighting other people's battles."

This seemingly more measured approach to social change – certainly less threatening than the marches and even civil disobedience that had characterized the struggle for suffrage – nonetheless met with considerable resistance. Many men either misrepresented or misinterpreted what occurred in the CR groups. Some of them felt excluded and feared that what was being discussed was inevitably critical of them as a group and as individuals. Some of the criticism took the form of trying to control what was discussed. As Sarachild tells it, "Whole areas of women's lives were declared off limits to discussion. The topics we were talking about in our groups were dismissed as 'petty' or 'not political.'" Not surprisingly, these often touched on the key ways in which women were being oppressed as a group, including housework, childcare and sex.

There was irony as well. When the topics being discussed were contextualized in terms of male chauvinism, "we were suddenly the living proof of how backward women are," Sarachild recalled. Despite the numerous ways in which women had taken action and would continue to do so, "suddenly we were just women who complained all the time, who stayed in the personal realm and never took any action." Issues that were deemed dangerous – concrete examples of discrimination and exploitation – were described as instances of "man hating" or "sour grapes." Rather than recognizing the issues as appropriate topics for study and debate, CR's critics attempted to both trivialize and marginalize the women participants and the groups themselves by defining the discussions as "psychological delusions."

As is often the case, the distortions about what was actually happening in CR groups led some women to resist participating, many of whom could have greatly benefited from the sisterhood and support. Nonetheless, those who did participate learned much from one another's lives and stories.

Interestingly, the National Organization of Women did not pick up on this growing wing of the movement until a catalyzing public action got its attention. Focusing on the issue of feminine appearance, a group of women confronted the Miss America Contest in 1968. As Sarachild described it, "We protested and picketed ... throwing high heels, girdles and other objects of female torture into a freedom trash can. It was this action ... which first awakened widespread awareness of the new 'Women's Liberation Movement,' capturing world interest and giving the movement its very name."

Once the original group of women experienced the radicalizing of their own consciousness, which had led directly to

31

the protest of the beauty pageant – an early example of the personal becoming political – their mission became getting the word out about CR groups and what they were achieving. To liberate women on a mass scale, CR groups would have to be known and available to all women, and that, in Sarachild's words, meant telling them "about how very political these so-called bitch sessions could be, suggesting what important information for our fight we still had to get from studying the experiences and feelings of women, describing some of the obstacles and proposing that women everywhere begin."

Not surprisingly, since the avowed mission of the women's liberation movement and the CR groups it birthed was to end patriarchy and male supremacy in order to give women full equality in every aspect of life, backlash was again intense and widespread. Anti-feminist men and women who felt threatened by the emerging women's movement made a variety of attempts to dilute the original efforts to prevent it from bringing about the long-overdue societal changes such an approach requires.

It was in this spirit that Sarachild and others sought to return CR to its roots, which she termed "the commitment to a radical approach, a radical solution," one which was seen as "both a method for arriving at the truth and a means for action and organizing." It was not seen as a stage of the movement, but instead as "an essential part of the overall feminist strategy."

These CR originators made several assumptions about their work: that it would be ongoing as a source of theory and ideas for action, that other women would be interested in the same problems they faced in their lives and discussed in their CR sessions, that having the courage to speak about the oppression they faced would be powerful, that women had a common interest in ending oppression, and that "anything less than a radical approach to feminism wouldn't interest other women any more than it did us." The belief was that other women would respond to this radical agenda, even though they would not see themselves as "radicals" because the word was being so widely demeaned and misinterpreted.

Consciousness raising, then, is not one particular method, but rather, as Sarachild expressed it, it is the "basic radical political principle of going to the source, both historical and personal, going to women themselves and going to experience for theory and strategy.... One of the exhilarating and consciousness-raising discoveries of the Women's Liberation Movement has been how much insight and understanding can come from simple honesty and the pooling of experience in a room full of women who are interested in doing this."*

As to the methods involved in running CR groups, Sarachild strongly believes that such basics as hearing from each woman present were less about being "nice" or "tolerant," or even developing listening skills, and much more about "getting closer to the truth." This was not about individual therapy, but rather to hear what each woman had to say in order to be better able to analyze the situation for all women, not just the woman speaking. It was also not about internally changing one woman or the women in the group. It was about changing the conditions women face as a result of male supremacy.

In keeping with CR's co-construction of the conditions women face, the idea was not to end generalizations about women's lives, but to produce depictions that more accurately reflected the real-life experiences, feelings and necessities of women. Once this had occurred, CR was not satisfied with simply increasing awareness and knowledge. No, uncovering the truth is critical, but in and of itself it is not enough for making changes. In fact, with increased understanding of the plight of women comes the necessity for action. Theory and action need to be joined for substantive change to be able to occur.

As for the type of action that best serves the goal of undoing

* These same "discoveries," together with the principles discussed below, apply equally to the evolving men's movement and its use of CR groups, as will be pointed out in the following chapters.

male supremacy, CR requires deliberation, not precipitous responses. Time needs to be taken to learn which methods of organizing and taking action are going to work most effectively. One enormous piece of the unfolding puzzle was to gain deeper understanding of the "connections between the oppression of women and other systems of oppression and exploitation." When this did not happen sufficiently, the movement has become fragmented and divisive, which obviously undermines the kind of progress required. Since this was the first major movement aimed at liberating half of the world's population, it has undergone an enormous learning curve, in terms of engaging all women regardless of race, religion, class, gender identity, sexual orientation, age, etc. The CR movement, along with the Women's Liberation Movement in general, has come to this awareness over time, after some inevitable missteps.

It does not require a giant leap of thinking to see how the CR groups of the '60s and '70s have evolved into a wide variety of support groups for women over the last five decades. This evolution has been accompanied, thankfully, by cultural shifts, in large part due to the actions and efforts of the previous generation of feminists – itself a word that is continuing to evolve. Some of the guiding principles of the early CR groups remain intact, even as we see the emergence of a variety of support groups – for incest survivors, for PTSD victims, for eating disorders, for divorced or single women – but the goal of changing the culture has not necessarily remained. Chapters 15 and 16 will address the question of how support groups affect the culture. It will also be worth paying much attention to the impact that the #MeToo movement has on relationships and the workplace. Regardless, we owe much to the originators of CR groups, most of whom have aged gracefully and begun to depart the stage.

One of them is Gloria Steinem, originator of Ms. magazine and life-long crusader for equal rights. Ending this chapter with a piece of hers, from 2014, seems a fitting way to update the ongoing struggles women – and men – face in getting to true equality. It also serves as a compelling segue to the next chapter, on the history of men's support groups.

Why Our Revolution Has Just Begun

First published in Ms. magazine, Feb. 27, 2014, reprinted by permission, ©1981.

If I had to pick a couple of myths about the women's movement that are most wrong, I think two might be tied for worst place. One is that this movement – also known as women's liberation, feminism, womanism (African-American feminism), mujerista! (Latina feminism), grrrls (strong younger women) and more – is only for white middle-class women.

The second myth is that women of the '70s did all that could or should be done, and young women can now relax; feminism was their mothers' movement. Even the abolitionist and suffragist era show how ridiculous this is. If it took more than a century for black men and all women to gain a legal identity as citizens instead of chattel, it's likely to take at least a century to gain a legal and social equality as everything from workers to candidates to parents.

Let's face it, such deep changes take time. That's why I'm glad that, as I travel, I see more diverse and determined young feminists than ever before in history. Yet I fear that my age – and that of all of us who started this work in the '70s – is an excuse to focus on the past.

So I'm listing here a few of the adventures that lie ahead of us. These are reminders that we're not even halfway there.

— In political campaigns and the media, "women's issues" are mysteriously separated from "economic issues." This conceals solutions. In the last financial crisis, for instance, the government propped up banks, Detroit, mortgage profiteers and other powers that are

35

overwhelmingly white and male, and rewarded greed or error in the name of economic stimulus. However, the most effective economic stimulus would have been – and would still be – paying women equally for comparable work done by white men.

— A woman's ability to decide when and whether to bear a child is not a "social issue"; it is a human right. Like freedom of speech, it affects everything else in life – whether a woman is educated or not, works outside the home or not, is healthy or not and how long she lives.

— Nothing else is going to be equal in a deep sense until men are raising children as much as women are. Children will continue to grow up believing males can't be loving and nurturing, and girls will keep believing they must do that by themselves. Women will go on choosing cold and distant men because those men feel like home. Also, we voters will go on associating female authority with childhood – the main time it was experienced – and thus be uncomfortable with women who lead in public and political life.

— The U.S. is the only modern democracy without some form of a national childcare system. The average cost of childcare here has surpassed the average cost of a college education. I rest my case.

— We're the only advanced country that saddles its college students with debt at the exact time when they should be most free to explore. Also, women pay the same tuition as men, yet are paid an average of $1 million less over their lifetimes, making it harder to repay those loans.

— The Digital Divide is a pretty good proxy for world power. It also tells us something here at home. Though men and women are only about 2 percent apart in computer use, 67 percent of white non-Hispanic households use the Internet while only 45 percent of black households have access.

— While we're celebrating victories for marriage equality, let's not forget that just 51 percent of people in the U.S. say that "homosexuality should be accepted by society," while 69 percent of people in Canada do, and so do 83 percent of people in Germany.

— Do enough people understand that racism and sexism are intertwined, and can only be uprooted together? Think about it: To maintain racial difference, you have to control female bodies. Women of the so-called superior racial group tend to be restricted to maintain "purity" – or at least visible difference – while women of the so-called inferior group are often exploited to produce cheap labor.

— Here's a final shocker: Violence against females in the world has reached such heights that, for what may be the first time in history, females are no longer half the human race. There are now 100 women per 101.3 men on this Spaceship Earth. The causes are everything from son preference to the lethal results of female genital cutting, domestic violence, sex trafficking, sexualized violence in war zones, honor killings, child marriage and much more.

How do we move forward? It's not rocket science. We need to worry less about doing what is most important, and more about doing whatever we can. And remember, the end doesn't justify the means; the means are the ends.

At my age, in this still hierarchical time, people often ask me if I'm "passing the torch." I explain that I'm keeping my torch, thank you very much – and I'm using it to light the torches of others.

Because only if each of us has a torch will there be

enough light.

Yes, much of this agenda is the same one that characterized the goals for the second wave of feminism dating back to the mid-'60s. That these remain unaccomplished to such a large degree, and in some parts of the world more so than others, serves as an undeniable reminder of patriarchy's power and its resistance to being transformed. It also means that large numbers of men need to be part of the transformation that has yet to occur. As you are about to see, I believe that support groups can encourage, promote and sustain commitments to the achievable goals Steinem describes.

CHAPTER 2
PRO-FEMINIST MEN'S GROUPS BEGIN

This chapter has a dual purpose. First is to provide a bridge from the previous chapter, to show the impact the women's movement had on the nascent pro-feminist men's movement that was emerging nationally in the early 1970s, by focusing on one such effort in western Massachusetts that began in the early 1980s. The second purpose is to describe my personal journey and evolution of consciousness that was occurring as a result of my encounters with feminism, which began in late 1972 and grew out of my involvement in both the civil rights and anti-Vietnam War movements.

Having ended the preceding chapter with Gloria Steinem's charge, delivered in 2014, which delineated the numerous ways the work of feminism and its allies remains unfinished, I will begin this chapter by focusing on a few of the areas she addressed that pertain most directly to the creation of men's support groups back in the '70s.

I want to emphasize that I am choosing to zero in on the role played by pro-feminist men and the pro-feminist men's movement. There are several other paths and organizations supporting men in the so-called mythopoetic branch of the men's movement, particularly in what have been termed "men's rights" vis à vis divorce and custody issues. These are not the subject of this book. I join with Rob Okun, editor of both *Voice Male* magazine and the book *Voice Male: The Untold Story of the Profeminist Men's Movement*, who writes that these "men engaged in an often painful emotional inventory in considering their personal lives (especially their relationships with their fathers and other men), but then failed to consider that their personal experiences were directly connected to the system of male dominance and the narrow definitions of manhood it produces."

In contrast, let's recall Steinem's words, which for me hark back to my earliest exposure to the principles, ideas and goals she outlines. As she puts it, "Nothing else is going to be equal in a deep sense until men are raising children as much as women are. Children will continue to grow up believing males can't be loving and nurturing."

There's a big challenge in these words for my fellow men, a challenge I thankfully encounter more and more men rising to face. It is a challenge predicated on being able to gain access to a fuller range of what it means to be a man, which includes being vulnerable, being willing and even eager to share all aspects of life with women – in the workplace, in politics, in sports, in the bedroom, in marriage and in raising healthy boys and girls who see their fathers and mothers equally committed to their care and welfare.

I take heart when I encounter men being fully engaged with their children and one another, as I did on a recent visit to Marblehead, MA, where I met four men who call themselves Maddie's Daddies, since they regularly dine at Maddie's Restaurant. They displayed awareness of their ten children – attentiveness, affection and warmth. I found myself envying their bond with one another as fathers, which I never experienced when co-parenting my four children, and simultaneously pleased to see such a hopeful sign for the future.

Steinem warns what is in store if the egalitarian treatment of women continues to be denied. If men throughout the world remain unwilling, for whatever cultural and/or personal reasons, to become partners with women in seeking equality, we are destined to keep repeating the failed behaviors that have resulted in the ongoing mess we're in. She connects numerous dots from the belief, on the part of boys and girls who are raised primarily by their mothers, that men are incapable of providing nurturance, that women will choose such men because that is what they're used to, and that men and women alike will not trust women to be the leaders they deserve to be because their authority only applies to the nursery, not the board room or the executive mansion.

In the mid-'70s an increasing number of men started paying close attention to the rights women were demanding as a result of their CR sessions and the "second wave" of feminism (the first having been the fight for suffrage). The need for men to not only support women, but to do their own work to change society, was being acknowledged. In 1975 a group of men taking a women's studies class – another result of the women's movement – at the University of Tennessee were inspired to hold what they announced as The First National Conference on Men and Masculinity, in Knoxville, TN.

The following year, a Second National "M&M" Conference was held at State College, PA. Over the next five years M&M conferences were held in Des Moines, St. Louis, Los Angeles, Milwaukee and Boston. There was little formal organization outside of the conferences, but what developed was an ideology which was strongly pro-feminist and gay-affirmative, while also advocating changes in traditional sex roles and the importance of developing men's personal and emotional lives.

It was attendance at an M&M conference at Tufts University in 1981, sponsored by the National Organization of Men against Sexism (NOMAS), that inspired men in the Pioneer Valley of Western Massachusetts. The organization they founded, at first called the Men's Resource Connection (MRC), now the Men's Resource Center for Change, describes that impetus on its website (mensresourcecenter.org):

> Several men who attended were moved by the ideas they heard about redefining male roles in healthier, non-violent directions. They returned home inspired to create an anti-sexist men's network. Recognizing that many men were keenly interested in putting old stereotypes of masculinity to rest, in 1982 these men founded … a grassroots organization … committed to developing a strong local network among men, and between men and women. Soon the men began taking their hopes and visions into the community.

The resulting vision that the MRC espoused and worked to achieve encompasses many of the values expressed in the Preface to this book. Although I never worked with or for the MRC, their presence and their efforts to undo sexism, homophobia and racism inspired me. I was supportive of and felt supported by the organization as it delved deeply into changing men's roles through work with fathers, perpetrators of domestic violence and young people. Here is the current vision statement that guides its efforts today, as it did then:

> The Men's Resource Center for Change is committed to helping bring about a more just and peaceful world by redefining masculinity to exclude violence and embrace trust and compassion. We envision a safe and violence-free world in which:
>
> - Men and women are equally nurturing and equally empowered;
> - People of all gender identities and all ethnicities feel safe and accepted;
> - Human rights for all peoples, including freedom from violence and abuse, are protected;
> - Egalitarian, nonviolent families and relationships are supported in all their diverse forms;
> - All individuals can peacefully reach their full human potential; and
> - All people share a respect and sensitivity for the earth and all beings.

Many of these ideas were offered to me when I moved to the Pioneer Valley of Western Massachusetts in late 1972. The woman I became involved with worked for the recently created Everywoman's Center at the University of Massachusetts and was raising a daughter, Annabel, by herself, having made the decision to keep her baby despite the absence of a father. The political analysis she was passing on to me regarding feminism's major goal of ending male supremacy in all walks of life, as well as the relationship of equals that she was expecting from our partnership, felt immediately familiar.

I saw innumerable connections to the reading and work I had done as a civil rights activist at Trinity College, where I had started a program for inner-city youth whose lives were circumscribed by white privilege and gross inequality. Fast forward three years and that's precisely what I felt when I started hearing and witnessing what feminism meant in my own relationship. In addition to seeking equality in such practical realms as planning our time together, what food to eat, what movies to see, etc., the major realm where I saw the need to be an equal partner was in the care and nurturing of the young child who was to become our daughter. Though it was challenging to break into their twosome-ness at first, since I had not been there for Annabel's first two years, once they both saw that I was not only committed to being with them, but also to sharing the parenting responsibility, we became the family we all wanted to be.

In 1974, we chose to marry, but I felt isolated at this point – isolated in terms of finding other fathers who had made the commitment to co-parenting in an egalitarian relationship. Here's where the CR groups of Chapter 1 come into my story. Having heard about such groups run by the Everywoman's Center, three other men and I were inspired to start our own. These men were at least ten years older than I, and much of what motivated them was the potential break-up of their marriages to women who were questioning their roles as wives and mothers.

Much of what transpired had to do with how these three men could save their marriages – or not. We did not have the kind of focused sessions that would have fostered deeper aware-ness of the ways in which we were affected by a patriarchal society, since the crises my fellow members faced took pre-cedence. Rather than being able to examine how playing the roles we were individually and collectively taught to play, which contributed to the dissolution of relationships with women who were not just seeking but demanding equal-ity, each of the men was trying to prevent a divorce through clutching in too-familiar and therefore unproductive ways.

It is with great appreciation and indebtedness that I am able to include the words of one of the men in my first men's group. Charles Sackrey, retired economics professor who taught at both Smith College and Bucknell University, kindly offered to share his memories looking back 43 years to some very difficult times he was living through. Even though our group did not examine the causes of the systemic struggles in which we were engaged, Charles identified aspects of our affiliation that are characteristic of core elements in support groups for men and women, and why they are so very worthwhile:

> I knew that we would offer each other conversation and the four of us were in circumstances where that kind of conversation with people going through the same kind of thing was not possible except in that kind of environment. What we were also able to do in dealing with our pain at the time was to share with each other all sorts of experiences of how you go through it. You're hurt and it hurts as much as anything you've ever gone through. So you could have a conversation with people going through the same nightmare.

> Each of us was there with his experience and knowledge. It was a kind of school for the broken-hearted. I certainly learned a lot. I came out of there with a different way of feeling about it. It was an early and a very good example of self-help groups.

Notwithstanding our relative lack of awareness and sophisticated analysis of the dynamics of patriarchy and the roles men and women too often play in marriages, Charles did reveal some of what our early group sought to unravel.

> Pat,* my wife at the time of our group, was very much an active and influential feminist in the area and I was dealing with that. One of the things that was useful

---

* Pat Sackrey, now Patricia Lee Lewis, was a founder of the Everywoman's Center (now the Center for Women and Community) at the University of Massachusetts in 1972. She was inspired to name the Center by having done much reading in the Everyman's Library in Scotland when she was a child.

when we talked about these kind of things – I would often think, "What would this conversation sound like to her?" I became more in tune to how much we and they (women) – given the change in the culture – needed to work on what that other bunch was doing and thinking. Listening to us talk about them and thinking about what they would think about this conversation added to my ability to become a feminist myself.

Pat was in favor of me being in a men's group. Our conflict and imminent break-up were much more upsetting to me than to her at the time. She was the one who first suggested that we forget it. We were at war with each other – not physically, but it wasn't working anymore. She was probably relieved that I had such a group to pour out my heart to.

It is still so exciting about what's happening with women now. How would they see that – me talking about them in what we might think are lovely terms. We know so little about their conversations. Any sentence that I may lay out there will likely be a different sentence for them.

As Charles's reflections and musings indicate, the fact that men and women experience so much of life so differently was a key element in my decision to enlarge my focus for this project. The two women's groups that have allowed me to interview their members are now part of the book, and it has been an honor and privilege to be able to include them. Having the opportunity to compare and contrast the male and female experiences of many aspects of group formation, cohesiveness, trust-building, impact on one's life and many other topics reflected in the chapter titles will hopefully only add to the awareness and appreciation of the role such groups can play in our culture.

Then there are the two younger groups represented here, which are enabling me to reach out to a generation of men and women who have had a very different experience of American culture. I've mentioned the joint meeting of the two men's groups in the Introduction – our weekend together that I've described as a "love-fest" as all of the men, older and younger, found so much to appreciate about each other. As previously mentioned, the article I wrote about this event for Rob Okun's *Voice Male* magazine is in the Appendix.

I'd like to make reference here to a difference in perceptions that reveals how men's support groups are evolving. Talking with my group after our weekend together, it was abundantly clear that we saw updated versions of ourselves from back in the day – young men like we once were who were politically savvy, dedicated to exploring intimate connections with one another and the people in their lives, open to us and each other and definitely pro-feminist. It was evident in subsequent emails from the young men's group members that they saw us as role models, pioneers of re-defining and expanding the definition of masculinity, abundantly available to their questions and their ideas.

The difference – no doubt a function of the times that have been changing – had to do with how our groups are perceived by others. In the case of my group, especially early in our evolution, we were considered to be doing important work on ourselves and one another, work that women in our lives appreciated, as Charles' comment above indicates. I know that the women in my life express both curiosity and admiration for our group's longevity and dedication. The men in my life who hear about the group often share their wish that they had such a commitment, and several have gone on to either start or join a group.

By contrast, the young men have expressed concern about how the people in their lives, especially some of the women, have responded to their participation in a support group. They say they have to be careful about what they share, because it is so easily either misinterpreted or misunderstood so that, rather than feeling encouraged, they have to work at not becoming defensive.

Is this because we are living in such a divisive and polarized society, where men's motives are more suspect and less trusted? I don't have an answer, but it is definitely a subject worthy of further exploration.

CHAPTER 3
HOW DO SUPPORT GROUPS
GET STARTED?

This chapter's title, like those of the following chapters, is drawn from questions I asked the group members I interviewed. Their responses, here and subsequently, form the core of the book. So let's begin at the beginning – how and why these four support groups were formed.

There are several layers to the question of what enables the men's and women's support groups to succeed. The first regards the impetus to start a group. What caused the creators to put their energy into forging such an experience for themselves and finding groupmates? The second pertains to the motivations for individuals to become and remain group members. This chapter will look into how the groups explored in this book came into existence. The next chapter will investigate individuals' incentives to join an existing group.

I will begin with my own experience, since it addresses both issues. I was involved in the creation of two different groups, one in 1973 and one in 1979. The earlier group, which I referenced in Chapter 2, was certainly inspired by women's groups that originated in the 1960s.

As for my early involvement, I was a child of the '60s, and social justice involving racism, poverty and the Vietnam War were part of my own consciousness-raising. I read African-American writings, from *Invisible Man* by Ralph Ellison and *Native Son* by Richard Wright to *Soul on Ice* by Eldridge Cleaver. When I was a law student at New York University one of my first acts as a member of the Student Bar Association was bringing the film about the "Chicago 7" conspiracy trial to the university. These experiences, and the civil rights movement in general, changed me permanently, and the struggle for equality for people of color has been front and center in my life ever since.

All of which is to say that when I met my first wife and her two-year-old daughter on a bus en route to Northampton, Massachusetts, I was comprehensively primed to learn about the oppression of women and Eliza was comprehensively predisposed, from her background as the daughter of activists and her involvement with the women's movement, to provide me with the awareness I sought.

Once I found out the ways in which women have historically been victimized and limited by male supremacy and privilege, and once I started to experience the ways in which my actions could contribute to a more equal relationship with my partner, it felt very important to meet with other men to talk about how each of us was negotiating our relationships. I've discussed this group in the preceding chapter and, as I indicated, the other three men in the group, who were all at least ten years older than I, were on the verge of separating from their partners. This was sad, but also served as a major caution light for me. All of them were struggling with their wives' expectations that their relationships change in significant ways. That mine was just getting started enabled me to learn from the struggles of my fellow group members. Between my partner elevating my consciousness about shared childcare, housework, cooking and household management and this men's group exposing the serious issues the other men were facing, I was given an invaluable course in how to forge a partnership based on equality.

The men I met with weekly were, in a sense, dealing with the fallout of their wives' explorations. This encompassed hearing about their partners' frustrations, disappointments and anger with both societal male privilege and the current state of their marriage. Our group soon came to have a very specific purpose – to offer support, consolation and solace as well as perspective to men who were being challenged to change in fundamental ways. There were power imbalances in each of their marriages, and the resulting dynamics had been going on for years, so changing was complex and demanding. We provided as much compassion and encouragement as we could for one another, given the times, our limitations in skills and awareness, and the personal struggles that required a great deal of reflection. We tried to encourage each man to see his marriage issues in the larger context of a society in which women were opposing the patriarchy they had all grown up dealing with in all aspects of their lives while seeking to re-define themselves and their relationships to one another and the men in their lives.

The men's group which I helped create in the late '70s emerged less from a sense of crisis and more from men feeling the need to forge and deepen relationships with one another that allowed for a wider range of emotions, greater intimacy, more trust and lots of support for many different challenges. Some of these were centered on romantic relationships, both gay and heterosexual, but others included issues involving the workplace, child-rearing, friendship and families of origin. The domain of our meetings was thus far broader than the earlier group.

Paul Richmond, with whom I began the group, had a rich background in working with men while teaching at College F, an innovative and boundary-pushing program at SUNY Buffalo throughout the '70s. In his interview for this book he provided much detail about how the experiences he had there came to inform his views about masculinity and his perception of the role men's groups could play. Here, too, the women's movement was the inspiration for much of what took place for the men who came together in Buffalo. His story parallels the evolution of men's consciousness in the country, and exemplifies some of the ways men's groups came into being during that period:

> The university set up 13 trailers (for College F and other alternative programs) because they didn't have any room in the regular departments for the new programs like Women's Studies. The classes were run out of these trailers. It was the '70s, so people would sit outside or, since Buffalo is cold, they'd sit inside. The group I was connected to had been doing a bunch of therapy. They were very political and had been involved in the Freedom Rides. They saw a big connection between people's personal lives and their political actions. They questioned whether their own responses – what was causing their emotional state – were about whether they were fighting the system, because they

were really fighting their dad and there wasn't really any issue with the state. The goal came to be clear about what was triggering you in relation to what you were doing.

With this particular college it was all men who were involved. There was a gay constituency at that time. Stonewall had recently happened in New York and people were starting to come out. It was a big issue that they were bringing up. There were also a lot of Vietnam vets coming back to Buffalo and nobody was dealing with the fact that there was a lot of trauma. There were no initials for it. There was no name for it. In fact, if anything they were being told to "suck it up" and "be a man." Those who had been in World War II acted like, "You're being wimpy. What do you think we had to deal with?" There was no place for people struggling like that.

Women's Studies was an incredible force at this time. For a lot of men, all of a sudden their girlfriends joined and started taking classes in Women's Studies and in the early days all men were considered part of the oppression. They'd been given all the rights so they were the ones doing it to women. The reality was that many men were experiencing unemployment in Buffalo, so self-worth related to who they were as breadwinners and just being able to get a job was not happening. They were coming back from the war pretty destroyed in relation to what was going on. Many of them didn't feel that they had any privileges. They were being portrayed as, "You're a white man. You have these privileges." These returning soldiers had become politicized because of the war so they were in some mode of questioning. Everyone respected Liz Kennedy, one of the founders of the Women's Studies program, and all those women who were advocating for changing women's status. Women used consciousness-raising groups to talk and to then try to put that in some political context. That became the model for us.

College F, being a place that had a little more experience with therapy, started to attract more people who didn't just want to go to "a Marxist college," which was one way the college was thought of, and discuss that it was just capitalism causing all of the problems in society. They wanted to look at why as a man they were actually feeling that they wanted to cry or they couldn't get out of bed or the depression was too much or they had a lot of anger and they were getting too drunk. The political folks didn't want to address any of that. So the college suddenly became this magnet. Women's Studies would sometimes joke with us – "You're going to have men's groups because we have women's groups?" or "You're the oppressor. Why would you do this? To learn how to oppress us more?" – because nobody knew why men would want to get together. Later Liz Kennedy and other women came up to us and said, "You were really onto something."

There had been no real consciousness about why men would want to have this discussion or what they were trying to figure out or what they felt having been pushed to achieve, only to have to face that they weren't the captain of the football team and what did that feel like? Nobody in the culture had the idea that women were oppressed when that started being addressed. When women started saying, "I'm an object," men responded by asking, "What do you mean? Don't you want me to tell you that you're beautiful? Or that I desire you?" It had all gotten very complicated. "What does that mean that I'm saying to you that I'm turned on by you?" They were then mostly reacting with, "Hey, I don't want to feel guilty because you're turned on. I'm not turning you on. That's your problem and I'm not interested." Or, "I am interested," and that was complicated, too.

When we started to say, "We're bringing men together," it was not taken seriously. Many women felt that "You guys should just be giving up your power. You should be working with the Marxists to overthrow the state. You don't need to be talking about how you want to be crying. You've got to be fighting the police." Such comments and attitudes were almost putting us back into the same traditional roles, but there was a different aspect of how we were supposed to be liberated.

I think in the first couple of years everybody was thinking, "It's because you guys are gay." There were some gay aspects. Men were expressing affection – hugging, giving back rubs – where that had not been considered masculine. People observed, "You guys always get together and you want to do that so you can find partners." That became complicated, because people thought men were getting together to talk because they were either gay or hoping women in their lives would want them more since they were trying to change.

It took a while. It wasn't until we befriended a Vietnam veteran who was really having a hard time. He came to some of our groups and said, "I really want to do this group work. But I don't want to do it here." So he put it out and the college was set up to say, "Anybody can do courses." We were trying to support him and he got about ten veterans who heard about the group forming. It was very intense. People broke furniture and punched walls in. They had a lot of anger and violence and didn't know what to do with it. They felt betrayed by their country, by people their age. They felt that nobody really understood what had happened to them in Vietnam. They'd gone to do service and look what happened to them. Another factor was the complication about whether men admit that level of vulnerability to themselves. Do men even admit that they have these weaknesses?

I was taken into the college in '71. I got in under the

auspices that they could hire people with expertise who didn't have a degree. It was like that in the Women's Studies Department – if you didn't have a degree you could still teach women's studies, but only if they thought you'd been doing organizing so you knew what you were teaching. My classes were on collectives and co-ops, because I had been in several communes. They wanted me to tie that into cooperatives that were in the city – food co-ops and others. I became one of the staff, so I got in on the discussions about creating men's groups. I was helping set them up and being in them.

As far as leaders for the groups, we were considered the "anarchist college," though we believed that there were people who came to the forefront to lead when it was needed – like the Vietnam veteran who thought there was a need for a veterans' group. He did the work. He created the group and we came and opened up the trailer. We were there if they wanted us in the room. As things got more intense we were there as buffers, because sometimes it would trigger the guy who had started the group and he wasn't in any facilitating mode then. These veterans didn't have any idea of what it means to be in a group and that's where I came in, because no one had any experience of being in co-ops or communes, where you have a bunch of meetings, and that all got tied into how groups function.

When we would hear Women's Studies talking about what they wanted and what they were accomplishing, we decided in '71-'72 that we wanted to do our own study group – Men's Studies. We started to ask how would we do this for other men and how would we even do this for ourselves? There were some books we tried to read. We tried to use novels that had men as the main characters. We tried a couple of courses, because we felt that men were not used to talking about their feelings. They would project very easily. If we read a book about a male character who was drunk and beating his wife, we would either get the reaction of "I understand why this guy is doing this," or "He's a bad guy." Sometimes people would have these very extreme emotional reactions and eventually you'd try to say, "This seems like it's tapped into something for you. Do you want to talk about that, because we don't know that much about this character," or "It sounds like a lot of projections about what this character actually felt. Is this how you feel?"

We then realized that in our own experience we'd never really sat with men discussing the range of topics that emerged – what their frustrations around their own sexuality were or taboos about masturbation. We'd never had a conversation with our fathers about sex or had a room or a space where someone would say, "We're going to allow a wide variety of questions to happen." Suddenly, you realize all kinds of stuff comes up. I think it was a time period when there was a lot of introspection. The emergence of women's studies pushed that. Drugs, music and different cultural aspects were making people look at what they'd always NOT looked at and start to ask questions.

We quickly formed our own support group. It became apparent that while we were doing this work with other men, more and more of our personal stuff was coming out. We started to take suggestions for themes. For instance, "Let's start tonight with what did your father tell you about sex?" or "Where did you hear about sex?" Just hearing ten people answer these types of questions gave you a whole different perspective about yourself. But we didn't know what to do. Sometimes we took on more than we could handle because we didn't know what we were opening up in terms of Pandora's Box. One example was that we took on that veteran's group and it was kind of wild. We soon realized, "We're unleashing enormous emotion and are we prepared to hold this guy down because he's about to throw himself through the window after he smashed the wall?" – which tapped into everybody wondering, "Am I skilled enough to do this?" and "What skills do I need?"

First we thought you need a coordinator and you need someone who's running the group and it's structured. Then we thought, "Why don't you pick Wednesday night and whoever shows up should come and we'd be there." We did this for a while and then we ran into centers being closed, resources not being there. We were pulling in everybody from those that should have been on medication and needed extreme help, to people like us. What that brought up for us on the political side was, "No, the society has left people on their own and as men there is no place for them and as men they're being allowed to become alcoholics or abuse themselves." That tied in with our political work, to always be thinking in that context, like Women's Studies was going at it – that everything first dealt with, "I am a woman and this is how everything relates to being a woman and I'm probably being screwed in more ways than one."

I think that's what gained us their respect after a while – that we weren't just trying to learn more and better ways to be oppressors. In the beginning there were some jokes that actually became a reality in some ways – "Guys, why would I want to join this?" and someone would say, "Are you having any sex?" and the response would be, "Well, no" and someone would say, "Well, after you get done having this conversation you might have better luck at getting sex." It was more about getting better at communicating and being a better person, which was then more attractive to women.

Later, because of so many years of doing the work, we could point out, "Yes, there's a woman being forced into prostitution and there's a man lying in the curb sleeping and homeless." Could we talk about the system that is destroying both men and women? Yes, the system sometimes favors men – in pay, in employment – but no, there's this guy in the street or there's this person getting drafted. Up until '73 our men's groups were different than after '73, when the draft stopped. We had a different sense of why people were coming in and what they were coming in for. It was much more accepted.

I had my own groups. We started to separate out a group for us that was much more personalized, that had nothing to do with the college. We ran two or three other groups that were for other men. Mostly we were just helping people facilitate and have them experience what a group could be like – encouraging them to make their own groups.

That's essentially what Paul was determined to do when he arrived in the Pioneer Valley of Massachusetts in 1979. We met one another through a mutual friend and after a couple of times talking about men and the value of men's groups we both put out the word to a number of men we felt could contribute to and benefit from such a group. We began our sessions with eight men who were willing to make a commitment to show up once a week for two hours to share as much as possible with one another.

That group, which ran from 1979 to 1989, will be discussed further below, and more will follow in subsequent chapters. But first I will focus on the formation of the group Paul and I joined in 1989, after the demise of the other group. It has been in existence since 1978 – 40 years and counting. That group has a unique story to tell, and thanks to a couple of archivist-oriented members, I have some of the documents from its origins, including the initial invitation that went out to the community via message boards – one way people connected before technology revolutionized communication. The flyer, with the header MEN to MEN (a copy is in the Appendix), was distributed by the three men who were hoping to form a group. They wrote:

We are looking for anti-sexist men who are interested

in forming a group that would concern itself actively with radical social change in the Valley area. We want to focus our energies on confronting patriarchy, sexism, heterosexism, misogyny/womon hating and homophobia. These institutions of male privilege are internalized in the US and need to be confronted simultaneously on personal and political levels. In addition to these major focuses we want to be constantly aware of the direct interrelationships with exploitative economic structures, racism, classism and ageism.

We would like to gather to get to know each other and develop a common analysis and strategy. We want to implement our ideas in a highly supportive atmosphere. We have a commitment to taking direct action against sexism. Possible projects include men's community nights, men's childcare collective, organizing workshops and discussions, men's caucuses within existing political organizations, working against violence against women, networking, initiating support groups, etc....

We would like to work in a collectively run group of 5-12 men, who are able to consider a long-term commitment. If you are interested and/or have further ideas you'd like to share with us please call or write.

Signed "In love and struggle," the flyer was circulated in the fall of 1978, and soon afterward the first session convened with a group of men, several of whom are still in the group – obviously willing to make a long-term commitment! One of the three founders, Gary Seldon, was in the group for the first ten years. Here are his memories of the group's birth:

There were all sorts of movements going on. All sorts of attempts to create change. This was one particular vein of change – feminism – that was just obvious to me. It was totally vital to my life, my perception of reality, my existence. And we needed to work on it. The thought that ran through my mind was that I had grown up hearing my father say, "Racism is a white problem." I was just barely a teenager when my father was saying that, and so this was me coming into adulthood and saying, "Sexism is a men's problem." We need to do the work to fix it.

Another author of the statement above, Alan Surprenant, is still in the group these many years later. He spoke to the question of why he wanted to start such a group:

> Gary and I had been friends for a while by that point and we both thought we were missing out on something that women's groups were having. We knew we weren't going to get it from a women's group so we needed to get it from a men's group. "It" was related to all the things that were in our friendship, including not being competitive and sharing stuff. But that was one-on-one and the idea was to have that level of sharing in a group. We'd actually seen a few little pamphlet-type publications about men's groups that were typed up and run off on a ditto machine, and that got us going.

The earliest men's group that formed, in 1973, was first and foremost responding to the changes wrought by the women's movement – changes in the relationship each man had with his significant other, in each case a woman for whom the movement and its urgency to question patriarchy and the status quo was paramount. We used one another as sounding boards as well as a solace source as relationships imploded and a sense of meaning needed to be redefined in light of the changes in our homes. Only rarely did the group turn and look inward at our relationships with one another, whereas the group founded by Paul and me in 1979 had the express purpose of building a close-knit community of men who would offer both support and the possibility of developing more meaningful connections amongst us. The scope of the later group wasn't limited to working out the ways in which we as men needed to evolve in our primary relationships, but rather had us examining our parenting, our relationships with our families of origin and our workplaces.

Not surprisingly, the longest-lasting of the three groups, the one that began in 1978 and that I joined in 1989, has gone through the most evolutionary changes. Having begun with the express, stated purpose of undoing patriarchy through actions, and thus not focused necessarily on "inner work" either within one's self or even within the group, the focus in the early days was on supporting women and challenging the system. This meant things like doing childcare for women at Take Back the Night marches and demonstrations as well as finding meaningful ways to protest against nuclear weapons or homophobia. The meetings, however, were rather characteristically male, with agendas, Robert's Rules of Order, even minutes. One of the men saw himself as "spying" on the group from his anti-pornography, pro-feminist position, to make sure that the group was acting as advertised in the invitation.

The group almost collapsed under its own weight, as political activism conflicted with really knowing, supporting and challenging one another in intimate relationship. As you will learn in a subsequent chapter, which deals with the construction of norms, ground-rules and expectations, it took a major shift in how the group constituted itself to arrive at the place originally sought, where the personal could be political – as was learned from the women's movement – and the trust that needs to be in place for really intimate sharing could be developed.

The older women's group that is featured in this book – which its members refer to as a "women's circle" – was founded in the mid-'90s. Two women who are still in the group after 25 years were the originators, Sara Elinoff Acker and Ruth Olsen. Here's how Sara described its origin:

> Being part of a women's group has always been important to me. Starting in college and throughout my 20's, I had been part of women's communities and circles. My women's collective household at college,

the lesbian/feminist community of Gainesville, Florida, my colleagues in the feminist health clinic and battered women's program where I worked.

I feel incredibly blessed that because of feminism, I really learned to value and prioritize my relationships with women. Go back a generation and things were really different for women. They certainly were for my mother and her friends. Women have always had other women for friends, but their primary commitment was to marriage and family. Their relationships with their women friends were always less important. Even though there was often great emotional intimacy between women, it just wasn't prioritized in quite the same way. I truly believe that women didn't value each other because of internalized sexism.

One of the greatest gifts of feminism for me was that it helped me realize how amazing women are, how powerful our connections can be to one another, that when we prioritize each other and we don't trivialize our connection, how remarkable that is. Women are important to me and even if I choose not to have my erotic intimate relationship with a woman, I want women to be primary in my life.

Once I settled in Western Massachusetts and realized I was going to spend many years here, of course I wanted to have a women's circle as an ongoing part of my life. My then-husband had his own men's group and truthfully, I was envious. His group was a rich and deep source of support for him and I wanted to have my own group. I started one women's group, but we were only together for three years. We were divided about what we wanted to do with our time together. Some women wanted the group to be focused on spiritual development, others wanted to focus on their personal lives and others wanted more lighthearted and playful ways of being together. I wanted a group that could encompass all of that!

Our group started to have some interpersonal difficulties and there was no safe way to process our conflicts. We never hammered out any group agreements, so there were tensions around basic protocol like coming on time or making a commitment to being present for the entire time, or how many groups to attend each year. But it was the tensions between some of the members that led to our unraveling. It didn't feel like there was any safety to work through those conflicts. So when we inevitably needed to process conflicts, people said, "I didn't sign up for this." There wasn't that kind of commitment.

I was really surprised and disappointed. I believed that working on our commitment and connection to each other was part of what any high functioning group was about.

The group fell apart. I took a bit of a break, but I still really wanted a women's group. I knew if I was ever going to launch a different group, we would need to have a shared vision and commitment to process right from the start. One of my best friends, Ruth, also had not had a great experience in her women's group. We were having a conversation about our experiences and then we both had the same idea: "Why don't we create a group together?" We both knew in our hearts that this was meant to be, that she and I needed to birth a group together! We became the mothers of the circle in that moment.

We wanted to incorporate all our past experiences: what didn't go well in our previous women's groups as well as what worked. So we crafted a vision statement of our ideal women's group. We wrote about the group we wanted to be part of. We included emotional depth, commitment to each other, commitment to working through any issues we might have to cover, an incredible safe container and then – fun, spending time outdoors together, creating ritual and ceremony and of course, in-depth sharing about our lives. We included the practical details: meeting for a whole day, one Sunday a month, commitment to communication, showing up on time, etc. We talked about loving kindness, a commitment to self-examination and to gentle and honest communication. We wrote it all up and it was so inspiring. We were so excited!

We came up with a list of my close friends, her close friends, women we believed would resonate with this kind of intimate group. We set a date and place for our first meeting and decided to see who would show up. It turns out that 24 women came to that first meeting! Eventually, that number sifted down to 11.

I'm blessed to have really amazing, deep friendships with all the women in my group. We love being together. Our women's circle is our way to prioritize our time with each other in our lives and accompany each other through the decades of our lives. It's been remarkable.

Ruth shared how she came to join forces with Sara from her own experience in a women's group.

Prior to the group that we formed, I was in a women's circle that was really hard. Actually, I would come home crying sometimes. It was soon after that that I met Sara. Sara looked at me and I looked at her and that's when we said, "Let's start a new group and name the qualities that we want that are important to us."

When Sara and I got together we said, "Let's create it from the bottom up." That felt safe, creative, interesting and exciting. Sara said, "Let's just write what's important to us in a group. What do we want in a group? What are our values?" I had never thought about it until she thought about it – until she said it. We wrote about all the components we'd played and imagined and dreamed and made it everything we could and sent a letter out. "Here's our dream and if it speaks to you, call us."

What I really wanted was a group that was filled with loving energy – positive and gentle and soft and loving and fun and joyous and playful and spiritual and honest, with integrity and authenticity with mature women who would always look to themselves and ask, "What part am I contributing to any kind of issue?" "How might I be unconscious and how can I get conscious?" – so that there is a shared value of integrity, authenticity, loving kindness. A fear might be that we might have that intention, but that somebody might not live up to it. However, with a shared foundation like we'd envisioned, the group always lovingly holds us all accountable. We all hold each other accountable to our shared values. That was really important to me.

In these origin stories, there are clearly some common themes pertaining to the need to come together as a group of men and women to deal with a variety of issues. But there are also some important contrasts, both in purpose and, at least during the early stages of the groups, in what took place. For the men's groups, these differences were functions of a number of variables, including the time period during which the group formed, the participants' ages and life stages, and the perceptions of the culture and the role of men.

The women's group had the great advantage of being able to build on the achievements of the earlier women's groups and the women's movement and thus they could give their energy and attention to supporting one another in their intimate relationships, their work lives and their parenting. They also sought trusting relationships, having experienced some of the effects of being in a group with women that did not have trust and safety as essential components of their group.

One of the differences between the men's and women's groups is evident in the invitations sent by their founders.

This difference can be seen as a function of the times in which they were written and shared. Almost 15 years elapsed between the creation of the two groups. The men were wanting to combine personal work and activism as a group, which made a great deal of sense in 1978, when there were so many causes to support with one's time, energy and commitment. The women were older when they began, in the mid-'90s, and had already made some of those activist commitments in their careers and their lives, so being part of a group that was centered on forging intimacy, making deep commitments to showing up, being focused, attentive and loving were the highest priorities.

Fast forward another almost 20 years and let's see how the next generation went about creating support groups. I'll begin with the women this time. Amelia Olsen is the daughter of Ruth, which means that she grew up experiencing her mother's group. If this book succeeds in influencing more men and women to become part of support groups, there will someday be lots more Ruths and Amelias who participate in such groups – mothers and daughters and, hopefully, fathers and sons..

Here is how Amelia responded to the question about how she helped start her women's group:

> I had just moved to New York City, and Naomi Lutra had just gotten engaged. It was because of her that we were all brought together. She and I were childhood friends, several others had gone to primary school together and still others met in college. She was our connector, but we all saw something in each other and immediately felt connected to this new group.
>
> After that we'd see each other every weekend. We'd explore the city and museums. It was that period of your life when everything is about expansion. It was our early 20's and we were exploring our world, expectations of jobs, boyfriends, and who we would become as adults. We were building foundational beliefs

and principles that would guide us. It took me until adulthood to find my best friends, and I was deeply moved, changed and grateful for it.

We had about eight or nine years with all of us together in the City and then life took us in different geographic directions. I feel that all of these women are exceptional. We all elevate each other in amazing ways, so moving away from them was scary and felt like a big loss.

I selfishly – what I thought was selfishly – sent them all an email saying, "I have this idea. I was thinking we could do a Skype call once a month and make sure we stay connected." They immediately said yes and we've now been doing it for six years.

I don't think we realized it was like a women's circle. It wasn't intentional. We naturally supported, counseled and cheered each other on. We are a sounding board, a sisterhood with deep history on each other and an ability to see what we ourselves sometimes cannot see on our own. As our life stages have changed, the fact that we are a priority to each other has not changed.

These exceptional women, who I get to call best friends, would have been in my life no matter what. But in creating an intentional organized call, a women's group, we made sure that as our lives changed, and continue to change we won't lose the fragility of connection.

Finally, there's the younger men's group. I first met Ben Blackshear and one of his groupmates, Kevin Quirolo, at a funky Chelsea café in New York City. This is how they described how their group began:

Kevin: I've been in a bunch of other types of groups. The groups I'd been in before were primarily focused on political organizing. In college it was all about turning out people for protests – pressuring the administration to respond to racial inequality on the UCLA-San Diego campus and fighting budget cuts and putting pressure on our administration to put pressure on the trustees. After that I was in a bunch of grassroots groups in New York. The organizing style, especially in college, was very focused on interpersonal relations. It helped me develop tools that come in handy in a more support-group format.

Ben: I had never been in an explicit support group where that was a primary part of the goal, but I've been in what I would call emotionally aware organizing spaces where the goal of coming together is to do political work, but it's done in a way that acknowledges everyone's wholeness and allows you to come to the meeting and really check in and say where you are. So there's space for that honesty and vulnerability, but it is not the purpose of the meeting.

Kevin: I'd been thinking about being in a support group for a while because I've been in different political organizing spaces and I've been exposed to a lot of ideas about feminism and anti-racism. What really motivated me was that I had a falling out with two different people about racism and sexism in equal measure around the time that I was seeking out people to be in a group with. It was a combination of a long-term thinking about it and then having a kind of crisis moment where I was like, "I'm making bad life choices and hurting people, so I need to do something different."

I had a blog before that, that was focused on white privilege, but also dealt with masculinity. I had been thinking about, "What if the theories become popular and prevalent in organizing spaces of intersectionality?" I thought, "Oh, well, if I use that to think about my own identity, I end up with all of these privileges at once." So what happens when you flip that analysis around because the people who developed it were queer women of color who were saying, "Oh, my God, we're oppressed by everyone," which is true, so if you flip that around and you're a white straight guy, what do you do? That was the abstract, analytical stuff that I was thinking about, and the more concrete experience was someone I was dating with whom I had a falling out said to me, "You're sexist and racist. I can't deal with this."

One of the things I learned from that relationship and reading and other things, but very concretely from that relationship, is the problem of asking people who suffer from oppression to teach you about it and to re-train you and re-socialize you to not hurt people. It is unfair and counter-productive because you're recreating the inequality, like, "I keep asking you to wash the dishes for me. Can you also help me deal with my feelings about feeling bad that you're washing the dishes?" In that relationship we weren't living together so washing dishes wasn't a real example, but it captures the moment. It captures the feeling that you're already putting this additional weight on people and then asking them to deal with your internalized superiority complex. That was a concrete impetus where I felt that the only way to break out of this cycle is to do it with other people who are coming at it from the same place.

I thought I was one of the creators of the group because I was coming from my own very personal perspective, but I think it was that a lot of people had the same idea at the same time.

Ben: Kevin's right. We had all been seeking this kind of group and thinking about it. For all of us there were some number of personal or logistical precipitating events that led to it happening. My main political involvement is with this group called SolidarityNYC, which is a collective of activists, organizers and academics, the majority of whom are women. They had gotten so frustrated with patriarchy in that organizing space – how it was just continuing to replicate itself, which was ruining meetings and throwing things totally off track. They formed a group called Everyday Solidarity for Everyday Sexism, which is a women's support group for women in that movement to come together to air their grievances, talk about the shit they have to deal with day in and day out and just support one another through that. I was on several email threads where people were talking about forming that group and I was in dialogue with people asking, "What do we do to get men to do this, too." Around the same time as all of that was happening, a friend of Kevin's had lent me a book that was Kevin's, entitled *Towards Collective Liberation*, by Chris Crass, which is a great book and then Kevin emailed me and said, "Heard you had this book and liked it. Do you want to meet and talk about it?" We did and talked about how to build a support and accountability group and what we'd both been thinking about recently.

That conversation was a generative one, because in fairly short order they convened their first group gathering of five men and so began their journey together.

It should be abundantly clear at this point that there is no single path to forging a group nor one set of reasons for doing so. Each of the groups depicted demonstrates some key ingredients for getting started, however. These include having at least one individual with sufficient motivation and awareness to inspire others to be connected to not just a single friend, but to a group of people. It also requires an openness to experiencing some degree of challenge to make the group happen, since the road to such a commitment is usually not without some bumps.

Finally, to create a support group with staying power necessitates bringing in people who express and act upon the desire for deep connection – the best part of what we mean when we say "family." The men with whom I am so wonderfully connected in our 40-year-old group often refer to one another as "chosen family." Not surprisingly, so does the young women's group. In fact, at least one of them, Charlie Evans, said she saw the group as being "chosen family" rather than a support group. It wasn't until our interview, when she spoke so eloquently about the group, that she saw her "chosen family" also being her primary source of support.

CHAPTER 4
WHY JOIN A SUPPORT GROUP?

As we saw in the last chapter, the reasons different individuals chose to start a support group are many and varied. The same is true for the range of reasons the men and women of different generations and backgrounds chose to participate in the groups profiled in this book

Although the reasons vary, a common denominator is the desire for affiliation with a group of people who have your back, know you well and accept you fully. The variations based on age and gender will be worth noting as the people I interviewed speak about their individual motivations. What else is happening in one's life and what degree of support is available outside of a group experience were other considerations for each person I spoke with.

When I wrote *Called to Serve,* about the Vietnam War draft, the interviews began with the subject sharing what was occurring in their lives prior to the experience of being drafted. In the interviews I conducted for this work I was eager to learn about whether earlier experiences with men's or women's groups were factors, as well as whether there were any precipitating events – emotional upheavals, a desire for more intimacy, a need for connection. Each person comes from a unique place and viewpoint, and being in a support group is therefore a kind of negotiation among the members, in terms of what is sought and what is offered.

In addition to these variables, there is also the point at which the group began and what stage it is at when the members join. Those arriving early in the group's history will have a major voice in the group's evolution, whereas those joining later on – in my case 11 years after the group began – need to be willing to adjust to the structure, purpose and gestalt of the group.

Of course, the group evolves over time as its members become increasingly comfortable with one another and, in the case of the two older groups, as the members themselves go through the various life stages. It is incumbent upon groups that hope to last, while meeting the needs of their members, that there be accommodations over time – for new members as well as for life changes. This will be a subject pursued in subsequent chapters.

But we begin with some of the voices from each of the four support groups, discussing their reasons for joining the group of which they are a part.

Older Men's Group

Stephen Bannasch: I saw a poster in 1978 describing a new men's group forming, but which had a feminist perspective. To me, it looked like it might be an interesting group. It was a perspective I already had. People hear all sorts of things, and they think of all sorts of things when they hear the word "feminist," so I'm going to define what it means to me. To me, it means realizing that, at a very deep level, there are power imbalances that have been in both personal, small-scale social interactions and large-scale social economics throughout a lot of recorded history. The system that included these features has created ways in which people interact.

People often use the word "oppressed" to describe what has happened to women. I don't tend to use that word. I understand it as basically seeing each other and interacting with each other with various kinds of straightjackets on that limit how people can actually be together. It involves trying to think about how you would like both your personal and social and large-scale society to change. Without thinking about the way that that kind of power and social imbalance has been around for so long and affected people, – not only in how they can relate, but how they can imagine – you're less likely to think about how change can happen and you're likely to be less effective. That's the basis of it.

So when I saw that poster, I don't remember specifically why I was drawn to it, because I was already in a household of men that had this intention. I didn't think I needed it because I felt lacking. I probably chose to go because it sounded interesting: "We'll talk about interesting things, we'll do interesting things, we're interesting people." I don't think I did it because I felt something missing in my life. It just looked really interesting. To me, "interesting" means that I'll meet people who I really want to get to know. What I mean is people I would find interesting on a very deep level – people who would have ideas, people who would challenge me and when we talk and think together and care together, that I'll change and they'll change and I'll have new ways of thinking.

Gary Phillips: I'd been in a couple of support groups. I was in what you would call a therapy group for a period of time in the mid-1970s. That was very valuable to me. I really liked it. There were eight of us and a couple of therapists who ran the group and a kind of intimacy came about inside that group that I really, really appreciated, a sort of basis of honesty that was outside my cultural scope at that point, growing up in a traditional society in the mountains of North Carolina.

My first touch with psychology is when I started meeting friends who felt that their mothers had ruined their lives. That was so outside any kind of cultural point I could grasp at the time, except through books. Psychology fascinated me. I took a couple of psychology courses and the opportunity to be part of this therapy group came up and I kind of jumped at it. I'm an intensity junkie and I really like intense relationships. I like conversation. I like to go deeper. This group was an opportunity to do that in a structured atmosphere and I was attracted to it. It was men and women. We had a very brief foray into a men's group in North Carolina in the mid-1970s, but it never jelled. We met five or six times with men who already liked each other and cared for each other, but we just didn't have the discourse or the discipline to go deeply into our issues. It became too much of a boys' club, and even then I knew the difference between that and creating a men's group.

I grew up in a matriarchal society and the women in my life were incredibly important to me – my mother, my grandmothers, my aunts, my next-door neighbors, the old women in our community. Even though I played sports and participated in male society and hunted with my family and all sorts of other things, often at family gatherings, given the choice of going out with the men to hunt or sitting inside with the women and telling stories, I chose to sit inside and hang with the women. I was frustrated, even as a teenager, with my male relationships and the limited scope of them. I was living in a communal household in Massachusetts for the first time, having come up from North Carolina with five other people on the strength of one car and one job. I was looking for community, and I like the idea of sitting with a group of men and talking about some of the issues of the day and creating intimacy. So I joined.

Dick McLeester: It was a combination of wanting to get more support with what I was dealing with in my life at a particular moment as well as wanting to hear what was really going on for other people on a deeper than superficial level. At that time, and since joining the group, I've run into so many men who have said they've got their relationships with women happening, but when it comes to relationships with men they're very superficial – talking about sports or drinking beers or degrading women. Various ways of men being together can be superficial or worse – putting each other down, putting women down. I knew from the men who were in this group that it would be very different and I wanted to experience that.

77

Tony Clarke: I think at that point in my life there was a lot of resonance in terms of looking at issues of men's and women's roles in society. How as men we could be less sexist and more supportive of women. The men's group had a very political consciousness, and I had been involved with a number of social-change issues for years already. Years before I had moved to North Carolina, I had worked to help organize a federation of food cooperatives in the Southeast and I had done other social-change workshops. I lived in Arizona for a while, where I first became involved in Movement for a New Society, which is the group that inspired the Life Center Association.* So it was kind of a natural outgrowth of all that for me. The men in the group were already moving in that direction. Some of them had done workshops with people that come out of LCA or had visited it. There were several men who had been really involved in the anti-nuclear movement. Early on we would go as a group and participate in different events. That meant a lot to me.

Before presenting some of the voices from the older women's group, there is someone whose motivation takes us back to the early days of consciousness-raising groups. My friend Lola and I have the same birthday, four hours and ten years apart. Each year we share a birthday sundae to celebrate. On one of those occasions, we began a conversation about my work on this book project. Within a comment or two I learned, for the first time in our 38-year friendship, that Lola had been in a women's group from 1972 to 1979. When

* The Movement for a New Society (MNS) was a network of social-justice collectives in the 1970s and '80s. The Life Center Association, an outgrowth of MNS, consisted of cooperative group houses and apartments. "These communities provided members an outlet to not only express their political views in their personal lives and in personal growth but to live the values of the future in the present. The Life Center sought to break down the language of 'isms,' which imposed limits on the understanding of a multitude of relationships (classism, racism, sexism, heterosexism, etc.)." www.lca.coop.

I asked her if she would be willing to have her reasons for participating in that group included in this book, she readily agreed.

Someone I knew told me that there were women's support groups starting up downtown, with Pat Sackrey (now Patricia Lee Lewis) facilitating. I'd become increasingly disgruntled at being an "appendage" of my husband, who had gotten his Master's and PhD, while I earned the money to support us and it was I who, according to tradition, did most of the cleaning and cooking. I remember clearly a couple of times, as long as several years before, when I became quite angry as, at the end of a long day of work, I was the one doing the dishes. I also spent my Saturdays cleaning our apartment. In the second year of our marriage my husband bought me a vacuum cleaner for my birthday! Even way back then, in 1963, I knew that was very wrong. So I had been questioning the "division of labor" element for a long time before this women's group opportunity came up.

The group, about seven of us who met weekly, brought to light many aspects of the need for women's liberation. We were one of many consciousness-raising groups which cropped up in the '70s, and it was an educational process: so many "light bulbs" were turned on so brightly, regarding the oppression of women in all aspects of our society, women as second-class citizens. Involvement in the women's movement was for all of us positively exhilarating, energizing, exciting. It was something like falling passionately in love.

Our group was somewhat unusual in that we used theater as a tool for resolving our difficulties with our partners and employers and once with the police who had harshly interrogated one of our members after she'd been raped. We would role-play a situation – the woman who was presenting the problem became

79

the person with whom she had an issue. The rest of us role-played the woman. In this way, we gave each other ideas as to how to approach the person with whom we had the conflict.

After the first couple of years, we went public with our theater and started creating skits about oppressive situations. We even used song sometimes in our performances. It was guerilla theater and our venues were varied: once in the hallway of the University of Massachusetts Education Department building, a number of times on various small stages at UMass and Hampshire College, and once in Holyoke at a very conservative women's club, The Junior League, who invited us because they wanted to know what this "women's liberation movement" was about. By then some of the women in our group were quite radicalized and the discussion after the presentation became contentious, to the embarrassment of the "softer" feminists of our group. I think that was our last performance.

My husband was definitely not super macho and, in fact, his resistance to my being involved in the feminist movement was, in part, because he felt he was not a typical male of that era. He respected women and did do a bit of housework and childcare, though I was still doing the lion's share. I think he felt the backlash against men as personally unfair and insulting to him. Ultimately, he felt he couldn't stay in a marriage where so much change was being asked of him, both psychologically and practically.

In fact, within a few years, all but two of the marriages had ended. Tina Krutsky's was one that survived. Tina recently wrote me: "To this day I see the world through eyes opened in the women's group. My husband has had to make this journey with me. That is how we have thrived, as a couple who share homemaking, work, and parenting children and grandchil-

dren. I have been happily married for 50 years."
In sharp contrast, a couple of years after the group's inception, two of the women declared themselves "radical lesbians" and as such adopted the code of not being able to even talk to us, their former close allies, because we were in relationships with men. Ouch, that hurt!

Lola's experience provides a bridge to the older women's group's stories. As such, her words are both historically significant and indicative of the evolution in consciousness that occurred for her and her generation, as well as, over time, for increasing numbers of men.

Older Women's Group

Diane Norman: I settled in Hartford, Connecticut, with the man who was to become my husband for 14 years. I was in a dream group in Connecticut with a woman named Dorothy, who was the leader of the group. Coincidentally, I met Dorothy through one of the women who had been in a women's consciousness-raising group with me years before, when we both were students at Vassar College in the '70s. This was actually the first women's group I had been in. Years later this dream group was formed and went on for about three years. We would meet once a week for two hours and one, two or three of us would share a dream. Dorothy would work with us individually, bringing us back into the dream to explore its deeper meaning. So it was like semi-therapy and semi-support group. It was an incredibly loving group of women who became important in my life at the time. We would sometimes have overnights together and intentionally "dream together." I learned a lot about dreams and how to work with dreams through that experience.

Several years later I moved to Massachusetts and after the birth of my daughter, I longed for another

81

supportive community of women like I had had in Connecticut. There were actually two different groups that were "recruiting me" to join them. I was already connected to many of the women who were in one of them, so I chose to join this group in 2003. They are my current women's circle. I recognized right off the bat that this group had an abundance of strong, wise women. Being asked to join, I felt honored, but also a little intimidated. If they invited me, I had to believe that I must have something I could offer this group. I wasn't quite sure what it was, but I felt if there was an opening for me, then that's where I belonged. I sensed I would grow more into the woman I was meant to be among these particular women.

Morning Star Chenven: I came to the very first gathering of the women's circle and then I decided that I couldn't be part of it. It was early in my relationship with Moonlight (Morning Star's partner) and I was step-parenting three African-American teenagers plus my own child and it was a big deal, so I just didn't feel like I had time. I came into the women's circle later – probably ten years after they had been going. Diane and I came in at the same time. I had a good long time to work with my parenting and get settled in my relationships with the children. I really wanted to be with women. I had been in small women's groups in college so it was something I was very familiar with. It was the time of women's liberation and everybody was grouping.

What women offer each other is a nest to come into – the nest of women's consciousness. It's like the mother or the sister – all of that wonderful energy that women share, and even though you can have that in the larger community, when you have a group of women who are focused on each other, you're receiving a lot. You're receiving the listening. You're able to give your heart to others. It's profound. It's deep.

Annette Cycon: I was thrilled when my friend Sara asked if I wanted to be in a women's group with her and some of our women friends. Having a soulful place to be with other women talking about our life journeys, what a vision! At the time my children were very little. I had a two-year-old and a four-year-old, so my world was completely consumed with that. I described myself this way: in a garden you have the rich, lovely soil where things are growing, and you have the paths in the middle that are beaten down and rock hard. That's what I felt like. I felt like I was the path and I needed some tilling. I had lost myself tremendously and needed that soil to fluff up so that I could grow back again. I knew that being in a group with women was going to be a place where my soul would revive.

Younger Men's Group

Dave Ratzlow: I met Joshua and he is such a lovely guy I just wanted to hang out with him more. One time we hung out for several hours and he told me about this men's group that he was in for the last year or so and I asked if I could come. A couple of months later I came to the first meeting – a little less than a year ago. A chunk of the time was spent checking in where everyone was at in their lives, what they were thinking about and doing. As it was presented to me, it's a group that's committed to undoing sexism and figuring out what men can do to do that.

Re-evaluation Counseling,* with which I have been involved for many years, has a policy where if you meet somebody in the group you guys are not friends. You can develop very intimate relationships – in fact, I have more love for some of these people than anybody

---

* Re-evaluation Counseling, or RC, is a "co-counseling" practice – peer-based counseling focused on mutual help and support, with an emphasis on bringing about social reform.

– and yet we're not friends. This means we don't hang out, we don't have sex, we don't engage in business together – only a counseling relationship and the logic is clear. You don't want to spoil that relationship or make it ineffective.

I wanted some more friends and particularly male friends. Most of my friends are women and part of the reason for that is that a lot of men are sexist and that's a real turn-off. So to have relationships with men who are at least looking at their sexism and consciously trying to subvert their sexism is a big bonus. The other thing about RC is that it is mostly women. I would say at least 75 percent women. So for guys to work on their sexism, it's very difficult in RC, because there are not a lot of guys around and things move very slowly. I needed a place to work on that and look at it and talk about it on a regular basis. Even if we're not friends – I only hang out with Joshua – just having that contact with other guys has been great.

Four more members of the group told me that what they find in the group is precisely what drew them to it:

Josh Latour: I see the group helping me with my own needs as a man and with being a better ally as well as with managing my relationships with women by being emotionally more aware. The group encourages me to be more emotionally available, to be a better listener, and to be more informed about how to be with other men.

Ben Blackshear: Our group offers the opportunity for structured reflection. We also come for the camaraderie. There are times when we offer one another advice. I have also received – and offered – emotional support.

Kevin Quirolo: I see our group as a space to develop emotional intimacy with other men, based on a shared commitment to anti-oppression politics. It also offers me opportunities to practice patience with others and myself.

Ben Fuller-Googins: The practice of sharing has been critical. One of the features of patriarchy and toxic masculinity is the feeling that a lot of the traits and habits are my own – thoughts about sex or about women or the inability to be in relationship. Then I pathologize my own issues, so coming together and sharing in a group lets me know there are others who have similar feelings and tensions, which is very healing.

I believe that, because patriarchy is a system, healing must be done as a system, collectively, so I joined a men's group recognizing that transformation is not a solo endeavor. It requires being in communion with others. The group has been a collective body to struggle, share, and practice together. Being with other men promotes the understanding that transformation and healing cannot be done solely on my own. I feel a heightened urgency and desire to connect with other men about how patriarchy shapes our relationships to ourselves, with others, and to the world.

Younger Women's Group

Liz Sharp: We met each other in different ways, but as life happened the group pulled us all closer, naturally solidifying us as a group of women who really enjoyed each other. Our weddings have been the through line. The turning point that drew us together in the way we're so close now, and what was so wonderful and special to me, was Amelia moving away and saying, "I don't want to lose this. I'm afraid that we're all just going to drift apart. So can we do a monthly chat?"

I thought, "Oh, that's a great idea," and then, "Is this

going to be something I'm going to be frustrated that I have to fit into my schedule?" I had never done a video chat before. It sounded like a great idea. I wanted to stay in touch with everyone, but was it going to really work? I never anticipated at the start that it was going to turn into something that would be so steady and so necessary. I'm so thankful for it now.

At the beginning we sometimes wouldn't get it together for a couple of months, or one of us would be unavailable, but it never stopped or drifted off. Someone would always bring us back to center. I wish I could pinpoint when it took a turn, but I can't. It's more that all of us came to realize that we were getting much more from it than just, "Here's what's happening in my life... Alright, see you in a month." It was very organic.

Naomi Lutra: My motivation is about being and staying connected, staying up to date on what everybody is up to. In this world of social media there is the veneer of updates that you can get from a very wide network of friends, but this is less about, "Let me tell you where I traveled," and more about, "Let me really talk about this experience that I had," where we ask for advice.

When we were still living in the same area, we would try to do dinner. Almost without exception, by the time it got to be that day, I'd think, "I'm so exhausted. I have to put out all this energy to go to this dinner." Then I would go and get so much energy back from it. I would feel so rejuvenated by how inspiring these women are and how connected we all are and how we know each other in such a deep way. The video chats also really feed me and make me feel rejuvenated. Yes, it's one more thing on the calendar, one more commitment, but it really does give energy back and that's a hard thing to find.

Heather Price: The group provides a constant and consistent support to me in my life. It's a source of friendship and encouragement. It's wonderful to be able to stay connected with everybody in this way. Some I get to see in person more often than I do others, just because of distance. Even aside from those meetings in between, it's so nice to know that we all connect on a regular basis and talk about our lives and what's going on and encourage and support each other when each of us individually needs it. It's hard to identify what it doesn't provide because it provides so much.

Men and women join support groups for various reasons, based on our individual experiences in this culture. Seeking intimate connection and striving to create and be in a place where such connections are dependable and satisfying are foundational to the reasons for joining offered by all the members of these four groups. Within that impulse there are noticeable gender differences in some of their reported motives. Men committed to undoing sexism personally and societally is a key motivator for both of the generations of men's groups. Women finding a place to feel safe in this sexist society is true for both women's groups. In the end, everyone I interviewed sought a loving community – "a chosen family," as almost all of them expressed it – in which to give and receive heartfelt compassion over time and with the same people, who accept them for who they are.

CHAPTER 5
WHAT MAKES A GROUP TICK?
WHAT ARE THE NORMS?

It is necessary, as each of the group members interviewed has expressed, that a group have **agreements** that each person adheres to in order for the group to last. Some of the norms that will emerge in this chapter have similarities, most particularly those pertaining to confidentiality. There are also significant variations that have much to do with the makeup of the group, as well as when it began and how it has evolved over time.

Another key component that transcends the age of the members or the duration of the group is **commitment**. Each group determines what is required for membership, insofar as "showing up" and being present are concerned. But regardless of the specifics, the degree of commitment is definitely a source of a group's strength as well as a source of potential conflict when one or more members waver in their commitment.

Since the groups I have studied are leaderless and have been created by one or more of the participants, the structures that are in place are the result of evolutionary discoveries as well as experiences individuals have had in other groups and other organizations. Seeing what has and has not contributed to group cohesion, shared vision and mutual satisfaction has resulted in each of these groups standing the test of time, from the three years of the younger men's group to the 40 years of the older men's group.

In addition, identifying a **purpose** for the group that the founders and those they reached out to could agree on has helped immeasurably in sustaining the groups. Whether this purpose is political, social or spiritual, or some combination, being as clear as possible from the outset provided a reference point to return to if the group felt it was beginning to stray from the original vision.

Ways of relating to one another are predicated on mutual respect and trust, as well as providing sufficient time for each person to feel like their needs are getting met, and in the case of the two older groups, enjoying a meal together. All these elements contribute to a shared sense of **belonging**. This is the ultimate goal – to create that sense of being part of a well-chosen family.

Here are some of the ways in which group members see the role of having a set structure with specific "ground rules" that inform that structure.

Older Men's Group

Alan Suprenant: We all came to experience trusting one another. I feel like the trust kept building. When the group started, we didn't necessarily jump to trust. I try to extend trust in a lot of situations first, and then be prepared to have it taken away or not. I try to hold that up as something I do in general – assuming the better of somebody as opposed to the worst of somebody. It's giving them the benefit of the doubt. I think the group did that. We took something of a risk to put ourselves out on another level with people who wanted to do that same thing. We fed each other. I like the sounding board aspect of the group when we do a go-around. I don't feel like it needs to be everybody, but I've gotten a lot back from that. I just need people to listen and to talk about something I'm experiencing. For myself, when I'm doing it, I don't always feel like it's "reporting," which I know a couple of men in our group feel. We don't do it every group, and I like the mix. I wouldn't want to give up the five or six people who do the go-around, even three. I like that attention, which I learned in Re-evaluation Counseling. I like that from the group. Getting that from eight people is very healing and very supportive. Even if you don't need healing, you do need to be supported.

A big change needed to take place in the older men's group when it was starting to get bogged down with meeting too often, but not feeling the connection that had been one of its key purposes. As the group was on the verge of collapsing, one of its members had an inspired notion that, looking backwards, made the next decades of group cohesion possible:

> **Stephen Bannasch**: I think it was about a year after we started, and it got more and more difficult to meet every week. People felt as though their lives were full and this was an obligation and they weren't getting as much out of it as they wanted from putting in that much time. They still liked it, but it seemed to me people were coming with a lot of stress. When you come with a lot of stress, your attention is not as good. So you may be thinking, "I should be doing this. I want to do this, but I'm stressed about doing this," which also means that the value you get out of the time you're spending every week becomes less.
>
> People had gotten to a point where we were thinking of stopping. We were just meeting too often and we were not getting enough out of the sessions. I said, "Well, I think the solution is to meet more, but to do it less often." I remember suggesting we meet once every month for a whole day as opposed to every week for a couple of hours. It was pretty clear to me that this was an interesting reversal because people felt like they were becoming over-obligated. If I can, when I make a point, I often like to make it in a way that has an interesting pivot. I can imagine myself saying, "Let's meet more." And then the pivot is, "Let's do it once a month." I can imagine myself doing that intellectually to get people engaged, because people will first say, "What?" and then, "Oh..."

Digging a bit deeper into the testimony of another older men's group member, Gary Phillips, it turns out there was another factor in the recommendation that Stephen Bannasch made for the group to meet less often for more hours. Here's how Gary remembers the evolution:

> **Gary Phillips:** Our basic group jelled pretty quickly and we met to great excitement. It was a group that at

the time felt very diverse to me because it was diverse in age, diverse in background, diverse in class. So that was very exciting and people inside that group were excited to meet and the basic group that still exists was that group. I felt frustrated because in our early times, at the end of every meeting, I felt like we were just beginning to get into the meat of what we were doing and that was a frustration to me that I expressed several times. We found our own way out of that and it's a way that I have used as a model for the rest of my life in working with intense groups, which is that we decided to do a weekend retreat. During that retreat, we gave our personal histories. Every single person in the group got a good concentrated, carefully listened to time between an hour and a half to four hours. Time to lay out everything they could possibly lay out on the table to very, very good attention from eight or nine other men and it transformed our relationships in such a dramatic way that two evening meetings a month were no longer viable for us. That's when we chose to begin working with monthly meetings and pretty much all-day meetings.

To say it ended up working would be classic understatement. Stephen Bannasch provided the framework that took the group from the doldrums into a world of possibilities and the group has never looked back. I remember when I was invited to join the group in 1989, having just left my once-a-week group of ten years' duration, that I questioned as a very involved husband and father to my 19-year old daughter, my 14-year-old son and my one-year-old daughter, whether I could make the commitment of a whole day each month. Needless to say, I found a way to make it work, which included bringing first my daughter, Madeline, at one, and later my son, Stefan, when he arrived in our family, to men's group.

Then there is the eternal question of how much structure is enough vs. too much.

Tony Clarke: When a group has been together a really long time, some things change and some things stay the same. There was a lot more endless-feeling talk about process earlier on. I think that talk has decreased a lot in recent years, although I don't think a year goes by that it doesn't come up in some way, on some level, in terms of how we focus our attention. Should there be an agenda? Should our time together be free-form? Should we let what happens happen, or should we have a focused topic? Should there be a dedicated sharing circle time where everybody goes around and has so many minutes to share or should it just happen spontaneously in the course of spending the day together? These issues I don't think will ever be finally resolved, because there are always people who lean in one direction instead of the other. I've always been in the "let it flow spontaneously" camp.

Now for a major disclaimer. It turns out that it is no accident that both the older men's and women's groups allotted an entire Sunday once a month to their gatherings. One of our men's group members used to be married to one of the women in the women's group. To facilitate their schedule, when the woman started her group, she requested that it meet on the third Sunday of the month for most of the day, as ours did. Given that mirroring, what follows is an example of how the time gets divvied up so everyone feels heard.

Older Women's Group

Susan Loring-Wells: I really appreciate how when we arrive we get organized as to how we will divide our time for the day. Some people have their agendas and that's fine, but it's never pushed or not worked out. When the group makes a decision, it's a consensus for how we break up the time. One thing I love in this group is having our meal together. I love the eight-hour block of time we give ourselves each month. We do lunch together. In general the check-ins are spacious. There's an opportunity to have feedback or not and I like that. You decide whether you want feedback in your allotted time. If you're in a vulnerable state and you don't feel like getting feedback in that moment, it doesn't mean you won't talk about it during lunch or at another point in our time together. Sometimes you just need to release and talk the whole time. We put on a timer and ask, "Do you want the full, let's say 20 minutes to talk or do you want to stop the timer at 12 minutes and then decide if you want feedback." You get to choose. There are people who are heavy on the feedback – they need to have time-keeping there at the feedback end. Sometimes it's easier to have that part of the conversation at a meal. During the meal the interaction can break off and you can get the feedback from one or two people or it can happen on the walk we almost always take.

Here's how other members saw the evolving awareness of time that the older women's group developed:

Diane Norman: By the time I got there in 2006, there was a desire by some people to do less talking and more moving, so half the day was devoted to some kind of outdoor activity. Then we share a meal and everybody contributes to that and then there's time for just checking in, long sharings, deciding if there's a topic we want to talk about and how to use the time.

I think this structure started right about the same time I came in. Sometimes people skip part of the day because of other priorities, but we have tried to commit to being there the entire time. There have definitely been issues that have arisen regarding coming late and leaving early, so there continue to be ongoing discussions reviewing and revamping circle norms and expectations. It is always a work in progress as we change individually and as a circle entity itself.

Annette Cycon: It's evolved in the women's circle. We were much stricter in the beginning. We had much stricter guidelines and commitment requirements, which for me was actually kind of hard, because my kids were little. A couple of people didn't have kids at all. Leaving for a whole day when you have a three-year-old and a five-year-old is not an easy thing to do. That kind of commitment was hard. Now that we are all older and have been together for 22 years, we try to be more flexible, while at the same time not losing the commitments that make a container strong.

Sara Schley: I remember in the early days, for me, we didn't move enough. We would sit and have long check-ins and just the way I'm wired I'd start getting antsy. Over the years, partly because I would give voice to that, we now get outside for some chunk of every time that we're together and I like that.

Our women's circle has offered so much. It offered the predictable structure, the consistency of that and the rhythm of that. The clarity of what was happening, so we could make space was really helpful. And it's been a long time now. It also offered connection, a place to be witnessed, a place to share the whole range of feelings.

Younger Men's Group

I interviewed Kevin Quirolo and Ben Blackshear together. Here is their dialogue about their group's structure.

Kevin: Our structure is like post-Occupy Wall St. No megaphones, lots of screaming. What I mean by that is that everyone has a cooperative movement background so there's a lot of horizontalism and facilitation and consensus-based decision-making. That's what everyone is comfortable with.

The way it is set up now, one of the limitations, especially if we want to plan more logistical things and do support work, is that we often don't have enough time built in to do that and do all the kind of deeper check-ins.

Ben: We've always done a check-in. In the beginning it was pretty short because we didn't know each other. If you were to do a graph, I think you'd see that the check-in takes up most of the meeting now. In the middle space we would do a check-in and we would do a workshop of some type, usually taken from Chris Crass's *Towards Collective Liberation: Anti-Racist Organizing, Feminist Praxis,* and *Movement Building Strategy.*

Our idea of what our structure would be for a while was that we would meet and do different types of workshops with the idea that after trying out a few of these in our group, we would then organize and facilitate some public workshops. There was a group called the Challenging Male Supremacy Project. We had dinner with one of them at one point. We read through their curriculum and picked a couple of workshops we wanted to do. We've really only done one of them. The workshop idea has instead morphed into more personal check-ins, and it's usually been that there is something pressing in the check-in that we should process together.

It's been frustrating at times, but it always feels like it's O.K. What's most frustrating is the time issue. We want to do all of these things and we end up doing what's most pressing. Sometimes that's more satisfying than others.

Our group started off as a Sunday morning thing. It's always been two hours. That became hard. It's been really ad hoc for the last six months.

Kevin: When we meet we try to figure out the next time we can meet, which is just a random day of the week, usually a Monday. It's mostly been weekdays from 7:00-9:00 p.m. We snack and it's usually at Josh and Dexter's house in downtown Brooklyn. It's been almost always once a month, but some months we do twice a month.

Ben: We've tried to establish a more regular schedule – like the third Monday of every month now. We're also trying to have a second thing, like we all do a social thing together or we all do some sort of political thing together. Kevin and I attended a Showing Up for Racial Justice (SURJ) meeting together, which was great. Ben* and I did a march one time. We've had exceptions to the structure a few times where it's gone to four or five hours and those were amazing conversations – in some ways our greatest successes.

Younger Women's Group

Amelia Olsen: We are more fluid than what I understand about my mother's group. Our agreement is the first Monday of the month at 8:00 or 8:30 p.m. who ever can make it makes it. Sometimes it's four of us and sometimes it's all 6 of us and sometimes we reschedule. It's organized talking. Whoever is bubbling over starts and it naturally leads to another thing and we'll talk about that.

We know each other's rhythms. If someone is quiet, we know how to reach out. If something feels unfinished we'll keep going. We go like this until we start falling asleep.

Michelle Chanson: It's important that each person gets her moment to share whatever is going on in her life – whether it's just a simple update of how her week has been or if there is a particular challenge that she's having for which the group can provide advice and support.

---

* Ben Fuller-Googins – yes, there are two Bens in the group, as there are two Stephens in the older men's group.

It's not a formal structure. We just want to ensure that everyone gets their moment to share and

to shine. We're not a shy group, so everybody weighs in. Since everyone is spread out geographically, we really dedicate time to catch up and hear what's going on in everyone's lives. Since we use video chat, we can always see each other's faces, so it allows for more of a human connection than just a phone call would.

Amelia sometimes brings her kids on the call, depending on their bedtime. As more people have children and we want to see those children, they will be brought into the calls where it makes sense. I can see that becoming something that is more a part of it.

Liz Sharp: In the beginning one person would start the conversation and we'd each get ten minutes to talk. We set it up so we were each going to get a platform to talk about everything that was going on and then the rest of the group would respond and then the person who initiated the call would say, "Alright, we need to move on." That just gradually fell away. It was a useful crutch in the beginning: We want to talk, but we're not sure how to in this format. It was less confusing and gave it some trajectory. Then that didn't feel necessary after a while, although we do in a way still follow it in that all of a sudden someone will say, "Alright, what about you? What's happening with you?" and the spotlight is turned.

Recently a friend whose four-person men's group has met for almost two years shared their ongoing debate about how much time needs to be devoted to checking in versus how can each man delve deeply into his life. Lack of or too much structure can clearly make or break a group, but the essential ingredient in being able to stay together, as the older groups have done, appears to be the combination of trust and commitment – both of which need to be on full display when negotiating potential changes to the way a group runs.

CHAPTER 6
WHAT DO YOU CONTRIBUTE TO THE GROUP?

Being able to accentuate one's own positives proved to be a daunting task for virtually all of the folks I interviewed. Serious pauses following the question, "What do you contribute to your group?" characterize each taped interview. It certainly required thinking about the role one plays in a group that has so much significance. No one wanted to answer perfunctorily. I was invariably pleased with what ultimately emerged, as participants acknowledged what sounded like essential contributions to the group's functioning. Their thoughtful responses were also a great complement to my next question, what members feel they receive from the group. That will be explored in the next chapter.

Older Men's Group

Tony Clarke: It's hard for me to be self- reflective, in terms of what I bring to the group. I think, if I look back, I bring a sense of caring to the group. I think all the men do. I think part of me is a caretaker kind of personality. When I see things that aren't being done, I'll step in. As an example, one of my pet peeves with the group is that most of the men are horrible about cleaning up. You go to somebody's house, we get through dinner and seven out of nine are out the door and whoever's house it is gets stuck with all the dishes. I think that's really rude and nasty. And I've brought it up before. It doesn't change. But I always tend to stay and help do some of the dishes because that's who I am.

I think there are other ways in which I care-take the group, in terms of thinking about people and speaking to the different issues. Then there's our retreat. I have a camp in upstate New York. It's a very beautiful, special place. I've been able to share that with the group in a way that has now become a yearly retreat that we go to for four or five days and spend some time in a very beautiful place together. I've been lucky in my life that that very special place, on one of the 1000 Islands in the St. Lawrence River, has been given to me through marriage and I've been lucky to do well in life to be able to afford that kind of thing.

Stephen Bannasch: I bring a deep interest in other people and how they think. I think I bring a very interesting combination of logic and creativity. I think it's often pretty easy for me to think abstractly about many different patterns and how they relate and how levels of patterns relate. I think a lot of people don't think that way. I think I contribute that to the group, but I contribute hopefully where it's helpful. I'm not describing some great way of thinking. It happens to be the way I think, and sometimes it can actually be very helpful. The way I spoke about changing our time (from bi-weekly for two to three hours to monthly for an entire Sunday) was a reframe and it's also a different way of thinking about something.

Another thing I think I'm really good at in the group and in other places is listening really well and being able to see something from multiple people's perspectives and come up with something helpful that connects the two or three or four. One of the things Steve (Trudel) has often said is that we have a group mind. When I hear that statement I think, "What does that mean?" Part of what it means to me is that I have a lot of trust in the thinking and feeling we do together. I actually will tend to rely on it, though "rely" is not quite the right word, but what I realized is that that is the way I think. Other people have possibly said things like that, which doesn't mean I didn't think it, but at this point it's harder for me to pull out and see what was actually my idea, and what are other people's ideas, because they combine.

Robbie Leppzer: In terms of giving, I feel like I give myself. I give my own story. I give my perspectives, my experience. I feel like I give my compassion, my wisdom. We are a collective group of entities so it's the contribution of each and every one of us that creates the collective whole. I feel like we all contribute ourselves and in doing so we create this collective whole.

Gary Phillips: I believe I contribute a political discourse from another plane of existence. I contribute, and I've always contributed, a particular spiritual and poetical discourse that I love. I'm also emotional in a very Southern way that I think sometimes helps ground the group. I have an extraordinary love and admiration for every single member of the group. Even if I tried to shield myself from those feelings I wouldn't be able to, because it is so powerful in my life. It is such a powerful gift in my life. I hope that that shines through when I am with the group and participating in the group.

Older Women's Group

Susan Loring-Wells: I am a good documenter. I take a lot of photographs and I just love the part of going outside together with intention. Also, it's not just going for a walk when we're out there. We usually do something, a kind of gratitude or singing together. For me that's my sort of spirituality and church – Nature. I was brought up Unitarian and I'm not really a believer too strongly in God, but I appreciate all my Jewish friends in the circle and how they have a relationship that way. My dance with spirit or God or however I want to call it – I love the reverence with which it is held in our circle and I am really happy to have some of the Jewish tradition in the group and to be part of it. It feels really good to me. I didn't know much about Judaism growing up. I had one Jewish friend in my class. So I'm loving that part.

I hold back in sharing with the group, much as I do in general. I was in a book group the other day and I said nothing. That's just who I am. It's a tender subject. I don't think of myself as a deep thinker and it makes me sad. I don't know how you change that at this point in life. The group has definitely helped me be more interested in a bigger range of subjects than I was before.

Diane Norman: Occasionally I bring an edge of challenge to what someone may be saying, which may not always be welcomed. I know there are skillful and not-so-skillful ways to give feedback to one another. Obviously, the intent is to be able to hear and say things in a way that we can help each other understand ourselves better and maybe even change. But sometimes the uncontested support gets "old" for me and I have this fantasy that someone might just come straight out, unedited, and challenge my own stuck patterns, if they see them. It doesn't feel like there's a lot of room for a certain type of "raw" honesty.

It is like there is a level of "editing of truth" we do, when we blanket our feedback in only traditional words of love and support rather than, perhaps, challenging the beliefs or stories any one of us might be telling ourselves. I don't always feel there is a place for this other kind of loving support because, as women, we are conditioned to be non-confrontational and mostly agreeable. Are there not ways to give uncomfortable feedback without fear of shaming or alienating one another? I believe this is a growing edge for me in relationship to this circle of beloved friends.

Nancy Knudsen: I bring whatever my own resources are – my wisdom, my way of being in the world, my heart. My thinking of myself as a therapist is there with me, but my role is not there with me. I'm not facilitating. I'm not in charge of guiding whoever is struggling. I may have some things to add. In that way, sometimes I can struggle a little with how to find my voice because it's a different role. The way our time is structured, there will be a limited time for feedback and then somebody else is going to be sharing in a few minutes, so there really isn't anything I'm going to do with this. I'm just going to hear it and witness it and offer a presence.

Sara Elinoff Acker: First and foremost, I show up. I prioritize the group in my calendar and work hard to fend off other commitments, so I can be there for my women. I also bring my organizing and planning energy for outings to beautiful places and creative projects. But really, it's about what we all bring collectively – leadership, love, listening, wisdom, humor, presence. I think what I contribute, which we all contribute, is that we listen really deeply. And we share a commitment to help each other grow into the best people we can possibly be. We have so much intimacy, which includes being aware of each other's flaws and our own. We can be fully human with each other and still feel loved and accepted.

Sara Schley: There's times when I show up and I bring a lot of "joie de vivre." I'll bring a lot of humor and a lot of blessing – a lot of energy and a lot of "Let's do this and this and this together." Get outside... And uplift. I have done shadow work,* so I can also bring my skills as a shadow work facilitator if that's needed – the concept that all of you is welcome here – all parts. A lot of times over the years I would end up informally facilitating a piece of work for our group. If somebody had something up big, the group would say, "Let's give her time." For example, one of the women was about to have both of her ovaries removed, so we did a shadow-work piece where her ovaries got to talk.

I also offer unconditional love of everyone in the circle. I'm holding that – whatever is going on for them, blessing them, loving them. I think all of us do that, but it is certainly something I bring – kind of

---

* Shadow work is the conscious effort of exploring one's "shadow," as expressed by C.J. Jung – the dark feelings, often ignored, that bring up shame, embarrassment and fear. Many of these shadow feelings are not on the surface and reside in the subconscious.

showering people with love so it's a safe place for them to show up. The group offers connection, a place to share the whole range of feelings. We reach out to each other a lot – both in the group and outside of the group – in good times and bad times. We've got a text stream going now.

Annette Cycon: I think I bring to our circle my groundedness and stability. I try to be steady and positive, loyal, a classic Taurus. People know what they can expect from me. I think people know they can expect a really good meal from me, a really big hug, an insightful, deep conversation and a huge belly laugh.

Being with my women's group gets me in touch with Spirit, Love and my Higher Self, so I'd like to think I bring my best self to group.

Younger Men's Group

Ben Fuller-Googins: I feel that generally in my life I am a good listener, a good listening presence. That serves the group well, because for me one of the functions and benefits of the group is to have a safe space where men can really open up and feel vulnerable and create intimacy around sharing things. I like to think that my presence of being very attentive helps that happen. If someone is talking, I'll direct my presence to them and I'll notice if other people are checking their phone. If someone is sharing, to me that is very sacred. So that is one of my offerings.

Kevin Quirolo: I think the things I contribute – everyone else is kind of flowy, as Ben said, and my posture is that this group needs more structure and direction, and everyone needs to be kept in line and put in containers. I'm also wary of that because it can be counterproductive, but that's a contribution. I also feel like I try to judiciously ask pointed questions of people when they're telling some story. I'll say, "That's interesting... Why did you do that?" I try to do that. It's a skill I'm working on. Or I am someone who tries to flag the things that people don't know to flag, like, "Oh, you thought that was an incidental detail, but actually that's what you need to talk about."

Younger Women's Group

Liz Sharp: I do try to be a really good listener, an empathetic listener, but I think we all do that. I laugh a lot and that's something that is often present on the calls. I think about the call and there's something there beyond who I am. It's a connecting point. I'm not thinking about the things I do well and that I can offer. It's just about showing up as I am, where I am, which is sometimes dead exhausted, especially when I was working early-morning hours, and as soon as I got off the call I'd rush to bed. Because of that, I bring more honesty. When I started my cooking work, I was just more tired and I think we're more honest when we're tired.

I like to listen and to hear where people are and to give advice from my viewpoint and experience that I know is sometimes really similar to what other group members are going through. Sometimes it's not at all similar, because we've taken such different paths and experienced such different things in our working lives and our personal lives and we're really open to all of that with each other. We've all had unique situations in dealing with difficult things and I just try to be as honest and helpful from my perspective and my experiences as I can without assuming that my experiences are going to be just like anyone else's I'm talking to in our group.

Amelia Olsen: I think that the others would say I am very pragmatic and the one who is the most direct. When we're all on the phone thinking something, I'll be the one that says it. It would be so interesting to hear what they would say about me. We all are listeners. We all are problem solvers for each other and cheerleaders.

That comment of Amelia's, when I interviewed her a couple of weeks before I was privileged to join one of the group's videophone sessions, planted a seed. I wondered if other members would also be interested in one another's perceptions. It turned out that when I was speaking with the whole group, I asked them if they would be open to sharing their view of another group member's contributions to the group – and to my great delight, they were. Were they ever! All six jumped at my suggestion that they each give voice to what they believe one of their fellow groupmates contributes to the group's functioning. What ensued was an extraordinary outpouring of insight, emotion and appreciation. Here are those reflections:

> **Naomi about Amelia:** This is not about just in this group. This is how she operates in the world, but it really comes through in this group. Amelia has this incredible superpower of being able to say exactly what somebody needs to hear in a way that you might not be able to hear from anybody else. I've heard her say it to me and I've also heard her say it to other people. I wish I could have been brave enough to say the things she says. There's a sense that when she is offering her support and her perspective, that it comes from truly wanting the best for that person and wanting the world to be a better place and wanting all of us to be operating with honesty and kindness and full-heartedness at all times. It's such a superpower. There are times in my day when I think about the group, "What would this person do in this situation?" but in particular when I need to truly stand in my values and kindly and gently urge someone towards a harder truth, "What would Amelia do?" is my go-to.

> **Charlie about Naomi:** For the record, Naomi said verbatim everything I was going to say about Ame-

lia and a lot of what she said holds true for Naomi as well. She has this wonderful ability to step back and see your situation, your issue, your challenge, your blessing – whatever it is you're going through – and give this lovely, kind, objective perspective on things. She doesn't always do it for herself, but she's great at doing it for us. I think that she is able to look at things from a different angle when you are wrapped up in your own world and you can't always see things from a different perspective. She always has this perspective of moving forward, not staying still and never waiting to see what happens, but making your own path. She's able to verbalize that in a way that makes sense, that helps you feel like you figured it out on your own, but you didn't because you're doing exactly what she suggested you do, but with such gentleness and kindness, but also with this fierceness of, "You can do anything. You can absolutely do it." She's always been that. She's been that way since she was 12. She takes on the world with this vibrant spirit and very rarely stops to rest. Our calls give her the stillness to see herself and to see what an important role that she plays for us – independently and for the group.

Heather about Charlie: I've known Charlie since elementary school. Putting aside all of the amazing memories we've created and adventures we've gone on over the years, the thing that she brings to the calls and to all of our lives is this incredible sense of selflessness. The thing that I love the most about Charlie is that any time in my life when I have really needed her, she has been there. She has always been there for all of the important things. She will drop everything and come be by your side when you need her to. She has been there for graduations and weddings and family events and reunions. She prioritizes us.

A lot of us do get caught up in the craziness and business of our everyday lives. I always have a million things running through my head – "What are my plans for the week? What meetings do I have to pre-pare for?" These calls help ground me and slow me down. They make me stop, take a break and focus on the parts of life that are more important than my to-do list. Charlie has this wonderful ability to always make time for you and show unconditional support and love. Her heart, her selflessness and the way in which she prioritizes her friends really stand out to me.

Amelia about Heather: Heather plays this dis-tinct and special role in my life, and in everyone she touches, of being the center. She has this gravitational pull that draws everybody in. She creates a welcoming protective cocoon, a home base – even in New York, where nobody creates a home that people come to. It's her nature, her essence as a creator of community and safe space. She's nurturing in a way that is motherly and has this equality to it. "Motherly" doesn't quite capture it – she's naturally, for me, the place you always want to go. You always want to invite yourself over to virtually be with Heather or physically be with Heather. And because of that fact, she has the biggest birthday parties you've ever seen.

But whether it's to have a party or to sit and be girls, have a lazy Sunday or put your head in her lap and sob – it's this chameleon quality of safe space to me. She brings it with her natural intuition about people and compassion and I don't think there is any other person that I've experienced this with – both physically and emotionally. I don't think she can help but bring it. I think that's why so many people are just drawn to her.

Liz about Michelle: Michelle is a superstar – truly. She talks about how busy she is, but I think Michelle is busy on a level that goes beyond anyone I've ever known, and yet she accomplishes all of it with such grace. There are so many things. She's a world traveler and yet is the fastest responder whenever you need something, whenever you have a question, whenever anything is going on in any way, whether it's dinner plans or if you want her to look at something you've bought. When I'm working on things and I want to be successful I think, "What would Michelle do? How would Michelle jump in and solve this right now and move on to the next challenge and not get bogged down?" She's incredible at that – just incredible at being an explorer and a woman of the world, a true powerhouse leader.

Heather (can't resist chiming in): And so consistently so! Michelle has this commitment to her friendships since the first day that I began calling her my friend, quite a few years ago at this point. It is unwavering – her support and her dedication. She is also the only person I know who always writes a handwritten thank-you note.

Michelle about Liz: I am so proud of Liz right now, because she is in the throes of starting her own business, so I feel like I'm getting a lot of inspiration from her as she starts to navigate this world. We've spoken about a lot of people on these calls just exuding warmth and kindness and gentleness and Liz just epitomizes that to the nth degree. She is always so openhearted. Every time you talk to her you feel that she is really listening. She is really interested. She cares. She is considering what you're saying. She's thoughtful about it. I've never seen her be anything but lovely to the people around her. She treats people with such respect and kindness. I've never seen her waver on that, which is really impressive. We all have moments where the world gets to you or something gets you and you snap at someone or you say something that comes off as really curt and you don't mean it in the moment. Liz is the most consistently warm person, and I am so excited to see where the next leg of the journey takes her, because I think that she is going to be an incredible business-person. I am sure she will build a wonderful community around her, because people will want to invest in her, not just because of the delicious food she makes, but because of who she is. I think that will be the key to her success. People are going to be drawn to her and to the persona that she exemplifies as she goes about creating this business. I am really excited to see where it takes her.

As previously mentioned, I interviewed Kevin Quirolo and Ben Blackshear, two members of the younger men's group, at the same time in in a Manhattan café. When they were discussing their own contributions to the group, as quoted above, Ben asked if he could tell me what he thinks Kevin brings to the group – a fortuitous supplement to the younger women's reflections on each other. Here is what Ben said about Kevin's contributions:

> **Ben:** I think Kevin brings a knowledge of theory and a history of applying that to his personal life that is really helpful for the group. I think part of what he is saying about pointing out what we don't always see is a reflection of that. It feels like he's done that a lot and he's read a lot and it helps us all bring that lens in. I also think he's good at admitting his own mistakes and being self-deprecating when he needs to be. That helps encourage everyone to be vulnerable, because we all have deep histories of messing stuff up. I feel like Kevin is often the first to share in a way that helps everyone be willing to do that. It creates that container for vulnerability. I really appreciate all of that.

In reviewing the various group members' comments included in this chapter, it occurred to me that the deep knowledge of each other gained over time from profound sharing, and the resulting love and devotion, make these relationships akin to a successful marriage. Although these last testimonies accentuate a whole host of positive qualities expressed so beautifully and devotedly, accepting the totality of each person – in a group as in a marriage – means also knowing their struggles and even personality traits, which can be challenging both for individuals and the group as a whole. Conflicts can and do arise from time to time, and this will be the focus of Chapter 11.

I hope that what emerges from this chapter above all is the variety of skills, talents, perspectives, awareness levels and emotional intelligence of the group members. The broader the range of these qualities a group possesses, the richer the interactions and the group's life will be – and vice versa. In subsequent chapters mention will be made at various junctures, by interviewees and myself, of the limitations of homogeneity in terms of race, class, sexual orientation and even the notion of single-sex groups. None of those comments, however, are meant to diminish the value of what the people in these groups give to one another.

CHAPTER 7
WHAT DO YOU RECEIVE
FROM THE GROUP?

As I mentioned in the previous chapter, many of the participants, asked to articulate their contributions to their respective groups, were hesitant at first, before movingly offering
their self-evaluations. Now let it be known that all of the 27
men and women I interviewed had not a moment's hesitation
in offering what they receive from their group experience.
Time and again I was the receiver of great appreciation for
the group's combination of love and challenge, and the challenge was always predicated on feeling safe and supported.

It definitely didn't matter which group the interview subject
was in – older or younger, male or female – when it came to
feeling that the value of being a group member was undeniable and worth whatever effort was required to make the
time and space in one's life to participate. The range of examples of when the support extended by the group felt so very
valuable and essential is broad, but the common denominator with each member was the trust they felt they could count
on when asking (or sometimes without even the need to ask)
for what they needed.

Of course, trust at the level these groups fostered was the
result of a process. It started with the shared desire to know
one another and to be known, and from there it grew based
on commitment. If and when individuals wavered in their
commitment, as we shall see in a subsequent chapter, it was
not simply skipped over, but rather the group sought ways
to address the issue. Without establishing the level of confidence in the group's wherewithal to give each member what
they needed, there would not be the staying power necessary
to building the kinds of compassionate and very present community each of these groups aspired to being.

I was moved by the level of emotion I heard throughout the
interviews when this question, "What does the group give
you?" was asked. It was also one of the topics that many
subjects came back to when I asked what insights the interview had provided. Here, then, are some of the responses this
question elicited:

Older Men's Group

Paul Richmond: During one of my harder break-ups I feel the group created a safe space. I went to a therapist during this particular time. I think I went twice and that therapist ended up telling me, "You don't need me." When he asked me what I was doing, and I told him about the men's group, he said, "You're doing it. It sounds like you have your support system. I'm here for people who don't have a support system.

I can remember the group allowing me the space, because I went through a stretch after that relationship ended where I couldn't stop crying and various things would bring up the crying. It wasn't a big deal. I could just go over to the corner and cry and they could keep having their conversations and I didn't have to feel like I was interrupting them, and they didn't act like I was burdening them or that I should just suck it up. I appreciated the group allowing me these various sessions during which I didn't have to explain, I didn't have to worry that I'm crying too much and that I could get disgusted with myself and say, "I'm crying now because I'm tired of crying. I don't know why I'm still crying about it. It's just there. It just really hurts somewhere deep."

To me the group tries to help and clarify and give people perspective that sometimes you might not even get in therapy. I learned that my pain over this relationship ending was connected to my fear of no one wanting to love me, that I will be alone. To acknowledge that and to love myself and not fear being alone and to acknowledge the pain of feeling alone and rejected made me stronger. I was given that by other men creating a safe place for me to be.

One other idea that really stands out in my mind comes from when you have a group that has a long time period together. It's almost like the old communities. People really know each other and I feel having that history enables you to talk to folks and say, "This is what you had hoped for and this is where you are." There's value and meaning in being able to offer each other that.

Gary Phillips: The group has been a platform for my entire life. In the film that was made of the group back in the early '80s, we were all asked to make statements. My statement was, "There will be a kiss in my heart for every man in this group forever," and that has absolutely held true. So there's been a thread of affection. I call up people in the group and I ask them their opinion of stuff. When I have interactions with them I take notes. I remember books that people are reading and I get those books. Like you and I – every time we talk there's a swath that happens in our minds. "Oh, I've got to think about that," "I've got to see that film," "I've got to get in touch with that person." That happens at all kinds of levels in the group that I absolutely love.

In the past year almost all of the members of the group have been at my house in North Carolina. They are definitely a part of my family. There's a certain kind of integrity of communication. I'm not saying it's absolute because nothing ever is, but we developed a kind of integrity in communication that I think we still try to abide by in all the ways we can.

In North Carolina, when I did a Bill Moyers project and helped create the Chatham County Political Reform Group across difference and brokenness – a multiracial group with an age span from 18 to 64 – I demanded that we begin by having a retreat and giving each other our personal histories. I promulgated within that group a kind of emotional honesty that became what the group was most famous for. It became a springboard, an incubator for a lot of things that happened that were very significant in my little county. I really give a lot of honor to the men's group for the maturity with which I could interact with that group, and also how I could form that group into its most powerful self.

Dick McLeester: The group has given me lots of support. When things were falling apart, when my relationships were ending and new relationships were beginning, the group was there for me. It feels like the men's group is part of my process – my two marriages, finding both partners in another country, unusual things about my life that sometimes make me wonder, "Am I totally crazy?" It feels like the men's group, even though there's been plenty of caution and concern expressed, has been a place where I can talk about my evolving process. I can count on being heard and to a certain extent being affirmed. I've heard, "Good luck with that," and "I hope the next check-in is a positive one for you," and "Communicate with us when you're in Peru. We're all curious as to how it goes." That's meant a lot to me.

Then there have been physical health challenges, like my issue with prostate cancer. That was huge. I felt like the medical establishment was giving me really negative energy and I was taking the steps to say, "You're fired. I don't want to work with you anymore." The men's group was a major source of support for figuring out my own way to make it work. I got a lot of inspiration from Llan,* who was taking care of his health in his own ways, as well as from everybody being able to share and talk about my process.

At times the group has challenged me, too. That's definitely true about my ongoing issue on the balance between work and the rest of my life, how that impacts my life and how it affected my first marriage, which

* Llan Starkweather, one of the original members, who is no longer part of the group.

ended in divorce. That was very difficult, and I am very grateful I had the men's group's support before, during and after going through that. The group has kept me from being more isolated. My tendency has been to overwork – to focus on my work and get cut off from other people and other things. Without the group to go to it could have been worse.

Steve Trudel: The group gave me the experience of being able to let go and realize that whatever happens is going to be O.K. We want to go to the Cape, then O.K., let's do that. Not think about it, not worry about it, but realize that I need that feeling of safety from a group experience with men.

I certainly like the longevity of the group in the same way that there's a way that you experience your own development and maturation.

Older Women's Group

Annette Cycon: In the decades that we have been together, this group has been through all my changes with me, supported me, given me tender advice and witness. I would not be who I am if it were not for them. They're my security, my sisters, my church, my safe haven, so even if I'm in a hard place in my life, I immediately get into a happy place when I'm with them. When I go to my group I feel like I'm in church. I feel like I'm at Thanksgiving dinner whenever I go to group! I go to group to eat a big yummy turkey dinner of love. I just love being with them.

I don't really go to group to fall apart emotionally though. Partly because just being with them makes the hard stuff disappear, and partly because I need a longer period of time to check in, to get to the deeper emotional stuff. We get 15 minutes to check in with five extra minutes for reflections from the group. So I often don't feel like that's enough time for me to delve

118

into deep stuff. That being said, I often leave group having gotten exactly what I needed, even if didn't expect it.

Morning Star Chenven: When we tell our stories to each other, we are met with deep listening and meaningful, constructive feedback. One time when I was having a major crisis in my family with one of my kids and I was desperate for help, the group was right there with me, helping me take action, calming my fears, holding me gently and strongly.

Things might be very intense for one of us, or it can be that we bring our more daily issues to each other and people offer their wise and loving advice. Getting together and exercising – walking, canoeing, hiking, biking, swimming – is also a wonderful thing that I receive from the group. Being active together is just plain fun and also encourages me to keep moving in my own life.

Sara Schley: One of the roles I play is as a facilitator. What I do professionally is facilitate circles, so I can do that for everybody, having a place to offer that kind of service – and then, on the receiving end, when stuff is up for me, having an opportunity to be held and seen and witnessed. So I can play the vulnerable one. That has happened for me at different times, where there's a lot of hard stuff going on for me in my life and people have just shown up for me, and that's wonderful.

One of the more challenging issues for me over the course of my time in this group is that I have a depression cycle. It shows up in the world as the two poles – one of feeling very empowered, very capable, very much a leader and a facilitator and very much a lot to offer. Then on the other hand, when I have had some really dark down times, what I call the "to hell and back club," the circle has really been there for me as a huge lifesaver. We've all been through stuff, where we've held each other in various ways.

Nancy Knudsen: I get seen in a way that I don't in other parts of my life if I'm sharing something about myself, because it goes deeper than a conversation with somebody. The structure allows for a kind of focus on one's self so that you can try to get to the heart of what's going on in your life. You have a little space to let that unfold. So I get seen in a different kind of way. In an hour of need I'm not alone. This year more than ever before in my life, when I found myself in a health crisis, it became very clear. I never had a chance to doubt that they'd be there for me.

Sara Elinoff Acker: I am being mothered by my group in a way I never got mothered. I grew up with a mother who was very wounded and didn't know how to see the good and offer blessings or delight in anything I did. She was all about seeing what was wrong, what wasn't happening and what wasn't good enough. She focused on the wrong things – how my hair looked, for instance, rather than on what I was feeling and thinking. I'm in my fifties now and recently I was with my mother. She was still making comments about my hair and weight, which is not just ridiculous and infuriating, but deeply sad. I feel she's always missed out on who I am on the deepest level.

But in my group, I feel seen and cherished for who I really am at the deepest levels of my soul. For those of us who grew up with wounding and wounded parents, we're re-parenting one another. We're creating a really intimate experience of loving, mothering, nurturing, blessing female relational energy. I know these women love me unconditionally. If I make an error and I'm not my best self, they will both hold me accountable and totally love me. When good things happen in my life, I know they're celebrating alongside me and are joyful for me. I feel seen. I feel known deeply. I feel honored. I feel protected. I feel nurtured. I feel blessed.

We've spent a lot of time talking about our relationships with our mothers. At least four of us had really negative, critical or depressed, toxic parents. Another woman in our circle lost her mother to cancer. The other women also had complicated relationships with their mothers. I think we've all been affected by how our mothers developed and by their own internalized self-hatred. The difference between their generation and ours is seismic. We're the women whose lives have been transformed by feminism. We were able to interrupt our self-hatred at an early age. We didn't judge our bodies or appearance in the ways our mothers judged themselves and other women. We developed beyond simply being wives and mothers. We were far more independent. We are able to talk about traumas we experienced, rather than keeping all that internalized and believing we were to blame. There are just so many things we were able to understand and do that our mothers didn't. That was the gift of the feminist movement. It's a gift that keeps on giving, by the way, as we age.

Younger Men's Group

Ben Fuller-Googins: My tendency is not to share. I'm usually someone who wants to give other people the opportunity. The way the group is structured I have uninterrupted time to share and that is very good for me – to have the opportunity to try to go a little deeper than I normally would around particular issues I have some shame around.

Kevin Quirolo: One of the things I take from the group is that I've learned a lot about group dynamics. It breaks out of the give-and-take distinction, because it's been created with the group. I also take a lot of peace of mind, because the process is sort of therapeutic. I've taken a lot of – actually instead of "taken" I'm going to say "learned" – I've learned a lot about dealing with the fact that everyone is in a different place in their understanding of themselves on a very basic level, their understanding of sexism on a very basic level, and their politics. You can't just send out a mass email and say, "Everyone who's read five books by bell hooks, we're going to have a meeting," and have a bunch of people show up, because everyone would have taken different stuff from them. So I've learned a lot about interacting with people and negotiating differences and priorities and visions.

Ben Blackshear: I value having a space for men to do emotional labor together and to process things. There was another thing that I was really looking for around the formation of the group. I was in a long period of being single, which I hadn't been for quite a while. I had been coming out of a lot of relationships where it had been my emotional home and I was wanting to find a place for emotional support and vulnerability outside of a romantic relationship. I think the group has really provided that.

In addition to trying to find other friendships, I've opened up a lot more with my roommates in that way, but it's really nice to have the group as another example of that. It allows me to be more balanced throughout my entire emotional life and less needy and dependent in the romantic relationships I have now, because I know it's not this be all and end all thing. I know that there are lots of people who can support me and I can tell things to.

It's been really helpful to have a safe place to do this emotional processing. It's really important for me to be doing that with other men and building the skills to do it well. It would be really fun for all of us to share how we feel about each other. We're really good about appreciating one another in our check-outs oftentimes, but it would be nice to do a structured reflection on that. One of the reasons that I am so happy to answer all of these questions with you is that we had talked about doing a big check-in at the end of Year One – what the group has meant to us – which we haven't gotten around to, but which would be really valuable, and this interview is getting me to think about our group.

There are things I've shared with these men that I haven't been able to voice with other people. Sometimes it's been about digging up some buried ghosts I have, in terms of how I've been socialized. I wasn't raised as an evangelical Christian, but I chose it for a while growing up and it was a big part of my identity. There was a lot of self-imposed sexual repression that I've been able to unpack with the guys and it's been really helpful to have a space for that, since I don't know who else I would have talked to about that part of my life. It was hard to do and it's been really valuable. There have been several meetings where I've ended it feeling like I've said things here I've never said before. That's how I know it was a really good night.

I think that the group has also provided a sense of accountability. Knowing it is a space to be emotionally vulnerable, when I know we have a meeting later that day or when I'm on the train going to it, I think through and reflect more than I would be likely to do if I didn't have this sort of thing. I think that's really important. It makes me check in with myself to see where I'm at, how I'm feeling right now, my commitments, how I'm really feeling. It's been valuable to me in certain times when I've been really low. There was a time earlier this summer when I was down in the dumps, because the people I was close to were out of town. I was feeling really drained by work and a variety of other factors. Meeting with the men's group and feeling held in those friendships and talking through it with the men's group – they were the first people I told I was feeling down - and just to have that space to share that with them was really valuable.

I feel very close to them now...

Younger Women's Group

Michelle Chanson: I'm a very social person. However, I tend to be the person in all of my friendships and relationships who is offering advice and rarely seeking it. I tend to problem solve in my head and keep moving forward. I don't have a lot of time or patience for getting hung up on things. This group is really good for me, because it forces me to share whatever challenges are on my mind. Because I run a business I'm used to thinking that when I have a challenge, I'm going to solve it, just work through it and get it done. So it's nice to have a group of people who are very open to saying, "Hey, we're here. Tell us what's going on. How can we help you troubleshoot this?" Sometimes you can think you're burdening people with things or you think, "No, I can fix this on my own." This group has been very therapeutic in that way for me. I don't know that I would proactively seek that sort of support on my own. I tend to be a person who is doing 50 things a day, just moving forward, making decisions very quickly, because I have to in my career. I sometimes forget that it's O.K. to rely on other people in those moments where you actually need advice and that it's not a burden. They're your friends and that's what they're there for.

Naomi Lutra: Certainly the group offers a variety of perspectives to situations I am grappling with. The group, but definitely each of the individuals in the group, is so gifted in knowing what a person needs to hear. I get both the soft feather bed of support and I also get pushed out of my comfort zone in really healthy ways.

When I took on a new job, they were there for all of that, even down to talking about salary negotiation and about what kind of money to ask for – asking for my value. We talked about how to balance following a passion in work and getting compensated. That is so taboo to talk about in society generally, especially for women, so to have a group of incredibly competent, professional, successful women having those conversations in a really open way is something I don't get anywhere else.

Amelia Olsen: It's this endless flow of support and inspiration. They keep me hungry in parts of my life that don't include my family. It's easy for me in this life stage to focus on being the best mom I can possibly be, get my kids into the best daycare, to take them to the park, to be the best wife and partner I can be, keep everyone healthy and create a joyful home. It's easy for those things to have the bigger balance of my attention. This group reminds me that we are whole complete people. It creates a space to remember that and to be inspired by that.

It's also a safe and productive place to vent to people who understand, especially about family and relationships. Challenges will come up in a long-term partnership and marriage. I am extremely careful about the privacy of my partnership and the complexity of it. Bringing something up in this group, the first reaction is going to be from a place of understanding, of perspective, not just "being on my side" or jumping to validate my reaction. We are invested in each other's partnerships.

This is the chapter that speaks most powerfully for itself and requires little by way of summary or conclusion. It is the chapter that is intended to provide the most compelling "sales pitch" for readers who are not already in a support group to join one. I hope the testimonies you've just read confirm that such a group can offer you meaningful benefits on many levels to make your life more satisfying.

CHAPTER 8
HOW DOES BEING IN THE GROUP AFFECT
WHO YOU ARE
AND
HOW YOU ACT IN THE WORLD?

As you've seen, many of my interview subjects said they joined their group to learn more about themselves through the closeness and intimacy of being in such a group. It feels immensely worthwhile, then, to discover how this effort has turned out. What does it look and feel like to have uncovered and unraveled the proverbial onion-skin layers of one's self in the group?

Obviously, this will be at least partly a function of the age and gender variations I've already mentioned. For my group, now in its fifth decade, there will be depths of self- and other knowledge that will be the product of our decades-long commitment to showing up for ourselves and one another for a whole day every month. The older women's group is in its third decade, and their bonds have been steadily developing through innumerable gatherings, crises and joyous outings. The younger, newer men's and women's groups have already experienced gains in self-awareness, and the contrast between their experiences and those of their older counterparts – as well as the influence of the different times in which we've come of age – will be interesting to observe in what follows. But there is a constant. Everyone I spoke with felt their group experience has enabled them to not only gain added perspective on themselves, but also to navigate their lives outside the group with the wisdom and compassion gained through the honest, supportive and challenging feedback they have received.

Older Men's Group

Tony Clarke: The group provides a good balance for me in terms of keeping me a little more socially conscious and attuned with thinking about issues of social change and how in little ways I might contribute to that. More than most people in the group, I have pursued the path of being the capitalist entrepreneur. My partner and I have built up a business that has been fairly successful and employs 40 people. Now it has its own building – the American story of going out and starting with nothing and building this business up.

127

In pursuit of that, it's pretty much consumed my life. When I joined the men's group I was in those early years. I worked as a carpenter doing odd jobs. How I allocated my time was very, very different. I was much more actively participating in events, going to protests and dealing with social change. As I got swept up in having a family and having a business, it all kind of faded into the background. Without the men's group, I think my heart would still be there, but I don't think I would be as actively thinking and talking about a lot of social change issues as I do.

People have friends in life and I have friends in life, friends that I have in common with Margot (Tony's wife) from different circles that we connect with. But both Margot and I can be somewhat insular. We always talk about how we want to entertain more and have friends over and six months will go by and it's like, "Oh, we were going to talk about having a little dinner party and we've really got to do that." We'll say "Yeah," and then another six months will go by. We tend to hang to ourselves a lot, because we like each other's company and my life and my business are pretty all-consuming. Without the men's group I think I would be even more cut off from the social politic.

Robbie Leppzer: Being in our group affects me tremendously. I feel like I have total validation for being the man that I am, which is a non-macho man, a non-violent man, a feminist man by being in the group. We get constant support from each other. I have a place in my life where I can share things with other men. I think that's really healthy, because so many men hold things in and don't share intimate emotions with other men. If they're in a heterosexual relationship with a woman, that might be their only place to share that, but I feel like a healthy relationship is to be able to share your deep emotions with a number of different friends and men and women in your life rather than have it be just for one person, your most intimate partner. I feel the group has given me a healthier perspective on myself.

Paul Richmond: I think that the group has given me a language, a form of communication to help me distinguish what to expect. I can tell within a few sentences of hanging out with a new man I meet whether we are only going to talk about sports or politics but we're not going to get any farther than that. And that's O.K. There are a lot of great relationships that you could say are a little more surface.

It has also given me the ability, and I don't announce it, that when I talk to someone and I start realizing they're going to start telling me about what's happening with their wife or something else, I can say to myself, "By the way, I am counseling you." It's given me certain skills, and there might be some confusion about this, because some would say, "All guys get together and they just bitch about their wives and partners." But when you've been in a group like ours there are two parts that you realize the group helps you do. The first is we all need a space to complain and even blame, but you're with this group that doesn't judge you and then says, "What's really going on?"

So the group is not reinforcing your perception, but instead it has given me the skills to help me pinpoint questions I need to be asked and to ask myself about my role in what happened between me and anyone I care about.

Stephen Bannasch: I bring a certain perspective to work sometimes that comes from my time in our group. We often have meetings at work and I often have strong opinions about things, but I actually don't mind at all being wrong. It took a long time for me to realize most people aren't like that. In meetings I'll present an idea and someone else will present something else. It's very easy for me to say, "Oh, well, that's a really great way of thinking about it," or "Oh, of course, we're doing this to get better ideas and combine them together." I find that a lot of people don't do that, even though that's nominally often the purpose of this kind of a thing. I think that's partly how the group has affected me – and the kind of ethic we have, the concept of how all that takes place. That is a good thing and we actually do it and recognize it. Often it's not just doing something. It's also that meta part of recognizing what you're doing and giving words to it, a description to it. That helps you remember it. It also helps you carry it into other situations

Older Women's Group

Nancy Knudsen: In our group I have such a sense of being held and that is such a blessing. So many people don't have that. It allows me to move through life with a lot of gratitude and a sense of connection.

Ruth Olsen: My women's circle changes the way I see what is possible in my life and my approach to taking risks. For example, when my father passed away it awakened me to my calling at age 45. I was drawn towards playing the harp for the dying, and the support I received from this group on this long journey was essential to my ability to bring it to fruition in the second half of my life.

When a beloved one dies, you have the chance to see that life is too short. For me, when my dad died, I began praying for my soul work. Someone showed me a video on playing harp music for the dying. I instantly knew that was what I was called to do. I didn't know that the process would take me 15 years and four schools of learning how to use music as medicine. The group helped me keep it together to get through to live my life's purpose.

I had never played music, let alone been able to read

it. I didn't have a harp, let alone a teacher. I was taking on a life-changing journey. It was really challenging for me. When I would fall apart or go into self-doubt or self-judgment the women's circle would just build me back up: "You can do it." "You're O.K." In some moments they would say, "Ruth, you're done. Just be done." And I would say, "No, I've got to graduate."

The community bought me a harp – my community of women. For my 50th birthday, they organized a GoFundMe before it ever existed as a formal thing. It's hard for me to put the spotlight on myself. I don't naturally make a big deal of my birthday. I am more comfortable in the background, being of service. They had a 50th birthday party for me and a 60th and it is always this deep authentic amazement and appreciation.

I don't think I ever fully and truly appreciated myself, or knew how to appreciate myself, so when I get this reflected back to me, it resonates. I think we revere each other. We admire each other. To be in each other's company helps us all live up to our potential.

Susan Loring-Wells: I feel like I'm surrounded by incredible role models. There's so much to learn from each of them. The way they all do family inspires me. I also love to be connected not just to the person, but to her extended family. I've really enjoyed when I've met the parents of these women. It moves me just to see their other relationships of mother/daughter, father/child. I feel like I had a very sheltered upbringing, very safe. I felt adored by my parents, loved, and yet there's so much that I didn't get. Not that it's bad – that's just how it was for me. I really appreciate walking into the other women's lives and seeing how they've done and it influences how I do my life with my kids. It's eye-opening. I look forward to sharing holidays and traditions and the kids' milestones and just knowing the women's circle is there. We cover each other's back.

Annette Cycon: I believe so strongly in the power of groups to strengthen and change lives that I built my entire adult career around it! As a social worker, I founded a non-profit, MotherWoman, and a business called GPS (Group Peer Support) to give other women the gift of a women's circle in their lives. MotherWoman was started soon after our women's group began and focused on creating safe spaces for women to talk about the realities of motherhood. It was something I needed so much and got in my women's group that I had to share it with others.

I designed a structured group model which incorporated many of the elements of our women's group: an opening meditation, discussion of guidelines, check-in, reflections and closing. When we offered these groups to women they were amazed! They grew so much that 22 years later, I still hear from women who tell me their lives and their parenting were transformed because of MotherWoman.

We began training other women to lead women's groups, both here in Massachusetts and across the country. The movement grew and grew, to include training medical providers, social workers and community leaders. Hundreds of leaders have been trained in running groups and countless women impacted.

Now my co-leader and I have developed GPS, which offers an improved trauma-informed and culturally sensitive group structure to populations of people beyond new moms, to parents struggling with addiction, bereavement, incarcerated moms, trans-parenting, high-risk college students, teen parents, men, fathers, etc. I have also trained community health workers in Guatemala to incorporate groups in their work with rural mothers.

So, yeah, my women's group changed my life and in

turn, changed the lives of many others.

Morning Star Chenven: It's like having a very strong family. It's helped me learn more about listening, about deeply listening and responding. There is nothing like having the sense that it's not just you in the world, but you're with a "chosen" family, on a deep level. You can't really fall too far, because you're going to get caught.

A lot of the things we do in the group I bring to the community choruses and workshops I direct. A piece of feedback I get from my choruses is that we're not only learning and sharing music, but we're getting to know each other in an authentic way. We are loving each other and listening to each other, creating an experience together.

I have learned to bring this sense to whatever group I am facilitating. When I teach classes to Personal Care Attendants, I work hard to hear people, to bring them out to each other and have them participate as people on an emotional level.

Younger Men's Group

Ben Blackshear: It has heightened my emotional awareness and provided an increased willingness to be vulnerable. It has helped me to know that vulnerability is difficult and to seek it out because it's always a growing experience.

Ben Fuller-Googins: I think it allows me to be more open in the world of my other relationships. I don't have the need to compartmentalize, because I have this space where I know I can say things and I can process things, because I know people have my back. That really grounds me in myself. I feel supported and when I feel that way it manifests in my other relationships. I know that in all my partnerships I am much more open – with my family and my romantic partnerships.

The practice of sharing has been critical for me. One of the features of patriarchy and toxic masculinity is the feeling that a lot of traits and habits are my own – thoughts about sex or about women or the inability to be in relationship. Then I pathologize my own issues, so coming together and sharing in group lets me know there are others who have similar feelings and tensions, which is very healing.

Josh LaTour: For me it's about being more intentional and talking about different things – like what it was like growing up as a boy and all the pressures society sets to be tough or being talked down to if you showed emotion. It's about talking about sexuality and how to be a better lover. Like so many men, I've been affected by the phallocentric view and it was all about penetration and not how to pleasure a woman. I grew up hearing phrases like, "Did you get your dick wet?" No, I don't want to be that way. Being in group allows all of us to talk about our sexual identity preferences. We don't have to identify as male or female. Seeing the group through a queer lens. We want the group to be more inclusive for people of all sexual identities and orientations, and the group is very open to that. It helps to inform our language.

Younger Women's Group

Charlie Evans: It has identified me as a human being in the choices I make – in how I identify myself as a leader, as an activist and as a lover of the earth. I'm a Mama Bear.

Heather Price: It is so grounding. The feeling of grounding, and the feeling of knowing how consistent support and love in your life is, makes me more grounded and happier in all other aspects of my life.

Amelia Olsen: It's a safety net – the calls and our text-message chain. We cover a lot of the little things like, "I'm going in for fertility treatments today. Wish me luck!" or "My grandmother is sick," or even updates while I was in labor. We just give each other a shot in the arm.

Naomi Lutra: I notice that there are many different circumstances where I'll be saying, "What would Amelia do in this situation?" or "What would Michelle do in this situation?" or "How would Charlie approach this person?" It reminds me of that image of people who have angels on their shoulders. These women are my touchstones. They are people I really admire and if I'm stuck in certain situations, I think about how each of them would approach it.

Staying connected to the group is deeper than, or transcendent of, other ways we build our identities in the world. I am somebody for whom a lot of identity is wrapped up in my work life. That's true for a lot of people in my field – that somehow your job title communicates all these things about who you are as a person. But these women who I admire, who I see as incredibly successful and inspiring in totally different fields – they don't care what my title is. For them, our relationship is not about who I am presenting to the world, or who my professional career says I am. It helps me stay connected to who I actually am.

This chapter could have been titled "The Support Group Dividend." It captures the ways in which being a member of such a group has benefits that extend beyond the group experience. It can become a template for relating to others in your family, your friendship circle or your workplace. It can assist you in making changes to your circumstances by challenging assumptions and patterns. It promotes an authenticity that is lacking in these days of social media and moving through life at hyper-speed. The skills and insights offered by being in a support group are priceless.

CHAPTER 9
HOW HAS THE GROUP IMPACTED YOUR RELATIONSHIPS?

A key element of support groups is providing an opportunity to gain perspective on one's life. Nowhere is such perspective more important than in one's relationships. In the interviews I conducted I asked about relationships in the broadest sense, which enabled my subjects to focus on a wide range of possible responses, from their relationships with partners to their relationships with parents, children and friends.

It became clear that the group experience provided the opportunity to process decisions about whether to remain in a relationship and how to navigate difficult issues. As participants came to know one another well and to become sensitized to the core struggles they each faced, the combination of compassion and challenge was the goal when members brought their struggles to the group.

There is always a fine line between how any individual perceives compassion and challenge. Once the trust is established that enables group members to bring their central struggles with others in their life to the meetings, the next question is how well can he or she articulate it and also articulate what they need from the group in response.

Of course, it's not always smooth sailing when it comes to confronting one's own role in what is occurring in a relationship. There are times when we are and are not ready to express how we are experiencing the struggles that are occurring, or to take in feedback. A group becomes more and more aware of these variables as members develop trust in one another, as well as knowledge of what makes each person who they uniquely are. Over time, trust and knowledge facilitate a more profound conversation with a greater likelihood of the kind of understanding of and learning about ourselves – and one another – that we all seek.

It is my hope that what you are about to read will show the variety of ways individuals have felt that their group experience affects their relationships outside of the group.

Older Men's Group

Gary Phillips: The group really helped me long, long ago process my relationship with my first wife, Gail, before we left Massachusetts. That was a relationship fraught with intensity and all kinds of emotions. She and I had begun our relationship very briefly as lovers in the mountains of North Carolina, and we moved to Amherst, Massachusetts together. We were no longer lovers, so even though we lived together I didn't want to be perceived as being in a relationship. We spent several years re-sorting out our relationship and then became lovers again and then became partners. Some of that was very confusing and the group was really helpful in a beautiful way – helping me muddle through that.

The group's acceptance of and caring for my current wife, Ilana, has been a blessing to both her and me. The first time I came back and did a retreat with the group (having moved back to North Carolina) it was an intense weekend. I loved reconnecting with the group so much. When I came home, Ilana took my head in her hands and said, in a kind of wondering way, "Somebody has been taking really good care of you. You let me know who that is." She immediately understood that I had a need for these relationships. It was a really important part of myself that I had shunted aside for a long time and that welcoming it back into my life gave me something that was really crucial. I feel like I can bring up my difficulties to the group and not have to have them all sorted out and that's very valuable to me.

I've tried with my three sons to bring a lot of lessons from the group to them. All three of them express that in their lives. They're all emotionally dependable in ways that people in their lives are really glad for and I consider that a legacy of the group as much as anything else. I consider the group has given me ground to act like a man who doesn't have to act like a man. All of my sons have that as part of their characters, part of their lives, and as one of the reasons they're loved by the people they love. I think there is a direct connection back to the group in that.

Robbie Leppzer: I was going through my healing with my parents, in particular my relationship with my father. I had a lot of anger against my father and the men's group helped me to develop a more compassionate understanding of him and of my relationship to him because he's stuck in anger, and so was I at an earlier point in my life. It's not helpful to be stuck. It's an important stage to acknowledge and go through, but to stay stuck in anger is not very helpful. I remember when I wrote this letter that was totally blasting my father and I really wanted to send it and the advice of the group was, "No, don't send it. It's a good thing that you wrote it! Express the feelings, but it's not a good idea to send it." That was a good thing.

When something's going on in the rest of my life, there's a place I can share about it and get really good feedback and support. When I talk about being in this group with other people, people are always very blown away. They'll say things like, "Wow, you've been in this men's group for so many years?" or "Wow! You have this support for each other?" It feels like one of the ways that I am in the world is that I can share my experiences as a man and really point to the reality that there is another way that is very viable that men can be and I know it because I've lived it. I'm with this group and that gives people hope and inspiration. Both men and women who I've talked to about our group say there is hope for men. I'm a product of it and my men's group is a product of it and I know this to be true. I can speak with absolute confidence. That's a way that the group has allowed me to be in the world and allowed me to be a continual kind of change agent around how men can be in this different way from the stereotype of being macho and holding in their feelings.

Since this issue, how the group impacts one's relationships, comes so close to the heart of this book, I would like to offer the response I gave when I answered the questions I asked of the others:

Tom Weiner: Since those closest to me have heard about my current men's group for decades and my participation in such groups for almost 45 years, there is definitely an association they've formed between men's groups and myself. I try to live the values the group espouses, especially in terms of treating women with respect and equality. Since I make no separation between who I am, insofar as values and behaviors towards others are concerned, someone watching me teach for any period of time would see that I seek to impart similar values to my students – being able to question the dominant paradigm, especially when it comes to learning about America's past and the importance of fighting to achieve equality of the sexes and how connected it is to all other struggles for liberation, whether they be racial, sexual orientation, age-related, ability-related, etc. I know my parents, being from such a completely different life style and even value system, had some difficulty understanding what the men's group means to me. I believe they saw it as another manifestation of how "different" I was and I don't know if they ever got what I was seeking in terms of intimacy with male friends and support for the rough times we all experience.

Having nine other men in my life who value being an actively engaged, equal sharing partner in all aspects of a relationship is incredibly significant for me. Being able to bring my two younger children to the group when they were infants and feel that the men welcomed their presence and assisted me if I needed it was incredibly important for my wife to see and for me to experience. I also have gained perspective on marital issues by talking them through with the group and this has enabled me to be more empathetic, more willing to acknowledge times when I was less than considerate and became defensive, and to be more forgiving when that was what was essential to preserving my relationship. Having such a forum to express a wide range of emotions and to know that I was safe, that I could trust both the confidentiality and the honesty of the group and that I could count on responses that came from a deep knowledge of me, and from a deep-seated appreciation for what women confront in this culture, all served to strengthen me as a husband and father.

I also used the group to help me be a better parent for one of my children who was struggling with a variety of life issues. There were times that simply expressing the torn feelings I was having or crying about how hard it felt were enough. I respect the collective wisdom of the group as well as the analysis we all bring about how relationships are affected by so many factors – genetics, life experiences, friends, etc. When the group couldn't be enough to help me get through a crisis I knew it was time to find additional support through therapy, which I did, and the combination of my men and my therapist was very powerful.

Older Women's Group

Susan Loring-Wells: I've shared the depths of my relationship and my struggles there. There are a couple of people who've had divorces who probably look at me and say, "Why is she still with that man if it's that challenging?" That's what you do sometimes. Processing with the group about that has been so important. I feel the questions I get asked are good. I never feel pushed. There is this group of women wanting to know about my family. They want to know about my kids. I just feel like I can say pretty much anything. Raising kids, financial stuff, waiting for a house to be finished for years and years. I live with a carpenter/builder, a jack-of-all-trades, a brilliant man who works on other people's houses and takes care of other people's problems. Of course, it's much easier to look at other people's problems.

Some of the sharing I've done about my marriage took place in the Friends and Lovers circles.* There was a time when my husband wasn't around and I went by myself to an F&L gathering. There was one time when he actually left. He checked out mentally and got on his motorcycle and rode away to California. I didn't know where he was for a while. That was really challenging. He left me with our three little girls and there were no calls for two weeks. That's that flight response. He's a survivor so there's a lot of shit up. I think that requires a bigger heart from me, more com-passion. The women's circle helps a lot with that.

Sara Elinoff Acker: My husband is very supportive. He knows how important the group is to me and he can see how it makes my life better, helps me to get grounded and be better able to deal with life's adversi-ties.

Sometimes, he feels a little worried about what the women's group thinks of him. When I come back from the group he asks, "What did you guys talk about?" He knows that I talk very openly about my marriage – our strengths and joys and our struggles. But the women all have struggles and joys in their marriages as well,

* Friends and Lovers was founded in 1983 when six couples gathered at a girls' summer camp in Connecticut for a long weekend getaway. They had such a good time that they decided to make it a regular occurrence and invite more friends – and those friends' lovers. The core of the vision for the community was "re-villaging our lives within a spiritual context." This meant a shared desire to explore deep authentic relationship in a space that also supported and encouraged spiritual investigation, with an acceptance of the diversity and plurality of belief systems.

so I keep reassuring him that everyone loves and respects him, supports our marriage and no one is judging him or us.

We don't have the rule (in the group) that you don't talk about your marriage. You can talk about anything you need to talk about. The hope is that anything you're talking about with the circle – maybe you're using the circle as a sounding board – you're going to speak with your spouse about. The group has also been a model for my daughter. I think it's been important for her to see how I prioritize my friendships with other women.

The rhythm of me going off to the circle once a month is all she has known and grown up with. And what's so beautiful to see, now that she's a teenager, is how much she prioritizes and honors her friendships with girls as well.

Nancy Knudsen: Right now in this group, a lot of us are dealing with aging parents and sometimes ourselves and our partners' aging process. We have gone through the deaths of several members' parents and we have a number of us still with one or more parents left. There have been times where we've met one another's parents through social events. My mother lives around here now. Several group members chose to have an elderly parent live with them. I think it's been helpful to know how other people are dealing with their parents, and yet each of us has our own path around that. Dealing with this is a recurring theme. I think there is a lot of permission for each person to go through their struggle with some good support and advice and sometimes challenge. Everybody is seeing this life stage as a very deep and sacred passageway, as parents move on.

As for the partner piece, I feel like I'm in a pretty strong partnership, so I haven't needed to use the group for support, although a couple of years ago my husband had a back injury and couldn't move. He was out of work for a couple months and the role of caregiver that I played with him was different from our usual pattern as two very independent people. I got a lot of support from my women's group while moving through that.

My kids are grown, and I was not in the group while they were young. Still, young adulthood can be very challenging for parents to figure out how much to be involved in certain things and how much not to be. A couple of years ago my son was living out of the country and informed us that he was planning to get married. He was only 24 years old. He said, "I want your advice and your blessing," and I thought, "Which does he really want, advice or blessing?" That was a parenting dilemma that was tricky to navigate. Sharing in the women's group was very helpful, because some kids aren't that receptive to their parents giving them advice and others want it, so that whole process has been helpful to have people to talk to.

Younger Men's Group

Ben Fuller-Googins: I think it allows me to be in the world of my other relationships and to feel more open. I don't have the need to compartmentalize because I have this space where I know I can say things and I can process things. I know people have my back. That really grounds me in myself. I feel supported and when I feel that way it manifests in my other relationships. I am much more open with them and with my family and my romantic partnerships.

I think of it as almost developing a muscle – to have more vulnerability. It's a reference point that I can bring into my relationship with my partner, Courtney, and with my dad. It's a place where I can feel somatically if there is something that I want to keep, that I don't want to share or that I feel embarrassed about or I don't want to ask about. I think having some practice in having the actual repetition of meeting with this group where I learn and remember that I have the capacity to move through some of this stuff in these other relationships is key.

Ben Blackshear: It's been helpful to reflect and process ways that I've behaved, behaviors that I've enacted in past relationships that I'm not proud of and that I don't want to do as much of any more. Hearing other people share and name times when they were emotionally manipulative in their relationships helps me realize times when I exhibited that behavior and how I need to learn from that and not do that going forward. As Kevin was saying earlier, recognizing markers in someone else's story that are something they need to talk more about helps you bring up things in your own history that you maybe didn't process as an important moment or an important way in which you were embodying this harmful male ideal. It's helped me look at my past through a different lens and a more critical lens.

My current partner is very happy that I'm in the men's group. She thinks that it's something important that all men should do. She's asking me if I can recommend someone who's also doing this for her friends to date, because she believes that men need to be processing and working on this all the time. I don't think she has met any of the men yet. I think it would be good for all of us to meet outside of the group to strengthen the bonds of the relationships.

Kevin Quirolo: I think I've processed a lot of the initial crisis fall-outs that I had with two people that caused me to initiate the men's group. These were both women of color. One was with someone I was dating who broke up with me and among the many reasons why we broke up, was a racial and gender dynamic that she said was harmful to her. The other fall-out I had was with someone I was in a political group with. She called me out for being racist and sexist and I didn't really know what to do with that. I talked about it with the group, which really proved beneficial and when it's appropriate, every once in a while I still bring it up and relate it back to something someone is saying. It has helped me to understand what happened in those moments.

Since I interviewed Ben Blackshear and Kevin together, once again it is worth including what Ben had to say in response to Kevin's description of the impact of the group on his relationships:

Ben Blackshear: I want to say that part of what I think you've learned is the process itself. Coming out of those moments you just mentioned, you were seeking accountability in a group to process what happened with those relationships. What I remember you took from doing that with us is that you emailed one of the women and wrote, "Hey, do you want to explain to me or talk more about why this was bad?" They responded, "No," but in the group you found a place where you could deal with that. We all share stuff like that in our group.

Younger Women's Group

Amelia Olsen: When things are hard I retreat to these friends. They are one of my safe places – confirmation that I have friends and people for support. They had ideas and ways of pushing me to embrace being here in North Carolina. It was helpful to have them push me that way. In some ways I think I needed their permission or their positivity to do that. I was here with my husband. That part was covered, but friendships weren't.

Michelle Chanson: Sometimes it's just commiserating about life, because we all know each other's partners, families and siblings, job responsibilities, friends, etc. Because we know those closest to each of us we can offer insight from a real place of context and understanding. It's nice to know that we have some of the same frustrations with our partners or other friends. They're typically pretty minor, but just being able to laugh about them together makes a difference. We all know each other's partners' quirks, which I'm sure the men in our lives would roll their eyes at, but they know we have this call and that we talk about everything, so commiserating comes with the territory.

It was my own need to examine the role we as men play in the strife in our marriages that began my involvement in support groups. This chapter illustrates how the group augments that function with stories of sibling, parent, child and other relationships that are impacted by one's participation – the chance to vent, to process, to receive support, to be challenged and to challenge oneself, and ultimately to come to new awareness. Ultimately then, the gift keeps on giving.

CHAPTER 10
HOW HAS THE GROUP AFFECTED YOUR VIEWS
OF MEN, WOMEN AND GENDER ROLES?

All four of the support groups I interviewed have chosen to be composed of only one gender. In each case it was a conscious decision. We have apparently not yet arrived at a time when men and women are comfortable and open enough with one another to participate in groups of both genders – let alone able to readily find them. There are some exceptions, including a group that a member of my men's group has recently become affiliated with. I will have some words in the Conclusion about mixed-gender groups and their potential role moving forward in a post-#MeToo world.

It is worth pointing out, as I have already done in the second chapter, that the single-gender composition of each group is no accident, considering their origin and history. Women took it upon themselves some 50 years ago to seek out other women to share their lives, their struggles, their hopes and their fears, because they did not find sufficient opportunities to do so in their marriages or even their friendships. There was great intentionality in forging groups that were composed of only women with whom there could be deep sharing predicated on deep trust. It is not too much to put forth that these groups – along with political action, demonstrations, fighting for rights and demanding equality in workplaces and homes – helped change the way women saw themselves, one another and their place in the culture. That both of the women's groups I interviewed have chosen to maintain a women-only identity is thus no mystery.

Nor is the men-only aspect of the other two groups. In both groups there was, from their origins, the powerful motivation to address our masculinity with one another and not to expect women, as had been the tradition going back in history, to assist us in expressing our emotional responses to our own lives and our gender. We all knew we had work to do to dismantle the effects of patriarchy on our psyches, our emotions and our behaviors.

Not only is the commitment to being with one's own gender evidenced in the groups' compositions, but I would maintain that there are also both shared and individual conceptions of the roles men and women can and should play in our culture. That was the inspiration for the questions I put to each interview subject, regarding the impact the group has had on their awareness of their own and the other gender,* and how being in the group affects how they see, experience and understand gender and, in some cases, sexuality.

Older Men's Group

Gary Phillips: Our group deeply affects how I see myself as a man and how I understand masculinity. Absolutely and all the time. I am a businessman. I am constantly out in situations that are to a certain extent competitive. All through my life I've been able to say, "No, that's not the way to do things. I've been with men who do things differently. We can sit down and organize ourselves in a way that involves mutual support, even in the midst of challenge or having to make hard decisions." So it affects especially the way I see men. I'm not willing to accept a superficial relationship with men unless it is for a specific goal. I'll be affirmative and get through what needs to be done, but I am going off either to be with men who are as complex in their relationships with me as my men's group is, or to women who have that as part of the field of their life much more accessibly.

So the men's group gave me a standard by which to look at relationships that was a higher standard than I knew before, in terms of relationships of equality and challenge and love that has now been the standard for my life. That's what I want. If you're going to have a relationship with me then step up at least that high.

---

* I need to own that I have maintained a gender binary here, reflecting these groups' compositions. Were I to expand this study to include groups with transgender or gender-fluid members, there would be additional views, attitudes and awarenesses to investigate. That is the subject matter for another book.

Alan Surprenant: From the outset we all knew that men didn't just suck. Because we were men, and we weren't willing to accept that, even though at the same time we were gaining knowledge of the patriarchy and the society we live in where men are in power. We still are. So it was all about trying to cultivate the things that were positive, whether they were "feminine" or not, and the belief that men could be those other things, too. I spent a lot of time realizing, maybe a little later, how steep the learning curve was with 20-some-odd years of conditioning before that. And we are all still learning.

One neat thing about the age of our group, for me, is I'm still learning new things from these people that I've known for 40 years. It's kind of fun that things are still opening up continually. I get mostly positive responses to being in the group. One of the things I wanted it to do was to give people hope that men could be in a different role than what we were seeing. You didn't have to be playing football. You didn't have to be shooting people in the military. You didn't have to be corporate and competitive, stepping on others. All that divides people, all that competition – all the power over everyone all the time. That's a lot of what we're taught and what happens among men. I don't know if women always saw that. I'm making sweeping generalizations here, because the power of men over women is right in their face, and it expands to race and sexual orientation. But I knew that in the world that I lived in, it could be a very isolating situation – competition on whatever level. Whether it's girlfriends, grades, money, jobs, who's the boss, the person who can tell you you're not working there anymore. It's very isolating and our group contradicts all of that for me.

Once again, since this topic is so near and dear to the core of my being, I have chosen to offer personal reflections:

Tom Weiner: Being in three men's groups over 45 years has served to strengthen my notion of what is masculine. I was headed down this road before I joined my first men's group, but I have also felt encouraged, through the support of the men as well as through my observations of them at different moments, to express my feminine side – though I am hesitant to use the concept of our having two aspects to ourselves that divide neatly along gender lines. Being a fully involved parent for me is not expressing my feminine side, but rather more fully developing my maleness so as to include and incorporate being nurturing, which again is not a feminine characteristic in my view of people and their potential, though it certainly has been seen to be over the centuries.

So, yes, being in a men's group with other pro-feminist, anti-sexist men has fortified me in my efforts to be one and I hope to have been doing the same for my fellow men's-group members. If one believes, as I do, that inherent in each person is the potential to access a vast array of parts of one's self, then my way of being a man is now informed by these realizations – about the role I can play in the lives of my children, in the development of my students and in my relationships with the men and women who are my friends and associates. Given the level of toxic masculinity that has always been present in almost all cultures, having men's groups that actively work to first acknowledge and then undo the impact of such toxicity on everyone has been essential.

Paul Richmond: Being in men's groups has changed my view of women and sexuality. It made me realize how much the culture had defined that you kiss, you undo the bra, you do this, you do that and then you're done. That there wasn't really a sense of how can I be with this person and their body and how do I enjoy my own body and can I explain what I like to the other person and feel O.K. about that and be willing to allow that to happen – to be in the role of accepting that and not being on guard. Because of people talking about these subjects with each other and hearing other familiar stories and getting questioned on my own stuff or hearing that relationships can be done in different ways – all of this came from being in men's groups. The groups in the beginning were trying to define what is sexism, what is oppressing somebody else, what are male roles – including ones that could be positive in one situation and negative in another. It's been an unlearning and a learning experience and quite a journey

From early on in our lives, if you take the history of growing up in the '50s and even up until fairly recently, if someone was gay it would be like it was an archaeological find – "We found one in Buffalo!" It was as if there was this one anomaly and folks were like, "We'll try to deal with this guy and find out what happened to him and find out why he became gay," instead of the realization that there are millions of gay people and they've been around as long as there have been people.

I think that early on, with the men's groups that I was in at College F, it made me wonder and question, "What is my sexuality? Oh, I really do like hanging out with these guys as my friends and I do have a real love for them, but does that mean that I want to be sexual with them?" And then, "What does that mean, 'to be sexual with them,' since all those acts have been defined as being weird, dirty and whatever by the culture. Or that you're being submissive in a way that's bad or that you're being taken advantage of in the male roles." In that perspective it's not whether I didn't end up having a lot of male lovers or I wanted to be gay, but those experiences made me realize it's not just a clear-cut thing and there are people who feel these attractions from a very early age.

Older Women's Group

Sara Elinoff Acker: I've spent a lot of my career (as a clinical social worker) working with men, especially men who are abusive or violent. But I've never been against men. I'm just against sexism and male dominance and I do expect men to examine their own behavior and attitudes. This really is a powerful historical time to be a woman – women's way of working collaboratively, rather than hierarchically, our focus on relationship and cooperation. Our refusal to be silent about all the hidden abuses. I think that we are changing the world right now!

Annette Cycon: All of the women in the circle have empowered each other. We've all supported each other and ourselves in what's most valuable, including our relationships with the men in our lives. Being in a confidential circle with other women at different phases of life and with different lived experience allows us to get feedback that is invaluable! We have learned so much from each other.

When we support each other, it is not to the detriment of men or to compare it to the way that men work or the way masculinity works. It's more about female empowerment.

Morning Star Chenven: Coming to the Pioneer Valley has affected how I see women. There have been so many great relationships here. The women's circle just amplifies that. I get to see the strength and the power and the intelligence and the love and the fun – all of that. I get to see all of that with these women I'm with and I get to see real loyalty. There's none of that behind-the-back stuff. We're really trying to be as honest as we can with each other. That's a beautiful thing. There's not stuff that gets left unsaid – as best as we can. That's one of the things I see and have learned and experienced.

There's a commonality – ways in which we see men as being similar and women being similar. Women want this kind of emotional connection, of being seen and being known. And the men in our lives – even though we're always saying, "Why don't you get together with each other while we're getting together with the women?" – they don't do that. We're often commenting, "Men are not wanting that. Or if they want it, they don't know they want it." There are men that do want the emotional connection and men that know they want it, but I think for a lot of the men that we're connected to, they may have gone through New Warriors,* but that was it. They learned from it and now they're on their own. There's not that reaching out, of being seen and known. There's more fear about being that vulnerable.

Younger Men's Group

Ben Blackshear: The group has broadened my idea of masculinity, which we all, coming into it, had as a goal – a place where men came together to be able to express more emotions than typical concepts of masculinity would allow them to. That's something we were all hoping for. It has produced a heightened awareness towards seeing the patterns that don't work everywhere, like seeing how they're embodied in every interaction. It's on my mind a lot more now.

Ben Fuller-Googins: I was with my dad and his brothers for Thanksgiving. We're planning an "ancestor trip" to Ireland. They're all men, uncles and cousins. I don't have close relationships with my uncles. Even being around my dad for a day or so I would get

* The New Warrior Training Adventure is a modern male initiation and self-examination program that works for "the development of a healthy and mature male self. We ask men to stop living vicariously through movies, television, addictions and distractions and step into their own adventure in real time and surrounded by other men." mankindproject. org.

very annoyed. I think part of my growing awareness and appreciation of men's struggles is having an awareness around the lineages of patriarchy beyond just one generation. When I was there for Thanksgiving I noticed that I had much more of a gentleness with these men. They're not embodying the type of awareness I look for about whiteness and masculinity that is for me a liberating framework, but for most of my life I would just shut off to them.

Now I am feeling much more of a curiosity – seeing that their patterns and attitudes are really old stuff. I am excited about this trip to Ireland to deepen my relationships with these men in my family that are so very much surface level at this point. I do not think that I would have been in a position to say that let alone be excited about it without being part of my men's group.

The next response moves our discussion into the evolving sense of what it means to be a man or a woman in today's America. It arises in part from the impact of the #MeToo movement and the group's tentative role in offering a place to rehabilitate men accused or convicted of sexual harassment.

Josh LaTour: We've had different beliefs about the impact of toxic masculinity and we're finding such a group to be useful for men, and not just for men but for the movement. We have a system in place for when problems occur. We're not professional social workers, but we used to joke around and say, "Hashtag – Send us your men." We think we can work in tandem with some organizers to hold space for men who are being problematic. It wouldn't be like larger actions, but it would be very useful locally in projects people are involved in where inappropriate behaviors occur.

One situation involves an individual I'm friends with who taught a lot of people and now some individuals have accused him of things that, in my opinion, can be seen as just his being immature. You're dealing with he said/she said and then you're dealing with certain feminists and there's a counter-narrative that they are exploiting – "No questions asked, whatever a woman says, believe her." I understand the reason for that. I was part of the group that was trying to handle the accusations against my friend in a proper way, but with so much immaturity in terms of how people were trying to organize accountability circles* – both the person who was being accused and the people accusing him – there was no way for the people to come together.

When I started a catering company there was another issue with a member from North Carolina. He had been accused of doing something non-consensually down there and after he joined our New York co-op he let us know that he had some history. He was part of an accountability circle, and he didn't want us to be involved in his personal life. He was trying to work it out. Having a container where some of these outcasts could go – these pariahs – is an important part of healing. Toxic masculinity is not just someone's personal choices that make these things happen. It's our whole culture that is supporting the behaviors and it needs to be addressed that way, rather than just blaming men. I'm hoping men's groups like ours can play a role.

Younger Women's Group

Naomi Lutra: I hear some women say, "Oh, I don't have a lot of female friends," or "Women are catty," or other tired tropes about how women act towards each other. I feel really lucky that for so long I've had this counter-example of this group of female friends, so I

---

* Accountability circles are community-based groups using restorative-justice practices to work with sex offenders and their accusers.

knew from an early age that those toxic ideas about female relationships just aren't true. They're ultimately a tool of patriarchy trying to keep women isolated. This group has provided a grounding in the value and authenticity of female friendship.

Liz Sharp: We talk about the relationships with the men in our lives. It has given me a lot of faith in the power of women and a female approach – not that there's just one female approach. We all believe that women are equal to men, but I think there are a lot of ways in which women don't feel equal as we move through this world. And there are a lot of ways in which men have kept that pretty strictly enforced. We all have bounced up against that in various aspects of our careers and lives. This is a really powerful group of women with strongly held ideals and passions and the ability to make change happen in our lives. When the road seems a little bent, it gives me great inspiration to think about them.

Heather Price: Ours is a group of very strong women. I mean that in the most positive way. I think all of us truly believe in the power and strength of women and encourage it in each other and pull it out of each other. My view of women, being a woman, is a positive one. I believe we can do everything, and these women are such a great example of strong women. I don't know if the group has impacted my view on men and masculinity. It's such a great example of the strength of women and how when we support each other, it is not to the detriment or to compare it to the way that men work or the way masculinity works. It's more about female empowerment.

An important goal of the early consciousness-raising groups was to impact how women saw themselves and other women – in relation to one another, to men and to the society as a whole. That the groups in this study have carried this forward is clearly evident in this chapter. First, there are the gains in awareness about how each of us functions in our corner of the world. Then, since each group has a commitment to encourage critical thinking and analysis of sex roles and their impact, it is not surprising that many of this chapter's excerpts indicate much focused attention on the ways in which one's gender affects one's life – choices about relationships, careers, friends, where one lives, having children.

Of course, with regard to sex roles, the older and younger groups came of age in different epochs, as well as in various locations in our significantly divided nation. Nevertheless, hearing the responses to this question, and revisiting them while transcribing and editing them, affirms my conviction that such groups can promote gender equity, circumvent stereotyping and lead to greater insight into one's own and the other gender's experience.

CHAPTER 11
WHAT HAPPENS WHEN
CONFLICTS ARISE?

Put ten men or women together in a support group for 40 years, or even 25 years, and there will be moments in time – perhaps hours, days or weeks – when tension and conflict emerge. It is inevitable and it is also, on at least one level, desirable. Not only do conflicts offer us a chance to work through differences without recapitulating traditional power dynamics, but they also offer us a chance to recognize limits in our own vision and patterns in our own behavior that may do harm to ourselves and others.

Personality clashes, values differences, even such seemingly incidental issues like arriving on time – or not – can lead to difficulties. If these difficulties are allowed to fester, they can undermine the integrity of a group's functioning and lead to an accumulation of bitterness or resentment that then requires much more significant problem solving. Such conflicts, while challenging, afford unique opportunities to seek resolution in ways that maintain the dignity of each person through respectful efforts to acknowledge the conflict and give everyone involved opportunities to voice their experience and express their emotions in ways that first and foremost honor the shared group experience – even when the conflict is ultimately unresolvable.

I can, of course, speak most personally about the group I have been a part of for the past 29 years. During my time with the group, I have witnessed several significant conflicts, including two involving members who, as a result of these conflicts, are no longer connected to the group. One occurred shortly after I joined in the late 80's and the other 25 years later. Since both men were integral to the creation of the group and its functioning – in one case for the first 11 years, and the other for over 30 years – their respective departures were deeply felt by all of us. As a result, I believe, of the honest and respectful way these conflicts were handled, the two members who left the group remain a part of the network of people that includes several ongoing group members. I will attempt here to capture both the issues involved in these two conflicts and the spirit of the efforts to resolve them.

This chapter begins with some of the reflections that members of the older men's group shared with me in interviews, to allow readers to see more deeply into what occurred. I also reached out to the two men with whom the struggles arose – Gary Seldon and Llan Starkweather – for their perspectives.

Older Men's Group

Robbie Leppzer: The conflicts involving both Llan and Gary evolved into situations where both men actually stood apart from the group. They were trying to say something was red, but all of us were saying no, it's blue, and for whatever reason they became very rigid. That didn't work in a group like ours, where it's about being more open, humble and vulnerable. It was sad to see both of them get to this place where they ended up being separated from the group.

As for our process, I think that people went around and said what they could live with and what they couldn't live with. What we could live with was very reasonable, but for whatever reasons both of them at the time couldn't live with it. For a group like ours we need a consensus, which means total agreement by everybody about basic things, and really it comes down to respect for the group.

Stephen Bannasch: Gary would often get a hold of something and there would be a logical inconsistency. Sometimes it was just about an idea; sometimes it was about a process, or an emotional thing. And he would be stuck on it. He would just be very stuck. To me that was part of the essence of why we separated from him. It's almost sort of like OCD. I can recognize it in myself. I can keep a huge stock of different levels when I'm trying to figure something out. I recognize that quality both in myself and in others, but Gary took it to an unsustainable place with us, which made it not work in a group.

That was a difficult conflict. I felt like I could relate to him actually a lot, but it wasn't working in the group and while we may have tried, we couldn't figure out how to make it work. That was tough. I thought we did the best job we could in trying to resolve it so he could remain, so I don't have a complaint, but I'm disappointed. I'm not disappointed that we didn't try and that we didn't work hard at it. I would have liked it if it could have changed and he could have been in the group now. I like Gary.

With Llan, he took on a self-referencing, cult-like worldview* and I think there were a lot of things contributing to this. I see it as being mentally addictive. Maybe it's like the difference between crack and cocaine, you can get wrapped up in it faster. A lot of this gets wrapped up in your mind and takes you into this weird self-referential place where everything is defined in this circular way. I think when people do that – and it doesn't just have to be ideas, – there's an emotional component and there's probably a biological and chemical basis, too – but you can become disconnected from people. It's the ideas that are what matters, and the people lose more and more connection. I think Llan lost his emotional connection to us. I don't think he could relate to us without having all these ideas jump up and then he wanted to proselytize us. I feel sad that we couldn't help him more. We couldn't connect.

I think we've done the best we could. You reached out and talked to him recently and I really support you.**

* This involved apocalyptic prophesy, the existence of other dimensions, the Planet X theory, crop circles and other concepts defying modern science.

** Stephen refers here to my efforts to connect with Llan following his departure from the group. I could reach out more easily since I was not in attendance at the final gathering, where he declared his intention to withdraw from the group when those present told him he could not continue to try to convince them of his views.

I'm really glad you did that. The results didn't resolve in a way that helped us connect, but you tried. I would have a harder time doing that. I have less tolerance for that kind of a proselytizing worldview. I think what I was saying is, "Oh, if he could just accept us and not need to try to convert us." If he had something that needed fixing, I would go over and fix it for him. I would do it because I cared about him. I don't need to change him. I don't need to change his proselytizing views, but I don't think he's going to change at this point. I'm really glad that you tried doing what you're doing. Just because you didn't succeed doesn't mean you didn't try. That was a great thing to try and do.

Paul Richmond: I think we were at a point where what was happening with one of our members was emphasizing how we deal with the need for someone to change. Llan asked the group to believe what he has come to believe about our world and to come with him down this particular thought process. He was feeling that we were failing him in not going together after he asked for that, which was different from, "I need help" or "I'm feeling sick" or "I'm lonely." We've given people what they wanted around an emotional crisis. So I think it's important to ask, "What demands can a person put on a group?" If I say, "I want you all to try to become jugglers," that's a nice thought and you might all pick up my scarves that I use to teach juggling and then at some point say, "I'm not going to be a juggler and I don't want to be a juggler." That's a request or an invitation and not a demand.

There have been other times, if you're staying with a group long enough and you're having all kinds of conversations about a wide range of topics, it should be noted that now you're bringing in what your beliefs are – "I believe in Jesus Christ" or "I believe there's a planet coming by between the Earth and the moon." It never got to a place with something like Alan (Surprenant) saying about his tax resistance, "I'm leaving the group because you're not doing this with me." He put it out there. He hoped and he wished, but he didn't leave, and that is another thing about what makes a group survive. There are places where I need to decide, "Do I leave this group because I say nobody's interested in poetry because nobody came to this poetry reading I did?" They're glad I'm doing it and they have nothing against it, but it is not what they want to do and they wouldn't want me to say, "You have to have a poem next month to read." I might ask for my time to read a poem. That's different than someone saying, like Llan said, that they want the whole group time. If you want a group to succeed I think you're also dealing with the fact that each person has to be asking for their needs and realize that I am sharing the time period with other folks' needs. That stopped happening with Llan.

Gary Seldon: I remember the last time that I went to a meeting, and I can't remember entirely the specifics, but in my mind it goes into the category of my willingness to consider opposing views, different outlooks. Llan put forward some event that had happened recently in Springfield. I believe it had involved a gay man and it involved the police. I was just pushing some viewpoint that was not entirely what I felt, but I would just overstate it. I like to overstate things, which is possibly a big foible of mine. I was wanting to not go with the lock-step, politically correct perspective. I was considering other ways of conceptualizing the situation. I think that my voicing of those things was painful to Llan, on a gut level, because he was basically expressing hurt and outrage. And I expressed ideas that didn't validate that, that possibly contradicted it. And it was dreadful. It was dreadful in the group vibe and process and it was like, "Oh, there goes Gary again, being a pain in the ass." We'd been down that road enough times and tried just as much as we could to resolve that. I decided to take a leave of absence. I didn't think it was a permanent leaving of the group, but it likely wasn't tremendously specifically clear.

I felt absolutely horrible when it became clear that it was permanent. It was a huge, horrible loss – another instance in my life of losing touch with a group, through my own personality. It was a huge failing. Hugely painful. This was an incredibly big part of my life that I had started. I was a founder and I was no longer acceptable to the group. It was a huge blow. Two to five years after that time, I felt the anger when it started to become clear to me that I wasn't going to be allowed to come back, that I was going to be excluded without a hearing. I felt more anger about that.

Llan Starkweather: I'd been talking for years about other realities and I saw the group as not wanting to hear about it. That hurt too much. It felt personally rejecting. Not reading the writing I did meant that I didn't feel like the men's group was part of my soul family any longer. The way I see it, all forms of denying the existence of spiritual dimensions ultimately generates deceptive harm in our lives. I couldn't get the men's group to see this. It's what led to my departure from the group since I felt that what I was trying to convey was being rejected, which felt like a rejection of me. I felt a lack of respect for my ideas and that meant I felt disrespected.

In the end, it is my conviction that our entire life in the world is made up of beliefs, and beliefs by definition are things that are not provable, but you accept as true. They're all false, and religion is part of that. Once you just accept that your soul is eternal and you never really die, it all becomes simple. I couldn't convince the men's group of this and I will always be saddened as to what resulted.

I see both the conflict involving Gary and the one involving Llan as learning opportunities for each group member. I have selected a few responses to share and there are others. In the end the group succeeded in continuing despite the struggle that both conflicts entailed. I strongly believe that, although there was considerable pain for all of us, and especially for Gary and Llan, what took place was within the framework of the group's purpose as a chance for men to come together to express their emotions, their experiences and their views.

That each of us came into the group with our own childhood wounds, along with the wounds that our culture inflicts on our gender, made resolving these two conflicts so that Gary and Llan could remain part of the group essentially impossible. For each man to maintain his integrity and for the group to remain a safe and supportive place with no one person exerting control required that we communicate as clearly as possible – individually and ultimately collectively – that the ways in which both men were behaving and treating the rest of us could not continue. That the result – their departures – was much less than satisfying for Llan and Gary will remain a source of sadness for all of us.

Older Women's Group

Sara Schley: I remember feeling hurt that there were two people within the group that had been doing some talking about me outside of the group. I have a very strong norm. There is a Jewish phrase, lashon hara, which means bad speech and gossip and you don't do it. That's a strong personal commitment that I hold and so I brought that into the group, saying, "If we have an issue with someone, let's make sure we bring it here, not triangulate off in different pods, which isn't healthy." Everybody appreciated that. No one was meaning to be hurtful. It was, "Let's care for this person by talking about them," but it ends up being hurtful. We've done better with this over the years. I think it's been a lot better. I don't think it's never happened, but from my standpoint I felt good about how it's been dealt with. I don't think now that there are any issues of trust with one another.

167

One interesting thing comes up from time to time, where some women will say – ironically after all these years - they still feel outside the group. I don't think it's about trust, really, it's about inclusion/exclusion, which is people's own personal issue and they'll own it as their personal issue. Trust is really solid. Everybody knows we all have each other's backs and we all really support each other in the world. To the credit of the women and their skillfulness, they know when they are feeling excluded. They'll name it and say, "This isn't about the group. I own this as my piece." I don't know whether that's a norm of the group or just how our other experiences have played out over the years from whatever personal work people have done. I think people take a lot of ownership and there's a lot less projection and so that's very healthy for the group as a whole.

Ruth Olsen: We are human, so we will have misunderstandings and disagreements. We will project and misinterpret. When that happens we come to each other's side in support. We always benefit when we bring it to the group – when we sit in circle to hold both people, both sides compassionately. Sometimes that means making forward progress, sometimes it means calling something or some behavior out as not working. Alone, independently we can't see everything and sometimes we just react. With a group like this, they see what I can't always see in the moment. But bringing it to the forefront, showing up for each other and having each other's back, that is what's really helpful.

Sara Elinoff Acker: The biggest problem was that we had a longtime member who the rest of us were feeling less and less connected to. She had been in the group since the very beginning. She tended to be rigid and inflexible and, in my opinion, did a lot of projecting. There were a couple of women who felt that they'd been attacked and demeaned by her. There was a lot of tension to work out.

Most of us had friendships with each other where we saw each other between circles. We were in each other's lives in other ways. We had organic connections, but she wasn't part of that. We would just see her at circle and with the tense dynamics, it was getting harder and harder. It wasn't working for her either. But we didn't know what to do.

One of our group members left the area, so there was an opening in the group. Seven of us had one woman in mind that we really wanted to invite to join our circle. We were connected to her, but this other woman was not. So she vetoed it. I can understand her reasoning. She said, "I already feel that you guys are all connected in your lives and I'm not really part of it and I don't really want another experience of that." So we said, "O.K.," but there was a lot of tension, because the truth was we really wanted this woman to join our circle and I think we secretly wished the other woman would leave. It was very awkward.

Then we had this day together when we went paddling on the Swift River. I organized it and we all went with our canoes and kayaks. When we came back we got together and she looked at us and she said, "I've decided to leave the group." That was it. We said goodbye to her and we honored her and nobody tried to talk her out of it. The next month we invited the woman we wanted to join the group.

In these examples, as in my men's group, some serious personality differences necessitated finding considerate and sensitive ways to support one another. In this case I did not interview the women with whom the issues arose, so it is my hope that enough of a picture has emerged in what the women shared to give a strong sense of what they undertook in seeking to resolve their conflict.

Possibly because of their much shorter history, neither of the younger groups identified the kinds of seriously disruptive crises described in the previous interviews. In response to my question about conflict, most of the members focused more generally on the dynamics of relationships within the groups and the kinds of challenges a newer group might be more likely to encounter.

Younger Men's Group

Ben Blackshear: There's been tension with certain people, particularly at the beginning. Trying to figure out what we were doing and what we all wanted was quite difficult. Almost any time you get a bunch of men together there's some amount of posturing, which I think there definitely was. Fortunately, we kept it to a minimum when we were first starting. I think people saw this for themselves and there was a turn when the discussions focused more on relationship building within the group. It was like, "We don't need to talk about this any more."

Joshua LaTour: Some of the challenges revolve around our capacity to do the work we want to be doing. There was a woman's group doing some incredible work on a project called Take Back the Night. They had a series of events in bars where they were training a bunch of people in bystander intervention. They wanted to make nightlife fun and safe because that's where a lot of stuff occurs. We were working with them, but they were having their own struggles. They invited us to things that I showed up to, but we were never able to really connect. We were all trying to find outside activities to be a part of. The challenge was how to do both inner work and outer work. We tried to make it a requirement where, if we were trying to have more outputs, we would have to do something as a group and then do something with another group. That didn't work.

Truthfully, I think the biggest challenge is living in New York. The cost of living is so high. We're all hustling. We have our jobs. We have our personal lives. We just don't have that much time to be doing the extra-credit stuff we're passionate about. It takes a lot of fortitude, month after month, to set time aside for things that a lot of people in our lives just don't think are that important.

Ben Fuller-Googins: There is tension around how inward we want to be and how outward focused – the kind of questions your group has been grappling with for a long time. I think that's a healthy conversation, which is never finally resolved. There are certain people who are saying, "We need to get out into the world and recruit people and do more outward stuff," and I'm more in favor of personal sharing.

Younger Women's Group

Charlie Evans: I had just broken up and gotten out of a very unhealthy and emotionally abusive relationship. In that relationship, I had isolated myself and my ex-boyfriend had isolated me from my friends and I didn't recognize that at the time. Retrospection is a wonderful thing. I actually pushed the group away during that relationship. It was terrible. They did all of the right things and I told them they were wrong. Most people don't have perspective when they're in the middle of a situation. I was totally blinded. I said to them, "I just want you to support my choices, even if you think they're wrong. I don't want to hear that they're wrong," and they all said, "We can't do that." It's the best thing they could have said or done. I was mad at them and didn't speak to them for a couple of months.

At some point I became more receptive and the group changed their approach and how they communicated with me about it. It was a little gentler and more effective. When I finally broke up with him everyone came to my parents' house, including many of the partners, those who were or would become husbands. It was wonderful. It was ideal. They helped me figure out the logistics of the break-up. That was life changing. The thing that stands out the most for me is not what the group did, but what the partners did. They said, "Don't go back there to break up with him. You stay here. We will drive down and get all of your stuff." I didn't take them up on that, but that has stuck with me. They would have done it in a heartbeat. That speaks very loudly to the quality of the women in our group in terms of the quality of the partners that we ultimately chose. My husband, thank God, is nothing like that guy I broke up with. I call all of these guys my husbands. It's husband, not brother. It's kind of a joke, but kind of not. Any one of them, if I needed them, would drop anything and come to help me. And the same for me for them.

Amelia Olsen: (reflecting on Charlie's relationship) One of us had a boyfriend we all really didn't like. We didn't like the way he was with her. Everybody handled it differently and part of that was she didn't tell us exactly what was happening, because if you're in it all the time you have to distance yourself. Some people had to say, "I've had enough of hearing that today." When she finally left the relationship, we were all there to help her exit.

Heather Price: We are trying to figure out a way to all get together to be able to spend some time with each other in person. The challenge with that is just life and schedules. We're going to do our best to make that happen. I don't foresee other challenges. Maybe having friends move away and figuring out how to keep in touch with them regularly you could think of as a challenge, but it felt seamless to me to go from seeing each other around the dinner table to seeing each other on a Skype video chat and talking to each other. I don't want to really view that as having been a challenge.

Luckily, we haven't had to deal with too many challenges. The one I can think of is trying our best to see one another, trying to figure out schedules, especially with families and partners – needing to take all of that into account. Of course, the physical proximity is missing on our video calls. If someone is tearing up, I do miss being able to reach over and grab their hand, or just hug each other hello and goodbye.

Naomi Lutra: On our video calls, we have naturally fallen into a pattern of taking turns saying, "Here's what's going on with me," and everybody rallying around that circumstance or story for a while and then moving on to the next person. That totally works for this situation, but I feel a little bit gets missed. Back when we were all having dinners, the conversation evolved more organically because it could feel less like an around-the-table report.

One thing that hasn't been a huge challenge, but is something I think about sometimes, is the ways in which the economic realities of our individual lives are really different because of our range of professional directions and career choices. When it comes to figuring out the practical realities of life – including how, when and where we get to see each other – it can feel a little bit like we're not on the same page. It's the kind of thing where nobody would ever get left behind if we were all going to do something, but if we go out to a fancy restaurant it's just a bit different percentage of the family budget for different people. Still, I know if any of us at any point said, "You know what, I'm a little strapped this week. Can't we go to a cheaper restaurant?" everyone would be saying, "No problem."

So there will be conflicts and challenges. How they are addressed is key to the healthy continuation of the group. An essential element is agreeing to address such conflicts and challenges together during group gatherings, so that disagreements are aired fully and openly, making sure to avoid blame and to use "I" statements to express differences rather than the accusatory "you."

As we've seen, it is inevitable that there will be conflicts that not everyone experiences similarly, up to and including having to part company with disgruntled members who are not owning their own roles and/or actually stopping the group from functioning satisfactorily.

Acknowledging the role conflict plays, and that it is part of any group seeking to explore deeply one's self and one's connection to others, will enable a group to respond effectively, hopefully compassionately and with integrity. (This is also true in a marriage, which shares some important qualities of intimacy with support groups.) Of course, having members who are either trained in conflict resolution or who have dealt effectively with conflict outside the group can be enormously helpful.

Even then, some individuals may very well not feel supported. Commitment to healing such rifts is essential. Our group did just that with Llan before his death in the summer of 2018. Each of us visited him to express the abiding love and appreciation we all felt for him as a man who had greatly enriched our lives. Llan was an artist in all that he endeavored, from designing homes to making wine, and he was a mentor to many of us throughout his time in our group. We were grateful for the chance to bring him back to us, and for us to give him back his "chosen family" so movingly, tenderly, lovingly.

CHAPTER 12
HOW CAN A SUPPORT GROUP
CHANGE YOUR LIFE?

There was a circuitous route to this chapter. The title of a 2016 film, *Welcome to the Men's Group*, got my attention, but the trailer did not encourage me to believe that those viewing the film would be motivated to find a men's group, since it used comedy to satirize the experience and exaggeration to humiliate some of the men and their interactions. That trailer, though, led me to a blog by Karen Covy, a self-described "Divorce Adviser, Attorney, Mediator & Coach" and an article she called *10 Ways Joining a Support Group Changes a Man's Divorce*. It provided some thoughtful ideas on ways a support group could help men access the full range of their emotions, but it was predicated on her assumption that men are emotionally incompetent.

In this chapter, by contrast, it is my intention to honor the ways in which men and women can and do find in support groups the kind of sounding board, challenge and support that ultimately leads to a more satisfying life. I have mentioned the impact my group has had on me in times of extreme stress and crisis – the tragic loss of a beloved friend who was murdered and the numerous surgeries my newborn son and our family endured.

Here, I will present a wide range of situations that have been experienced by my study participants that reveal the power of support groups to transform such difficult moments into opportunities to receive solace and to experience being held by loving arms and spirits. It is my hope that some of the answers to this chapter's question will resonate and provide encouragement to seek the extraordinary affiliation that such groups can offer.

Older Men's Group

Alan Surprenant: My getting sick – having Chronic Fatigue Syndrome and being out of it for a year, and having young kids and the struggle that was. There was a lot of pressure that was putting on my marriage. Bringing it to the men's group allowed me to follow the course of my illness in the safety of the group over time. I would be having this sickness that doesn't show physically – that's one of the books I'm trying to write – and the men in our group gave me the support I needed to help me through it.

The other aspect was people knowing the struggles I went through in my marriage and raising kids and how that all panned out. I felt like the group understood it and I trusted the men's responses to my struggles, because they saw things happen over time. Also, they could call me on things that could have been done differently that, unfortunately, we don't get a replay on, but that I could still learn from.

Steve Trudel: One of the sea changes occurred for me in letting go of my need to be in control and to begin to experiment with trusting that other people would make decisions in my best interest. When I've let myself receive the support of my men, who did some essential work on my home when I really needed the help, what occurred at the time was that I realized that it can't be true that I don't deserve this – too many people who I respect and value so deeply were showing me their love.

Along with trusting that decisions the group makes will work out for me and for the group – that they will be compatible with what feels good – the group has made it possible for me to feel safe in challenging other group members. It was never safe for me to question anything in my family. It was not O.K. to say that I didn't go along with a decision, because, depending on the situation and my father's mood, I would be told that my views don't matter, that I was wrong and that he didn't want to hear that. I never felt safe to challenge my father. It was never about whether he could hear me, but rather what degree of awful will I get back from what I would say.

What I'm talking about is dropping down into a feeling state as opposed to how I think rationally. When I say this, I am allowing a sense of how I feel to be integrated with the words I am saying. In other words, I'm being holistic. As my 12-year old self I was wanting my father to be a compassionate adult who could tolerate dissent from his child, knowing that it's part of developing into a human being – that you get to say I don't like something to your parents and they can handle it. With the men's group, I never worried that I would be told, "Your ideas are unacceptable," or "Shut up! You have to leave the group." Instead it would be, "Thank you for letting us know what you're feeling," or "Thank you for taking that chance with us." How could this not have an impact on the rest of my life?

Older Women's Group

Nancy Knudsen: I'm thinking about the individuals in the group. I'm thinking that there's a relationship to the group and then there are relationships with the individuals in the group, some of which are much closer than others. Some people in this group I just see in the group or at a social event where everybody has been invited, including their partner. Having an illness last year actually brought me closer to some of those people who were in that category of just a member of the group, because they came and visited me and they took care of me. They made it their business to be there for me in a way that I hadn't experienced before. Something about belonging to the group made that possible. If I hadn't been part of this group and I got sick some people would come by and other people would hear about my illness through somebody else, but not see it as their business to actually show up. There's something about belonging to a group that opens up that possibility for more closeness as time goes on.

I think talking to you right now is highlighting for me the huge significance of being part of a group when somebody's luck is down, as well as when there are times to celebrate. Maybe that's the time when you open up in a deeper way, when somebody is in need.

Annette Cycon: I am so heartbroken when I see women who don't have a place to express their soul and have a safe space of mutual respect and support for the journey of their lives. I feel that our culture is where it is largely because we've lost connection with our individual and collective souls and with each other in an authentic way. Life is hard. It's complex. We simply cannot live in isolation. As humans, we need each other. Social support is the key to resilience, health and happiness. And so many people don't have that.

So that's why I created MotherWoman. I wanted to create environments where the average woman – not the progressive woman, not the lefty woman, not the hippie woman – but the woman who works at the salon, the woman who would never, ever be in a women's group could have that experience of personal awakening and loving support from other women.

Diane Norman: My women's circle has, over the years, allowed me the space to go and shine light on some really dark, painful and vulnerable parts of myself. For instance, coming out about my history of disordered eating. The group has been and continues to be a place of non-judgmental loving and support. There were all the years of sharing with my circle the tumult and ambivalence I felt prior to leaving my marriage. When I finally decided I was done "working on my marriage" and was ready to separate and get a divorce, it was my women's circle that really showed up for me. They gave me the courage to go through with it despite my fear at the time of the long-term ramifications on my daughter. The day of my divorce, four of my circle women came over and had lunch with me. Divorce, separation, illness, support with spouses' illnesses, these are all opportunities to show up for each other. And we do.

Younger Men's Group

Ben Fuller-Googins: One of the features of this ver sion of masculinity we have is that it is very patholo gizing. So my relationship to pornography or how to articu late desire in sexual situations – that's the stuff I keep very private. My attraction to other men is another. At the last meeting that was something I shared for the first time in any group of people. It felt very relieving, like, "What a relief to not have to keep this in my body." There's this sensation of lightness that I am able to experience by sharing a lot of things I keep private and have some either fear or shame around.

I specifically remember the last meeting, where Josh was sharing being in some sort of relationship with a man. Him sharing that – I wonder if I would've shared what I was going through if he hadn't. There are defi nitely men modeling vulnerability in our group, which is very cool for me to experience.

Josh LaTour: I've been able to talk about how to have better consent practices. I've been able to talk about a style of seeking consent and knowing how to stay within the realm of consent. I'm thinking of the Wheel of Consent*, which is an interesting concept. I've talked about sexual fantasies and this relationship I had with this guy, using that model.

One of the things I want to talk about more (in the group) and that I've talked about with one of the group members, is that I am in an open relationship

* The Wheel of Consent is a model of consent for exchanges of touch – an issue of renewed importance in the #MeToo era. An illustration is in the Appendix.

now and it's been very interesting to navigate. Like how to avoid toxic masculine emotions because there are things that come up with my partner and the other guy that she's developed a relationship with and we're trying to navigate that with her while getting to know her at the same time. It's definitely been a roller coaster. It's been a lot of emotional work.

Younger Women's Group

Heather Price: When I was going through a career transition, it was a bit of a tough time for me – a big event that was occurring in my life. Everybody in the group was incredibly supportive both on our calls and outside of the calls. I got so much love throughout that process as I was navigating my way through that transition.

Michelle Chanson: I can think of a couple of times when it's been really helpful just to be able to talk through things with the group. One was about some business challenges I was having. I was trying to figure out the right moment to do certain things, make hires, grow the business. I was also dealing with employee challenges and it's been really interesting to get other people's perspectives on how they work in their work environments. It's been re-affirming to know that you're on the right path – that these things happen and you're not alone.

Liz Sharp: My group has been really helpful on the career front. When I made the leap into catering, it was so crazy. I was working long hours and my body was dealing with all the stress that I was putting on it. I remember Charlie and Amelia being especially aware of some pains I was having in my fingers. They really were straight-talking me about getting a handle on it, going to physical therapy, getting some second opinions, figuring out what I could do so I just didn't burn my body into the ground right away. It was really helpful. Nobody else had been able to say, "You need to do this." I made the leap into the crazy world of trying to start my own business, and I'm finding the group to be incredible, providing me with cheerleading when there's no one else to provide it. I have co-workers now, but I don't have a team like the women in my group.

My grandmother died last fall and it was a really hard goodbye for me. She was a huge part of my life. Everybody just really listened so empathetically. There were follow-up texts and calls after I had a particularly rough time. It was a year ago exactly on the call, and I was just letting them know that I was struggling with it, that it was not leaving my head. The women really listened and kept making me feel very supported beyond that moment. It wasn't like just that sense of holding on in the moment. They really extended it through time and space in a really beautiful way.

They've also been great – and this is being really personal, but I'm not too shy about it – with fertility issues. There's been amazing support on that front – advice, empathy and listening – and it's so helpful to have that, because it's not something that gets talked about as much. I'm pretty open about it, but not everybody is, and you never know how folks will respond to having that conversation, but I can tell them where I am and whether I want to talk about it or not. If I don't want to talk about it, they're fine either way. But for me personally, these are some of the places where they have been incredibly helpful and there for me.

I would like to offer one more life-changing support-group tale, this time from a friend who, in an article for *Voice Male* magazine in 2005, cited his involvement in a men's group as one of the "several steps that led to the peaceful ending of our marriage and the effective beginning of the rest of my life." Writing anonymously as "David J." to protect his ex-wife's privacy, he said he sought out this group with his marriage in crisis – a frequent motivator for many who choose support groups.

> The morning after hearing my marriage might end, I was staring in the mirror and thought, I need to remake myself in my own image. Somehow I understood that I'd been spending my life trying to be what I thought others – especially the women I most cared about – wanted me to be. It may have taken me 47 years, but I was finally figuring out that that wasn't working. And my intuition led me to realize this was about being a man. For as long as I'd given masculinity any thought, from my teens onward, I had rejected the conventional stereotypes of manhood – the implicit violence, the denigration of women, the bravado – but hadn't replaced them with positive images of what it means to be a man. I knew in that moment at the mirror that I needed to connect with other men and explore the question of maleness with them.
>
> By coincidence, an article appeared in a local weekly soon afterward about an organization in Brattleboro, Vermont, called For and About Men, which held monthly forums on men's issues. I contacted one of the organizers, who put me in touch with someone who in turn told me about a group that met in Keene, New Hampshire. I began attending the group, where I found men I could trust, who would listen as I poured out my heart and my tears, who would hold me in their arms and hearts, and who would affirm my worth and even my courage. Later I formed a group closer to home, with men closer to my own age and life circumstances. I developed real friendships with men – a rarity in my life before then – and learned the meaning of genuine mutual support.

Ultimately, whether you're seeking deeper relationships or you're in a serious life-affecting crisis, support groups offer the opportunity to forge enduring bonds, examine your life in a safe, encouraging and challenging environment, and a host of other opportunities that can make life more meaning-ful, provide more connection, increase access to emotions and change yourself in perhaps unimaginable but invariably life-enhancing ways.

CHAPTER 13
HOW HAS THE GROUP CHANGED OVER TIME? WHAT CHANGES ARE STILL DESIRED?

Hindsight continues to be 20/20 and prognosticating remains a shaky endeavor at best, but, hey, why not? – especially when it comes to imagining and then maybe even articulating the ways in which one's needs have and have not, are and are not being met. That's what this interview question offered – the opportunity to reflect on how the group could have been different in an earlier stage and how it might change to be even more accommodating of its members' desires for intimacy, connection and challenge.

Of course, the groups that have been around considerably longer have had more time to make – or not make – some of the changes members individually or collectively have sought. Each individual I interviewed had the chance to think about what level of satisfaction his or her group provides and to reflect on whether that level is satisfactory. That meant considering numerous aspects of the group's life, as the following responses will reveal.

What is also evident, especially with the older groups, are the ways in which the culture and life stages impact a group's functioning, its subject matter and definitely its structure. As the lives of the younger groups' members have become more complex, with partners, children and work demands, a web of issues arises, along with members' visions for how their groups might develop. For all the group members, it will be clear that there are a variety of challenges that have changed them and their groups, as well as some changes they'd like to see, to further deepen their commitment and their enjoyment.

I shall start with the man who proposed our group's biggest change to date – the decision to meet for a full day one Sunday a month instead of two hours once a week.

Older Men's Group

Stephen Bannasch: Once we switched to our present structure we had more fun. We had more eating. We're weaving much more of the rhythms of life that I think are sustainable. The rhythms of meals together, of adventures together, of longer conversations. It could be individuals sharing or a theme. It's enough time that you don't have to have this idea that you're always efficient. So many of those things are so important for creativity and intimacy. So many different things worked better after the change.

Gary Phillips: The group certainly has developed a maturity in some way, almost a culture of its own, which in its younger years was raw and appropriating from anything it could and trying to work with the existing culture. We went through a lot of intense changes in our first years. We are individually very political now. We were corporately very political at the time. So we would do things like provide childcare for radical women's events in the Pioneer Valley. We became involved in helping teach a course at Amherst College on men's issues. For a while we called ourselves Men Against Patriarchy. We were very, very involved in conversations about feminism. I think we still are, but in looser terms.

At some point along the way, especially after the long retreat where we gave each other our personal histories, in our analysis we began talking about intimacy as a radical act – about men being able to be close and intimate and trusting and challenging of each other outside of the normal boundaries of male bonding, and to distinguish true intimacy from male bonding in a solid enough way that we could look at it and tell the difference and that we could express that difference to the rest of society.

So that became one of our political arcs that I think still exists. It meant that in the group we were challenging to each other. We wouldn't let each other get away with stuff, but it also meant that we made the bridge of affection between that difficulty and whatever needed to grow after that to make sense. I feel like that was a keystone event in our group, even though you can't really term it an "event." It wasn't like you just all of a sudden had some awareness and this happened, but our own process of being demanding of each other and loving of each other, of hard love with each other, became a really important part of our group and what the group actually did. It became tangible. I see that as a marker or a change.

The group is more reluctant to have intense four, five, six-hour meetings than it was when I was still much more involved in the group, though this weekend* we have twice already had such sessions. I'm on the side of members of the group who like that. There were some members of the group for whom it makes them nervous. They'd rather muck around in boats and tell stories than talk about things. I love having that time, too, but I really want the intense concentrating on each other, delving into each other's lives and revealing who we are to each other. Time – that I consider very, very crucial to my relationship with these men.

Robbie Leppzer: The group has definitely evolved over time from being more outwardly focused to being more inwardly focused. In the beginning, we were really revved up to do a lot of outward actions like supporting women's groups and various movements. In 1979 we all got arrested in a civil disobedience demonstration at a nuclear weapons protest, protesting the launching of a Trident nuclear submarine in Groton, Connecticut. When we did the anti-nuclear demonstration, we went there as a men's affinity group to bring a pro-feminist men's perspective. We handed out a flyer that made the connections between rape and the nuclear mentality. So we were there with a double purpose. We felt very exhilarated by that because we were offering multiple levels of awareness

---

* Gary is referencing one of our originally four- and now five-day annual retreats, where this interview was conducted.

and that felt really exciting.

We made this crazy movie called *Positively Men* in 1981 and we spent most of our time at the NOMAS (National Organization of Men Against Sexism) conference at Tufts University showing the film and holding discussion groups with other men about our experiences being in a men's group. It felt really satisfying because we had something to share that was firsthand and concrete and personal. After every one of those showings, men who we were talking to were clearly inspired. We really planted a lot of seeds. There was this hunger for alternative role models and our men's group, as shown in the film, was an alternative role model. It was really exciting to share that and to feel that my personal experience could be a catalyst for other people to think differently and to change.

Alan Surprenant: For all of us over time, a different amount of self-nurturing became more important. After the first actions that we did together, I didn't feel like everybody had to do everything I was into. We had a pretty diverse involvement in what we did for work and family lives. Grown children, newborn babies, all that. It was really nice for all of my kids when they were little to see all of these men hugging and kissing, like it's not just a family thing or a woman thing where people do that. They could just grow up with that as part of a natural thing. It was good for Willow and Micah (Alan's children) to see another role for men.

Older Women's Group

Annette Cycon: There was a time when we were getting tired of just checking in. I used to feel that the only legitimate check-in was one where you were talking about something going wrong in your life – that the only thing that was permissible or acceptable or expected to be talked about were our challenges. It's important to have a safe place where you can go to talk about the hard stuff. But there is more to our lives than that. We also want to celebrate ourselves, our milestones. There was a call for more physical activity and more lighthearted activity and celebration.

We are open to discussing our needs, or ways we would like to see the group change. I think that is one secret to our longevity. We dedicate time, sometimes many months, to chewing on and discussing a topic, such as group structure or inviting new members, until we come to consensus agreement. We speak respectfully together, even when we differ. We use a talking object, so every woman has protected time to speak.

I'm very proud of that. Our women's group has evolved and matured, just as we have individually, because of each other.

Sara Schley: We've changed over the years. We were in our 30s, now we're in our 50s. We were kind of hippies, now we're kind of grandmothers. In the early days we would always start with drumming and we'd start with smudging.* I actually really liked that. There was a way we were intentionally calling in sacred space. We haven't kept that so much in recent years. Every now and then we'll remember to bring out the sage, but now we start a little bit more by kibbitzing over tea. There's usually some kind of ritual that happens. We always check in with the rock or some kind of sacred object. For people around our valley that's not a ritual, that's a given, but if you're out in the world that's a ritual. Sometimes we use sage, sometimes we drum, sometimes we pick an angel card, sometimes we light a candle. In the early days it was the person whose house it was who would

---

* An ancient ceremony of burning sacred plants, such as sage, to allow the smoke to clear and bless a space.

facilitate and they would choose whatever kind of ritual practice we would do. It was more formal in that way. Now we just show up and co-create it. I think if you overlaid something like Gail Sheehy's *Passages* onto our developmental stages as 30-somethings and now 50- and 60-somethings, it feels like it's been an organic change for me over time.

Sara Elinoff Acker: We've never changed the one-day-a-month meeting structure, but sometimes we add on. Last week we had a spontaneous dinner at Annette's house. We've loosened up a little bit. In the early years of our group, we had the agreement that everyone was supposed to set aside the third Sunday of the month unless there was an unavoidable conflict – something of monumental importance. The idea was you'd come for most of the months over the year.

But life is complicated. We have other important commitments and sometimes they interfere with our circle. Some of us have been more flexible about that, but for a long time, I was on the more attached and rigid end of the spectrum. I really love our circle time and I got upset, because I thought other people were holding it as less important. I remember thinking, "Where are you? Why did you make that other plan? Don't you remember it's the third Sunday? What's going on? I set aside everything else and I showed up, so where are you?" I found myself feeling hurt and disappointed.

There's been some tension in the group around this issue. Sometimes people had to negotiate. We had one person who said, "I am just swamped, so I'm only going to be able to come four times this year and I need that to be O.K. with everybody. I don't want to feel judged." One woman took a sabbatical for a while and said, "I just need to step way back. I don't know if I'm going to come back." Over time, as we continue to talk about the issue, we've worked it out.

I would also say that what's really helped is that I have shifted. I am becoming a more flexible person who can just go with the flow each month. The truth, really, is that whoever does come and whatever we share is amazing. I've let go and realized it's delicious to be in the circle, whether it's all eight of us or just three or four. Our new agreement is that we've lightened up our expectation of the number of groups you need to attend per year and we've just let people come when they can come. We hope that people can make it to six of the groups each year, but nobody's really counting. If we're going to be together for the rest of our lives, then does it really matter? We're all just doing our best. The group is important to everyone, no matter whether they can come to most or only a few of our meetings.

It will come as no surprise that fewer changes have occurred in the two younger groups. Their shorter tenure certainly is a factor, but it also deserves to be pointed out that the women have already seen one another through many changes, because four of them have been together since childhood.

Younger Men's Group

Ben Fuller-Googins: I feel anything we go through is valuable. When we first started out we made a mission statement and did other things we were used to as activists. But we've really not returned to that, which is O.K. To me we've deepened a lot of intimacy and sharing.

Josh La Tour: I think it's been challenging for the group to change. We've had times where we started to become more organized and then we reach our capacity in terms of how much we can do in a group. We also tried to check out a curriculum at the beginning. It was somewhat useful. We met one of the creators of it and he acknowledged it was needing to be updated to be more inclusive. We keep feeling our way.

Younger Women's Group

Naomi Lutra: When I think about whether the group has changed since the phone calls began, one thing that was really a key is that we've all been allowed to change from each other and to even change from ourselves. There really is an unconditional love and support, so even though many of us have totally different jobs and totally different fields and might never run into each other if we were just meeting now, that's O.K. The changes that have happened to us as people and how we are continuing to change and grow – we all leave space for each other to do it.

Charlie Evans: Because we've been friends for so long, for so many formative periods in our lives, we were always together for things like getting your first job – all of these major milestone events in life. When we collectively became what we identify as this group – we were in our early 20s – I like to think we had greater perspective on our need for one another than the older groups in your project.

After asking all the group members to think about changes that have occurred in the group, I followed up by asking them to consider what they would like their group to be, that it has yet to become: What changes do you want to see that would add to your satisfaction and enjoyment?

Older Men's Group

Robbie Leppzer: I've been okay with the change to being more inward-focused. I feel like my own personal life is essentially all about outside change work, so I actually welcomed this sanctuary of having a place, a personal space in my life, where I'm with chosen family and it is about supporting each other. I don't feel the compulsion to have us do outside work, because I feel like I do that all the time in my own life.

I'm happy for the break the group offers from that in a certain way, but maybe once in a while I could see us doing something. We did a few presentations about the group with our group film (*Positively Men*) in the '80s with other men's groups or people thinking about forming men's groups or people wanting to check us out. We didn't want to take on new people, but we inspired some groups to form. I think we could still do that and lead discussions and be available for that as a resource in the Valley, because in some ways we are an example of what's possible for men to have by being emotionally intimate with one another. This group of men has been together now for almost 40 years. It's pretty unique, so I think we have a lot to share. Maybe when your book comes out that will be possible.

Steve Trudel: I would like there to be a topic more often. Like at the annual retreat on the St. Lawrence River, when I said, "Let's talk about aging." Did that happen? Hardly. I found it frustrating. That part of me has been there all along. I want us all to be together and to share something that's really stimulating. It's like Gertrude Stein's salon. That's what I imagine. That's what I long for – artists and social workers and political people coming together and talking about some issue that's really being discovered societally.

Gary Phillips: Just yesterday we had what was, for me at least, our first full discussion about what resources, financial and otherwise, people have to go into the future, and thoughts about what the future is going to look like. We're in transition time. We're at the time when we look in the obituaries because it's likely to have somebody we know. We're at the time where we are either dealing with parents who are dying or have been dealing with it – that's a fresh part of our lives. So mortality issues are around us all the time. Everyone yesterday spoke to diminished capacity, to changes in their bodies, to fear for their future, to all those things.

The next ten years is a reaping time, a changing time. Everybody acknowledged that – will we hold together, what will we hold together as, or what will drift away from us? It's been a long time since '78. That's a long period of time for the group to meet and to be very cohesive. Having nine out of ten (after Llan left the group) is still very cohesive, but it also gives an indication of some uncertainty and of people's lives changing, of circumstances changing. How will we respond?

The question of changes we'd like to see touched on a value that has motivated me in many other arenas of my own life:

Tom Weiner: There is one significant area that I wish we could change, though it seems increasingly unlikely with each passing year. That we have had two gay men in the group has been incredibly valuable, being able to experience reality through the eyes of someone with a different sexual orientation than mine. How a gay man sees our culture, our media, our relationships with women, etc., has added immeasurably to my awareness of my own life and of our society.

It is in this same spirit that I would have liked us to have found a way to bring in a couple of men of color, but we neither set it as a goal nor had it happen organically. That is sad for me, since the kind of enrichment having someone who had grown up black or Latino or Asian in America could have provided would have deepened all of our awareness of what such a life is like. Of course, had they been the only person of their race or ethnicity in the group that could have been, and still could be, very challenging for them and would require much awareness on everyone's part. Having said that, I would immediately add that the men in our group continue to strive to overcome our social conditioning, having grown up with privilege in a racist society, and several of us have chosen work that allows us to put forth our values about social jus-

195

tice and racial justice in particular.

Older Women's Group

Morning Star Chenven: Structurally, I like the ritual and nonverbal aspects of being together, and sometimes wish we did more of that. Music, movement, prayer and meditation are some examples of this. When I bring it up people say, "Yeah, that would be great," but things don't necessarily change.

There's a lot of sharing and talking. I'm not sure I always want so much of that. I have said to people that I feel sometimes when we're going around giving feedback to one another, that I just don't have as much to say as some others. We have several therapists in the group and sometimes I feel less capable of giving articulate feedback.

We make beautiful meals. Everybody brings a potluck dish and it's usually fresh and beautiful, but a lot of times we don't eat with a lot of consciousness. We're eating fast – talking, talking, get the dishes done, getting back to whatever. I actually would like to share more consciousness around eating.

Ruth Olsen: I wish we had more time together. I wish I had more time to connect with everybody individually and between the circles. It doesn't give me enough time. We'd love to have more weekends together. Life is just really full. I wish I had more time to be with these amazing women. These are remarkable women. These are exceptional human beings. These are women who are at the top of their field, dedicated to living passionate, quality lives of full accountability and open-heartedness – they blow me away, every one of them. That's another part of what they gave me. Because they're so fearless and so smart and creative and powerhouses, they brought that part of me forward. We've nurtured the potential of each other – to live fully empowered in what we're going to contribute in the world. I would say that's an enormous role that we've played for each other.

Susan Loring-Wells: I love everything that the group is. The only thing is I wish we lived closer. We do talk about as we get older and we lose spouses, we'd all live together, because we know each other and we support each other. We'd get to spend more time together if we lived closer. It would give the relationships more nourishing. I don't call people on the phone the way I used to, partly because we don't have a landline anymore and the cell phone gets terrible reception.

Sara Elinoff Acker: I always wish we could have more time together. A six-hour gathering that ends at 4:00 feels too short for me. I wish we could have eight hours together. Sometimes it feels like we don't have enough spaciousness in a day. But we've remedied that somewhat by having two trips a year. The summer trip is four nights and the winter trip is two nights. Those make a huge difference for me.
I just thought of something else I need to talk about, and that is the issue of class. There's an interesting and delicate class dynamic going on in this group. It's a bit of a taboo subject – something really difficult to address. I think that has been scary for us to bring up and to really explore.

One of the fantasies that I have for this group is that when we get old, we're going to be able to live in proximity to each other. I have the dream of us being in a townhouse complex together or in a neighborhood together, but really it's so unrealistic, because we have such different resources. As we age, our class differences become more apparent.

When our group began, we were in our 30s and 40s and now we're in our 50s and 60s. It will be really interesting to see what happens as we go into our 60s, 70s and 80s. Our hope is to be together for the rest of our lives. A bunch of years ago, somebody found this great article from the National Enquirer about a women's group that had been together for 66 years! They are these cute older women who play canasta and mah jong, but it's clear that they are very bonded. Since we read about them, we have this running joke about our 66 years together. We're only 21 years in, so we all have to live to be at least 100 so we can make it to 66 years!

Diane Norman: Our group is currently very much a heterosexual, a married and, as far as I know, a monogamous group of women. After my divorce, when I was single, I felt like the odd woman out. Everyone would talk about their husbands and I would say, "I don't even have a partner, let alone a husband." I'd have to remind them when someone would say, "How about we invite our husbands?" and I was like, "Yoo-hoo." So, this is certainly one place our group lacks diversity.

Also, a lot of us are of similar ages, which has a beauty, in that we can really relate to each other's life experience, post-menopausal etc. This is significant in how we understand and support each other through similar life stages. However, I am happy I'm involved in the lives of younger women who are friends of my 28-year-old daughter. I enjoy the balance that their perspective on the world offers me at this time in my life.

The one place there is some diversity in our circle is in our individual access to wealth. I believe this has become even more apparent as some of us retire or consider retiring and as parents die and certain ones of us inherit wealth and others don't. Interestingly, this is one area we rarely, if ever, truly delve deeply into to explore together. Like it's the ultimate taboo subject. As much as I might enjoy more diversity, I adore these women and they are a vital part of my life and well-being.

Younger Men's Group

Ben Fuller-Googins: I think we could – me included – get a little deeper around things going on in our lives. I think the group can help better equip us in the world in terms of our inner being when things are going on at work or in our relationships. There's a situation that I can think of where I was a bystander and I didn't take action. There's a lot of shame around that for me. Just bringing more of those kinds of things going on in our lives into the group. I think we could up the rigor in that way.

This specific time I'm referring to was about one of our board members (at work), and he was, in my opinion, making some inappropriate moves and gestures towards this younger woman who came in to make a presentation, and I felt very stuck and I wanted to say something, but I didn't. I didn't share that with the group, because I have a hard time mustering energy to want to bring that up again. There's a lot of healing and important work to be done there. Maybe I'll bring it up in tomorrow's meeting in the wake of all of these revelations coming up through #MeToo. There are also these stories from high school that I've never shared with people – things I've seen and didn't intervene, and I have so much shame around them. We've never gone to that level with each other.

Josh LaTour: If we had lots of time and money... A while ago I thought of this art project that would have been interesting to do. It was with this art venue called the School for the Apocalypse and they were making a call for working groups to make up a project. I pitched it to the group for us to do some kind of photo-documentary about men giving testimony about toxic masculinity and how it prevents men from even being able to cry with their kids. But most of the men in my life, including this group of men, aren't creative-focused – it's more of an activist mentality. That felt limiting to me in some way. If we wanted to have an impact, what better way to do it than with a creative outlet with a viewing of what we produced, in order to create a conversation? I accepted that it wasn't going to happen. I wanted people on board, but this was a group of guys that didn't have the interest or the time.

It would also be great to have more diversity, especially since with #MeToo and the women's movement it's become more acceptable to talk about misogyny within different intersections of racism.

Younger Women's Group

Naomi Lutra: I would love to make our recent retreat a yearly event. I think it will take some work to make a group trip a priority. We'll all have to balance schedules, time away from work, and family commitments, but I hope that just like these phone calls, once it becomes a tradition, it'll feel like a seamless addition to our lives.

Michelle Chanson: I hope that we continue to hold each other accountable and continue to be as invested in this group as we are now. Being able to set aside a weekend for a retreat when we can all see each other in person is really great. In fact, we recently had our first annual "girls' retreat" and it was incredibly rewarding.

Michelle's next words underline the point made earlier – that their group, although comparatively new, has already developed a high degree of mutual awareness, deep devotion and steadfast commitment. The life changes that the older groups have been experiencing for some time will inevitably occur, but these attributes will remain in place and serve these women well.

> Everybody really shows up for each other in a really big way, which I don't see happen often for people I know in other friendships. These are women who show up. I don't know a better way to articulate that other than to say, when you need them they're there and they see the importance of this monthly gathering, because they truly want to know what's going on in each other's lives. We miss each other and we notice and know what each other needs. If someone were to suddenly miss several calls, we'd reach out to them and say, "Hey, what's going on? Can we make this work for you, because we really want to see you? How can we make this more convenient for you?" There would be a discussion to make sure that person was not losing touch with the group.

> This is a really honest group of women and because we care so deeply about one another we're not just "yes" people. We're thoughtful about the decisions that we and other members are making. If someone came to us with something we thought was a bad decision that was going to put them in harm's way or someone they cared about in harm's way or it just didn't feel like it was going to advance whatever we felt they were capable of, we would absolutely say something. If we didn't want to address it on the call, we're the type of group that would convene offline and ask, "How do we approach this person to let them know that we feel this might not be in their best interest?"

Change is clearly essential if a group is going to both meet the evolving needs of its members and be sustainable over the long haul. My men's group is already facing some major changes since I conducted the interviews, as several of us have reached or will soon reach the traditional retirement age and are also dealing with various physical and financial challenges. Through all these, we are staying committed to being there for one another. The older women's group is also experiencing the changes of the life cycle – losing parents, dealing with health issues – and their commitment is likewise enduring. The younger groups are going through a host of different challenges and their dedication to the group and its members is powerful and empowering, as their words so eloquently express.

Changes pertaining to group composition – to become more inclusive of racial, sexual orientation, age, ethnic and class differences – have been harder to find ways to bring about. Many of those interviewed compensate for the lack of diversity in the group by filling their friendship circle with people who represent a range of differences. I've personally got a number of very close friends of different backgrounds and my cross-race dialogue group fulfills this need. But I, along with others, continue to wish this change in group composition might still occur. Sharing our annual retreat with the younger men's group provided stimulating interactions and efforts are being made to make it happen again. Time will be the ultimate judge of how much any of the four groups will be able to keep changing to meet the needs of those whose voices you're hearing. The longer a group stays together, the more they have to navigate one another's changes and find ways to accept if not always embrace those changes.

CHAPTER 14
HOW WOULD LIFE BE DIFFERENT WITHOUT THE GROUP?

For folks in a group with 25 or 40 years of history, responding to this question required major imagination. Our adulthoods have been largely defined by the association with our respective support groups. It's hard to imagine life without them. Many of the younger groups' members focused on the absence of such support in the lives of their friends and associates, and the difference it makes in their worlds to have the group identity and the support it affords. The question definitely gave an opportunity to reflect, and many of the responses addressed it indirectly by considering the value and the role the group has played in our lives.

As for me, I have been in three different men's groups since 1973, which means 45 years. All three have provided guidance, direction and wellsprings of support. Outside the group, I am also blessed with a number of very close women and men friends with whom I am able to share intimately, over long periods of time. Still, there is something unique about being part of a group that has such history, continuity and commitment that I have found nowhere else.

Here, then, are the imaginings of group members trying to conjure up what would have been lost without their participation in their group.

Older Men's Group

Stephen Bannasch: I can't really even go there. What life would be like without the group? What would it be like without me? I don't know! It's so woven into my life.

I can say something that might get a little bit of the flavor of it. I don't like to travel much, but I do sometimes travel for business, to meet with people. I find myself, when I'm far away from home and away from my family, feeling ungrounded after a while. Disconnected. If I sat and talked to somebody, that would be cool. I love doing that. It's only in the fabric of my family and my extended family – the men's group –

that I can work the way I do and work hard. It's hard to have the kind of motivation for what I do and why it matters on a larger scale without being embedded in that fabric. It's not as important as my family, but it's like that. I feel like, "What am I doing here?" without it.

Robbie Leppzer: I think I would still be who I am, but I'm a lot more confident about being who I am, because I get a lot of support for who I am from this intimate group of men. If I was without the group, I would feel confident in my inner self and from individual friends, but I have a solid foundation of this group that is really validating for who I am and how I see the world and how I want to be as a man in this world.

Alan Surprenant: I never would have experienced the energy of ten men that were all together with each other in a pretty non-hierarchical fashion. It wasn't like a platoon in the army, where men feel that camaraderie, and I totally understand that – those people have your back and they don't in the real world, in civilian life. Your close friends do for the most part, but the culture we're in is a competitive culture with a lot of distrust, and rightfully so. But it doesn't have to be that way, and I feel like the group has helped me see that men's relationships can actually exist differently.

Of course, we can't change everything. It just gives me the energy to interact in ways I feel strongly about in that larger world and not feel isolated totally. I may feel isolated on the day I am doing something, but certainly I can bring it back to the group. I think my life without that would have had a huge hole in it. I think I would have continued to pursue personal, one-on-one relationships with other men, but I never would have experienced our group's commitment and longevity. There would have been a fleeting energy for some group around something, some common topic. But it would be fleeting.

Our far-flung member, who comes once a year from his home in North Carolina to our annual retreat, put into words the "glue" that keeps the group together, and in so doing provided a blueprint for what would not have happened had he not been part of us:

> **Gary Phillips:** We all contain valuable elements that we each need. Through serendipity or synchronicity or some divine providence or fate, we came into each other's lives in a powerful, formational way that created ripples throughout our entire lives. We formed a relationship that is very difficult to find in the modern world of tribal identity – access to an intimacy that has a solid platform. We kind of fell in love with each other and there are many reasons for us to fall out of love with each other, but none strong enough to actually make it happen.
>
> For some of those who began with the group, it became so precious as a part of our lives that we protected it. It created almost a life of its own and that has held. Also, we've been willing to go into important emotional territory that is really difficult to find people to go into. You need a group to do that work. We've also moved, in the circumstances when we had enough courage and enough skill, all the way through it to the other side. So there's a certain "band of brothers" aspect from that shared experience. We've not just been a group of men celebrating each other. We've been a group of men also watching each other break down and still being in the same room after you break down to help build you back up. That is something very difficult to find in this world. That's something so precious it's worth coming to New England for.

Older Women's Group

Sara Schley: My mom, who passed last year – this will be a hard story to get through. When I got married – this is not from our circle, but it's a traditional Jewish thing – the women got together and the men got together. So we're in the women's circle before the wedding and we set it up by age. The oldest person went first and the youngest person went last, all giving advice to the soon-to-be-bride. My mom was the oldest so she went first. She has an acerbic wit and is very intelligent, but she is disconnected from her emotions. She has her emotions and her spirituality in shadow. She grew up in that kind of environment – Yankee. So she went first and said something you might say was superficial. We go all around the circle – and my mom has also suffered from severe depression in her lifetime, but never had a place to speak that.

We got all the way around and my mom asked to take the talking object we were using and I went, "Uh-oh," because she would generally have something slightly sarcastic or nasty to say. She stood up and she said (here Sara teared up), "You don't know how lucky you are. If I'd had what you girls have, my life would have been completely different." She was isolated in her pain. She couldn't speak her pain. You didn't share your dirty laundry. She grew up in that era – a 50s housewife. I think that's what my life would be without the group. I have a place. I have that support. I have a place I can go with my pain. I feel like they've kept me alive over the years during the hard times and I know a lot of us feel that way. My mother named what we have and I have and all of us have – a level of support that her generation did not have. Without it I don't know how I would have made it to this day.

Susan Loring-Wells: I feel secure in my connections and my sense of community. I would be pining for something like this. I would really be longing. I also really like the ritual parts that we do. I think I'm more introspective than I would be without the group. I feel that when I'm communicating about my husband or other issues in the circle I am respectful. As hurt or upset or whatever I'm feeling, there's a lot of respect in how I bring an issue to the table.

Ruth Olsen: We lift each other up. We help each other be the best we can be. When we're each falling apart we show up to share the human condition and the dilemmas and struggles to help us find a way to live, to breathe, to continue. Without the group it would all be so much harder.

Younger Men's Group

Ben Blackshear: I think the group demonstrates to us the truth that we need each other. It clearly shows that peer support and realizing our interconnectedness are important in a culture that is so built on individualism.

It's helped me learn how to be more vulnerable with people in my life who are not my romantic partner. I've learned that sharing ways I am working on improving myself, or things that I am struggling with, helps me do the work I need to do to make the changes I want and need to make. Being in the group makes me more accountable to myself – and the group. Without the group I don't know if that would be possible.

Ben Fuller-Googins: It fills the need for connection because it's explicitly rooted in wanting to both outwardly confront and challenge patriarchal violence and inwardly deal with how patriarchy shapes our relationship to ourselves. Since it was the intention of our group from the start, it changes how I show up for it compared to how I am with other men. Right from the start we were talking about pornography or violence or how we objectify women or how we can't cultivate a relationship with our fathers. It's been a consistent invitation for me to reveal more, and there's nowhere else in my life where that happens. I want to touch on sex. I think I have a lot of shame around sex and my body –particularly about male violence in sexual dynamics. It's hard for me to bring my full self in sexual romantic partnerships because I censor and police myself so that I don't express violence. One hundred percent of my female partners have experienced this and it impacts our relationship, because if I'm putting a lot of energy into policing and censoring my behavior, partners can't experience my whole self. So I'm seeking a balance between feeling my full self, but not replicating patterns of violence and dominance that are still the norm. Even as I hear myself talk about this, it's such a release to have a space to talk about with other guys saying it's hard for them, too.

Kevin Quirolo: I tend to avoid connecting with men outside our group because having to confront the sexism I encounter is stressful. By facing and dealing with our own sexism in a controlled environment, it's made me more confident I can deal with it outside the group. I'm quite sure I would not take such risks were it not for this group.

Younger Women's Group

Amelia Olsen: I think I would have lost their friendship. Not in an absolute way – they'd still be my friends and I would see them when I went to the City. There are some friendships where it doesn't matter how long it's been or what's happened, you feel like you can always connect and not miss a beat.

I have lots of friends like that and I'm grateful for those friends, but the lie underlying that dynamic is that life is all the little things that happen in between.

209

It's not just "We just bought a house." It's "There's a house that we saw today that I hated and my husband loved. What am I going to do with this man?" The reality is you just can't catch up with somebody in one conversation. What you get are the highlights, and the truth is in knowing someone and giving them the details. I am super grateful that I still have details on all of these women.

I remember that I was trying to replicate these amazing dinners at a new different restaurant that would last for hours. It would be most of us, but not really ever all of us. That was the thing – how am I ever going to replicate those dinners, because so much happened at dinner? I think that was the insight – that was at the center of our women's group and we didn't know it.

Liz Sharp: I think I would feel more untethered. When I was talking before about how these women ground me, if I didn't have the group I absolutely know that I wouldn't be as aware of what's happening with Charlie and Amelia because they live further away. I'm absolutely sure that it would be harder to have a handle on what's happening in their lives, and I'm so glad that I get to have that.

I think it would be a little lonelier, because I think that in my 30s, not being affiliated with an institution meant I was on my own much more. Once I broke off into the food world I was working with these intense groups of people who I formed friendships with, but who weren't the people I'd been friends with for a long time. I feel like my friendships would all feel more fractured if the group wasn't in my life. Not fractured within the friendships, but more like – there's a friend over there and there's a friend over here. It would feel not pulled together and like I had to expend a huge amount of energy to keep in touch with everyone.

That is something great about this group that makes me feel so much more centered. I don't have to have the same conversation five times. We just have it happen once all together and everybody knows that everybody can go back and forth on a topic. I feel like more friendships with these women would fall off. It would be really hard to keep all the separate conversations going, and this frees up some energy to keep investing in some of those other friendships that I want to invest in. If I was doing this with everyone, someone would fall off. I actually think it frees up energy in a way.

Not surprisingly, the longer the interview subject has been in his or her group, the harder it was on many levels to imagine life without such support. Forty years of group involvement means almost all of the men in my group were in their 20s when the group began, so virtually all of the major events in our adulthoods were shared, processed, celebrated and challenged at some point in each of our lives. Four of the six women in the younger women's group have been good friends since middle school, so again a life with their emotional ties is essentially unimaginable. Yet each person spoke of a sense of significant loss they would inevitably experience were they not to have had the richness, the depth, the quality and the devotion of the group. Yet another advertisement for belonging to one.

CHAPTER 15
HOW DOES THE GROUP IMPACT
YOUR COMMUNITY?

Times change, but do the basic needs of our communities? Is there a parallel between what was going on when the older men's group began in the late '70s and our current times, so that the two men's groups have more in common than might otherwise have been anticipated? Do the women's groups share any common threads of purpose? These are all questions that are engaged in this chapter.

The question of how the group affects the members' wider community was intended to take folks beyond themselves and their group membership, and to think about whether there is intentionality around the phrase from the '60s, – "the personal is political" – or social, for that matter. Inner work and outer work – that is the question. Can one successfully engage in both simultaneously, or must one or the other take the proverbial back seat?

You've already read about the early days of the older men's group, which was forged in political activism. When I had the consummate good fortune to attend a gathering of the younger men's group, I was asked numerous questions about my group's political consciousness and about how we manifest it in the world. When they came to our Valley for a weekend, for both groups to begin to bond and to get to know one another, many of the conversations centered around issues of race, gender and sexual politics, so it was quite evident that nearly 40 years after our founding, here was a group grappling with similar issues and concerns.

When the older women's group came into being in the '90s, its members were older than the members of our men's group were at its inception, and they were in the midst of a different political and social era. In addition, each of them had had considerably more time to determine how much activism would characterize their lives. Nonetheless, the members of both women's groups had been impacted mightily by feminism and the women's movement, both individually and collectively, so comparing their responses will be worthwhile.

Older Men's Group

Dick McLeester: I feel like our group is a really good thing and most of the time I feel like it's hidden from most people. We did do our movie, *Positively Men*, and we showed that to a bunch of people. But that was a long time ago (1981). There are some people who know about us on an ongoing basis. Most of the time I feel like it's a big secret. I was thinking, "Geez, I have all these photos. It'd be fun to put a little presentation up on Facebook: Here's my men's group." On the whole, I don't know if we want to make an effort to be more public. We'd like to influence things. Most of the time our main task is not to get too depressed with how stupidly things are going in the world.

We have certainly been more involved in different actions at times. We have individuals who are doing stuff and that may at any moment mean that more of us from the group will join their efforts. The edge of that is if anybody sees something that would be interesting and be good for us to act on, they can bring it to the group and see if the group agrees or gets a current of inspiration and wants to do something like that. It's in the realm of possibility, so it could happen. More often, though, we support each other so we can each go back out there and do our best to make a difference.

Tony Clarke: I think all of us have a similar social-political outlook about the world and what we see is wrong with the world and right with the world and what we'd like to change in the world. A number of us have worked in different ways at different points in our lives towards that end.

Alan Surprenant: These days, in the group sense, our impact is somewhat limited. In the personal sense, it's very expansive. I think that in the friendship circles of each man in the group, it's expansive. Talking about the group lets other men know that we have a lot of similar beliefs and lets them see that men can do this type of experience together. They hear that they don't always have to talk exclusively to women about emotions and relationships and not talk to men about it purposely and just keep it inside. They hear that we want to hear from each other.

A lot of times I've known men who've just put it all on women and expected them to listen to them, which they don't have any interest in at all after five minutes. They don't usually try to work on things with other men, because they assume nothing will happen, so whatever they're feeling just stays internal. It's not expressed, or if a man does reach out they're likely to get a blank stare from somebody and they stop right after that because they don't really know how to deal with it. Maybe over time they would, if they could be in an intentional group that welcomes that kind of intimate sharing, and that's a way our group models how it can happen for men.

Older Women's Group

Ruth Olsen: I think we contribute positivity. I don't underestimate "the personal is political." The more that we try to be in balance and in alignment in our loving hearts and not contribute violence to the world, the better. As I learn how to love myself more I contribute more to the world. I don't do violence to myself through self-judgment or self-criticism. That contributes to the world and to my home and to the energy of the planet. It's all about generating that vibration, that energy of contributing positivity to the world. Once you set a thought in motion it stays in motion.

So if my thoughts are loving and compassionate and kind to myself – that's the hardest for me and that's where the group helps me. I am in that place more often then I used to be. On that level, which is very intimate, we can contribute to the world, to the planet, to the moment and to the universe. We set the example that we need to hold each other. We can't do it alone. I am not the person I would be had I not had the group. Alone, I didn't know how to love. I didn't know how to have friendship. I didn't know how to have community until I had the group. The group shows me how to love myself and how to love each other. Us being in the universe doing this work, committing to integrity, committing to truth-telling from a place of love and compassion makes a difference for ourselves, each other, our families, our children and the universe. It shows up in the world.

I don't know if we have done a lot of political action together. Some of us are more inclined to do more political/global action than others. I do it more one on one, more intimately, through my psychotherapy work, my harp work, and perhaps that could be a goal at some point, to do it more politically.

Nancy Knudsen: One of the group members has created an entire nonprofit around women's support groups (Annette Cycon's Group Peer Support). That is a way that this group has had a huge impact on the world. It's probably had a very positive impact on a number of people's relationships with their partners and their families and parents. Our group has been an anchor for people to do what they do and there are a lot of people who do incredible, wonderful things, not as a group, but individuals will say, "This is what I'm doing, how about we all do this?" and some other people will come along. As group members we have gone to marches in Washington and Boston, and some of us have brought our children along as well.

Sara Schley: The organization I created, Women Leading Sustainability, is a big example of our impact on the culture. I think each woman in WLS is doing amazing transformational work in the world on environmental and social sustainability issues, whether it's climate change or up-cycling. On the social side of things, one of them was in 145 countries helping kids have access to fresh water. These are change agents. For them to have a place where they can let down their hair, be completely safe, talk about whatever is on their hearts and minds... My organization has evolved interestingly, because we met in corporate, professional contexts and the conversations now are always about spiritual and emotional needs. That's a direct result of my involvement in the women's circle.

What is also reflected in the Women Leading Sustainability circle is that we've many times talked about doing something together, but we've realized that we're each doing powerful things and we just need the safe space where we're NOT doing, we're being and I think the same is true for the women's circle. Different pairs and trios of the circle have worked together on projects, but we haven't done anything as a group.
I have another structure that I also learned from the women's circle, which is that I work as a sustainability consultant and I've used a similar model. I have a team – the "sustainability design team" I call them – and I have them meet every Wednesday for an hour, which is just not heard of in that company, just to have the consistent structure. Then we also meet once a month for a day. This team has been doing great things. Ironically, it's mostly women, by virtue of there being 80 percent women in the company. We started out as all women and I thought, "O.K. This is just my professional women's circle." There is one guy.

Younger Men's Group

Ben Blackshear: Taking more actions is something we've all talked about and wanted to do. Whether it's us supporting each other in taking additional action, like supporting each other's existing political involvements or going together, showing up for the racial justice movement or going together to a protest march. Or if it is more focused around the group's identity – running an event.

In the origins of the group we were calling it more of a study-into-action group, which is using the language of the Challenging Male Supremacy Project, where they ran people through this curriculum and then had them do some sort of solidarity action to spread the word and to enact the values they'd been learning. The most concrete example we've talked about a lot of times is that we would at some time do a public workshop. It would either be open to everyone or target recruiting from specific activist groups or listservs. It could be a deep journaling reflection on how you've been shaped and participated in shaping masculinity and white supremacy, and any number of other activities.

I think we all feel we're having an important impact in a very small way on the culture through our own lives – how the men's group is changing our behavior. We could go in the direction of saying, "That's all the impact we want to have," or we could try to have the impact of encouraging other people to do that work. Or we could have a more direct and public face with a more clearly articulated vision of challenging patriarchy, where we see it in specific ways through a targeted campaign, a series of workshops or something like that. That's still up in the air and something we've grappled with in terms of how to do that.

Dave Ratzlow: As soon as I joined I wanted something to happen other than just meeting, because I already meet with people. We were talking about ideas and I noticed that *I Am Not Your Negro** was soon

* A 2016 documentary based on James Baldwin's writings.

to be released on video. It was a movie that was clearly important for the culture, so I proposed that we screen it in Joshua's huge living room with this huge projection TV. Joshua has a huge mailing list of people, and we invited Josh's email list. I think we had about 50 people come. One of the two Bens in our group knew an academic at Princeton who worked in African-American studies and we invited him to moderate the discussion, which he did and it was great. What a great film and what a great time to be thinking about all that stuff and talking about all that stuff. The discussion was really lively and interesting.

The audience was a diverse group ethnically and racially. Age-wise it was mostly people in their 20s and 30s with maybe a couple in their 40s. Male and female. My only takeaway was that this kind of event didn't happen when I was 20. Nobody was thinking about this or talking about this or gathering like this. If they were, it was not a mainstream thing. My takeaway was that it is so great that people are looking at this, talking about this, and how much even liberal white people have to learn. Some liberal white people made some mistakes, which needed to be corrected. It was a cordial, lively discussion and I'm really glad it happened and how much interest there was.

Josh LaTour: I think that's really the long-term goal, in terms of having greater influence on our community. It's a little weird to say, but we're not in crisis management like people recovering from a hurricane. We have a lot of conversations about impact or about how to address things that are really hard and not so visible. We're not just running to the border with the Palestinians in Gaza and claiming solidarity with that or running out to the Dakota Access Pipeline. The frontlines of feminism are just much more hidden.

We definitely want to have an impact. Part of it is, I'm responsible for making more of that happen. I've brought up ideas of doing things and not followed up on them.

Ben Fuller-Googins: At our last meeting we experimented with having a longer session on a Sunday in January. We had brunch together. We met at Dave's house and we cooked together. The first few hours were him teaching the rest of us about peer counseling (Re-Evaluation Counseling) and we also had a discussion about #MeToo. It was a time for us to share moments in our life when we perpetrated or were the ones who exhibited harmful behavior towards partners and towards women. That was quite a moment of all of us sharing what were shameful actions in many ways. If I didn't have that space it is very unlikely I would have gone around afterwards to all my relationships and said, "This is a time I did this..."

We knew we were going to discuss this before the meeting, so just reflecting ahead of time about what I was going to share felt meaningful. It really underscored how perverted my conditioning to sex and romance is. A lot of the things I shared were middle school and high school experiences and at that time I had this detached viewpoint – I didn't really know any better. I could totally remove myself from having agency, but at the same time that was the norm and that was the culture, which I was inhabiting. There weren't too many alternatives. It was a very clear example of, "Wow, this is what I am being taught by the culture." Thinking about it and then talking about it enabled me to start to undo the damage...

Younger Women's Group

Michelle Chanson: This is a group that is socially progressive and cares a lot about causes and issues. I'm not sure I can identify a specific way in which we, as a group, make an impact on the outside world, but we certainly make a vital impact on each other. My work is very focused on working with organizations and individuals tackling some of the world's biggest challenges as they relate to social impact and sustainability. But we are all very socially conscious, fighting for justice in our ways. If we're in a workplace and we feel like someone is not being treated the way they should be or we feel disrespected in some way, this is a great group to hash that out with and figure out the best approach.

Nobody in this group is afraid to take a stand and to fight for what she thinks is right. Just by virtue of the fact that we're all women who have chosen to maintain deep connections to each other and make time to come together and support each other, we've created greater confidence among each other. We can go out into the world and know what we're worth and know the value that we bring to the table – whether it's in our relationships or in our careers – so we're willing to fight for what we deserve. We encourage each other to do that, whether it's taking a stand and saying, "I'm not getting paid as much as my peer," or telling a boss, "I'm not being treated properly with this maternity leave policy." We all sort of crowd-source how we approach that with each other and then go out and, ideally, pave the way for other people so they don't have to have those conversations.

With everything that is happening politically right now, people really want to take action, to make a difference. People are gravitating toward being a part of something, because they feel in some ways – and maybe I'm speaking from my New York bubble – like they are losing control on issues that they thought we all had a grasp of. At this moment, seeking out people with whom your values align is really important, and so is having those safe spaces where you can debate and discuss things, even if you're not making policy changes. Being able to process everything that's going on with friends who are thoughtful, smart and dealing with all of the same challenges is really important. I'm increasingly seeing communities and networks cropping up to have these kinds of conversations.

New York has a women-only co-working space that I joined. I'm on the fence about how exactly I feel about it. No men are allowed inside, not even for meetings. I'm not sure creating silos is the right approach, but some people find safety in that. However, I do think the popularity of something like this space says a lot about where we are in our culture right now. This group of women that I am a part of is a precursor to that. We've created our own little safe space. We know when we come to the table, we can be open, honest and we're not going to be judged. We're friends and we're here to help each other sort out the chaos. Sometimes we're exhausted from the workday, but we make time because it's important to keep this connection and see each other's faces.

Heather Price: I'll touch on the theme of feeling grounded and supported and having examples of strength and empathy around you. We bring that to the table. We encourage it and pull it out of each other. We all feel so comfortable and so much our authentic selves in this group, you can't help but carry that to other parts of your life. The more authentic, strong, empathetic and open-minded people we have will make for a better culture and society. Each of us, having this source, taking it away, carrying it out through our everyday lives as part of other groups, will help improve the general culture.

Charlie Evans: We talk a lot about current events, which in this day and age is a major concern. Everybody wants to do something, and nobody knows what to do. I think that is true in society as a whole. It's overwhelming and there are so many different elements and so much at stake that people don't know what to do. We actually talk a lot about, "Hey, here are ways to get involved..." Naomi and I went together to the Women's March in Washington. We talk a lot about ways to be supportive of people, in particular supportive of other women during a time when women's rights, women's bodies and values are under such threats.

We encourage each other to be activists. I think it's always been that way, so it's not that different, but now it's much more vocal and much more specific and much more desperate.

Many different ways of impacting communities surfaced in this chapter, all incredibly valuable and worthwhile. There will invariably be the tension between the personal and the political, and each group, unless expressly getting together to do actions, will have to determine where the fulcrum is. The society's challenges will have an influence, as will the politics of the group members. I feel these four groups are aware of this dilemma and have been wending their ways through the sometimes turbulent waters of "the personal is political" dictum the early consciousness-raising women's groups gave voice to in the '60s.

CHAPTER 16
HOW DO YOU SEE THE ROLE
OF SUPPORT GROUPS IN SOCIETY?

Needless to say, all 27 of my interview subjects have come to have a deep and abiding appreciation for the role their support groups play in their lives. As the preceding chapter indicates, much would be different – less fulfilling, more isolating, less intimacy – were it not for the "village" that their group seeks to emulate. Each person movingly articulated throughout our conversations their deep gratitude for their membership in their respective group, and no matter how similar or different each group may be seen to be, one major takeaway for me was that everyone I spoke with felt that such groups can have a significant role to play in what is increasingly a divisive, even frightening world.

Support groups can have very different purposes. Witness the ever-expanding, ever more diverse listings of such groups in my local newspaper. There are now groups for "Aging Gracefully, Dying with Dignity," "Grandparenting Creatively," "Male Survivors of Cancer," "Living with Multiple Sclerosis," and others, all of which are giving their members the ongoing caring and support from which all of us benefit.

The focus of the groups in this book is on giving and receiving the kind of support that fosters emotional intimacy and serious challenge to promote personal as well as group growth and well-being, so the comments you are about to read will have those purposes in mind. Although the subjects here are four cisgendered groups, my hope and expectation is that the ever-expanding and diverse spectrum of connections will only increase. I will spend some time addressing this in the Conclusion.

This chapter has a different structure in the presentation of the interview excerpts. In previous chapters they have followed the order in which I interviewed the four groups: older men, older women, younger men, younger women. When I interviewed the two younger groups, I included a question I hadn't asked of the others – how they view the role of support groups in society. Their answers, as you will see, were so compelling that I followed up with emails asking the same question to both older groups. When it came to ordering them, the two women's groups' answers seemed to complement each other, as did the men's. So the chapter commences with selections from the women's responses, and then the men will speak. The men's contributions are followed by a few additional responses from my interview with the two groups at the double men's group gathering in 2017 for the article I wrote for *Voice Male* magazine.

Older Women's Group

Sara Schley: I think as social structures crumble, families are separated by geography and more, and religious institutions are no longer relevant to so many, circles like ours take on huge relevance. Indeed, come to think of it, I don't know how folks get along without them. Our circle plays the role that family, church and community have in the past. A built-in, solid support structure that we all need to get by. Especially in these increasingly fraught times: socially, politically, economically, ecologically. None of us can navigate all this alone. The circle is essential.

Morning Star Chenven: I think that support groups are key to keeping our world's people sane. This is a difficult time to be alive. Our very planet, the future of all of our children and their children are at risk. The divide between people on different economic levels is huge. Racism and sexism are again, and still very alive. Medical distress is high. Global warming changes are creating more and more disasters. There are so many enormous challenges to people in this world. When we can face these challenges with a support group at our back, we feel that at least we are not alone. That feeling of belonging to a circle of people creates a desire in people to share their wisdom, their resources, their love and compassion.

The craziness that plagues our world has a lot to do with the attitude that the world is a place of "each man for himself" or even worse, "dog eat dog." This sense that each person must compete with others, and make sure to grab enough from the little that exists, has created a world where so many people suffer at the bottom of the heap and everyone else is trying to climb on the backs of those below. Yuck! We are "using up" our planet's beautiful land and water, animals and plants, because we keep grabbing and not giving back. When we are working with a group of people in a circle of support, we are engaged in a process of giving and receiving that encourages us to live more in balance with the earth and all its inhabitants. We do not have to fear that we won't get enough.

For me, support groups have been lifesavers. Ever since the women's movement hit my college and I began attending groups, I have felt that I was lifted out of the nuclear family mindset into a community/collective mindset. I also learned the skills of listening without judging – the importance of hearing what diverse people had to say. My pregnancy and mothers' support groups were vital to my sanity as I raised my children. I did not feel isolated, as many mothers and fathers do. The experiences were rich and fulfilling for both myself and my children.

My current ongoing women's group gives me the sense that I have a circle of sisters who will support me in all the different phases of my life. It also works as an escape spout from the danger of getting too insular in my way of seeing the world. I have a writing group as well, which has become invaluable to me in my artistic and personal expression.

I wish for all people the opportunity to sit in Circle and feel the support and love that is found in the hearts of our fellow human beings. Circles put people on the same level field. Sitting in Circle, listening without judgment, being heard without judgment is the first step in coming to peace within a partnership, a family, a community, a nation.

Diane Norman: Support groups can vary in their intention and their longevity, but the biggest effect I feel any group I've belonged to has had on the "larger society" is in its modeling of "meeting together with intention." I started support groups at Amherst College, during the 28 years I worked there, for young women with disordered eating or body issues. This was significant not just to the individual women that belonged to any one of these groups, but in how it affected their interactions with the other people in their lives or even, down the road, with their own children. They learned listening and talking skills. They practiced being vulnerable in a safe container.

I have heard directly from one or two of these young women, several years post-graduation, that they have started groups of various kinds themselves. I'd like to believe there was a "trickle effect."

My daughter, now 28, has seen me go off to my women's circles all her life. She has watched me show up for each of these women and their partners in ways that only cultivating deep intimacy could allow. Now she, soon to launch into married life, has begun meeting with four to five of her closest friends, all at different stages of newly committed relationships/marriages/young children, and they hope to meet regularly "like your women's group," she has said. I would like to believe I have modeled what it is to show up, communicate, be vulnerable and share your gifts with other people.

When I speak of my women's circle to people, especially those who live outside our valley, and share what we do and for how long we have met, I have heard women say out loud, "I want to create that for myself," and, of course, I encourage it. I believe the more we model having deep intimate relationships with people other than our primary partners the better. The more people there are practicing "intimacy":

listening well, respecting differences, working out conflict – all skills our world very much needs to cultivate – the better our future will be.

Younger Women's Group

Naomi Lutra: I don't really identify with the notion that our group is a support group. To me, a support group is people who may or may not already have a personal connection coming together around a common need for support on a particular issue, even if that issue is very broad, like "Navigating the world as a woman," or "Masculinity." Our group is just a group of friends who have somewhat formalized our process for staying in touch. But there is something in that formalized, slightly ritualized process of regular group check-ins, whether it's a group of friends or a more official support group, that really does remind you of what's important. It forces you to pause and connect with people and check in with yourself and be real.

I was never somebody who kept a diary or journal or blog, but I do feel like this group of women holds my history and my trajectory in a way that other people don't know me. Listening and vulnerability and being brave about sharing your own stories, or when someone else is being brave sharing their own story with you. I feel it's like this *Brigadoon** moment where that kind of honest and vulnerable sharing is the norm. It's usually not the norm in the rest of life, but you're practicing that in these moments.

Charlie Evans: I think that some people are intuitive enough and self-aware enough to choose the people that they surround themselves with, whether it's a support group or a chosen family or their social

---

* *Brigadoon* is a musical about a miraculous village that rises out of the mists every hundred years for only a day so that it will never be changed or destroyed by the outside world.

network. Many more people are not. I don't think they have that self-awareness as to what they need or are able to identify and verbalize it.

I think the people who are not aware are the ones who need the support the most and, unfortunately, they're probably the least likely to go seek it out. I do feel, however you define "support group," you have to seek it out. If you are seeking the specific things that come with a support group – a chosen family, a loving environment – then it's intentional. Ours evolved to be intentional from something that was always there, and that's wonderful, but as young children we were certainly looking for that.

Liz Sharp: It is more important than ever, because in this country and a lot of countries, we're becoming so fractured and unable to talk to each other. We're standing in our idea boxes. Even if you're doing it in concert with a group of people that is more likely to share your values and ideals than others and feel like family in many ways – if you're able to talk to other people, it's going to make you a more empathetic, kind person in the world at large, and that energy is going to spread. If you don't have a sense of safety talking to other people, it creates more anger and lashing out and breakdowns than understanding. It leads to destructive and sad behavior. The more people come together and participate in conversations, the more healing can happen.

Michelle Chanson: What's going on in the world has sparked the urgency to create spaces that are women-led and that bring women together to collaborate, to discuss. I don't intentionally set out to be a part of these groups, and yet I find myself continually becoming part of them, because when you're a woman and you have a certain network, you get invited to these kinds of things – women business owners, women networking – and I'm always interested to see how they operate and to be a part of them.

With our group it's different, because it's an organic friendship group that started coming together in high school, not a group that came together specifically to be women-only. If we had a really great guy friend from high school who asked to be a part of it, I don't think I'd say, "No, I don't want him in it." I sometimes wonder if by having everything be for women, we segregate people more. We make it feel like women have to be catered to in a big way and I'm not sure that does the women justice. I go back and forth on that. As a woman who runs a business there are certain things that make my skin crawl, like when people are writing "#ladyboss" and you have to be caveated as a woman. I think to myself, why can't it just be #boss? Why does it have to be caveated that I'm a woman? It shouldn't detract from the fact that I'm still a business owner and I'm competing with everybody else. That's where I draw the line on that. I'm still grappling with it because I don't know the answer, but I do think it's important to have those spaces for women, because I do know so many women who feel more comfortable around other women. I don't personally feel more comfortable around one sex or the other, but I understand people who do.

In reply to my request for responses to the question I had previously asked only the two younger groups, I received this email that briefly, but ever so poignantly, sums up this woman's experience of the group's role in her life:

Susan Loring-Wells: I love this question and I'm sorry I haven't been able to respond yet. I'm not sure I will get to responding, as my husband just had a stroke last week in California and as you can imagine I am living moment to moment. What I can share with you is that even across the country I feel the support of my beloved circle sisters and it's helping to sustain my spirit knowing they are there!

Older Men's Group

Steve Trudel: With the assumption that there is accountability and a willingness to both challenge and be challenged as well as to demonstrate love and kindness, I think the role is boundless. We all need, as people, to be understood and to be heard even when all our ideas are differing. A support group can provide the environment for these practices and principles to grow. Societally, we're starting to break down the divisions that have existed between men and women. I'd like to think that at a future time, all genders could be together, especially if it is guided by authenticity and loving kindness.

All the female partners of our group members that I've talked to like the idea that their men are having other ways to explore their needs – not just in their marriage or partnership – because men tend to not do that. They traditionally do that kind of exploration with their wives and then think that's the only place they have to do it. In my work with men who are abusive and controlling, it's pretty characteristic that men are isolated without networks of support. Men's groups like ours work to undo the isolation.

Paul Richmond: It's about being in a safe place to explore and be challenged to help grow. It's people who know you for a long period of time that can reflect along with you about what's happening, what you've gone through. Are you still telling us the same story that you were when we met you? Now we're all tied up in it, too, so what do you want to change? Plus, there's the commitment we share to really show up and to go deeper, to ask those questions.

I appreciate our willingness to let each of us experience the pain that we might be having in our lives and to realize that there's nothing else anybody can do besides letting us have a safe space to experience that pain and witness it. If you need to be held, that's available. Nobody is putting you down, telling you to suck it up. That vulnerability makes it possible to get through some really difficult stuff. Men continue to desperately need such safe spaces to be challenged, to learn, to grow and to access a whole range of emotions.

Younger Men's Group

Ben Fuller-Googins: A friend contacted me via email today about a space where people – predominantly white people – can really work on their racism. I think it's modeled after AA where you say, "My name is Ben, and I am a racist." I found that interesting. It got me thinking about our group, particularly at our last meeting when we shared about times when we were being oppressive.

In support groups, the act of sharing and realizing that there are other people who are feeling the same way, or who have practiced and learned similar types of behavior, is a critical piece in the transformative process. I think that it can also become a self-serving type of experience. One piece about our group that I appreciate is really being mindful that we're mostly a group of white guys getting together and thinking about what the implications are of that. If we don't have a lens of acknowledging our privileges and our social position, the potential for these groups is limited.

I was recently sharing about the men's group with two women friends that I have. We're very good friends and we can speak very frankly. One of the women had a partner who was in a men's group. Her partner was abusive towards her, and apparently his men's group was not holding him accountable. According to her they were condoning his behavior. It was a very clear example that just because these groups exist, it does

233

not mean that it will change people's behaviors. Her experience of a men's group was that it absolves men's problematic behavior.

The other friend was asking, "Why do we need separate groups apart from our friendship circles?" That was very interesting. As much as I love these four guys, they are not my best friends. So I ask myself, "Why can't I have these conversations with other men?" It's not that I don't with my roommate or my brother or other men who I care about, for instance, but it's definitely not as intentional, and that makes a huge difference in the likelihood that the conversations will happen and be sustained.

Kevin Quirolo: A friend of mine, who I thought would be interested because he is a feminist, isn't interested. I think there are two points here. First there's a suspicion of a group of men focused on themselves, and second there's a sense of urgency to organize outwardly. The first point is crucial to this work because sexism is so insidious it can (and often does) corrupt seemingly earnest efforts by men to support feminism. Any men's group of this kind has to directly address how patriarchy shapes who we are and how we relate to other men. The second point is understandable, but it could be counterproductive. Getting out in the world and working against oppression can be transformative. But urgency could be an excuse to ignore your own sexism.

When both men's groups spent our weekend together, I asked them to reflect upon how they saw each other's groups – one of long duration and one of recent creation. First, two members of the younger men's group:

Ben Fuller-Googins: I went into the weekend having some skepticism based on not having very positive relationships with older, white men. It was such a joy to see your group's friendships with each other.

On one level, "Wow, it's possible to have these friendships that are expanding, challenging and deepening over decades." The level of curiosity I experienced you showing about us – that was fantastic. I so appreciated that because it is not what I experience a lot in relationships with older men. I left very joyful and hopeful having seen that if you commit to such a group it can be rich in lasting joy and transformation.

Ben Blackshear: The biggest takeaway for me was an affirmation that this work is valuable and the "project" of men's groups is worthwhile. Seeing the deep bonds the older men have, their happiness, their political astuteness, their willingness to challenge each other, and the shared memories they've built over the years was powerful. It made me feel that the benefits of this work are ongoing and get even richer with continued time and emotional investment.

Older Men's Group:

Steve Trudel: I felt like I got to experience my wisdom and our collective wisdom from having been part of our group for so many years. I also felt a great sense of relief knowing that there are young men who are finding value in being with each other, supporting each other in the same way that we've had the opportunity to experience – that sense that, "Oh, good, our men's group wasn't just a blip on the radar screen that went away."

Paul Richmond: It felt like they are a younger version of ourselves. In this time and place they are political guys who are questioning and working on issues that they think are important – whether it be about issues of race or climate change or the environment. They are being confronted with how they are being men in the various organizations to which they belong. They are being supportive of each other and trying to be different from traditional masculinity in

235

what they're doing.

Robbie Leppzer: I was so delighted and amazed that men's groups like ours are still forming in the 2010s because it's a very different era than when we started our group. To know that there's a lifeline of consciousness about men's groups and that young men are aware and feel the need and see the importance of forming a men's group is heartening because I'm generally somewhat disheartened that the consciousness we helped to develop has experienced a backlash against it.

One of my major contentions since conceiving of this project has been that support groups can play an active role in enabling members to achieve their potential as engaged, loving, kind and nurturing people. I believe that this chapter validates that premise – and then some. Whether the group is enabling women to be more empowered self-advocates and feminists at home and in the workplace, or supporting men to be more present in their relationships with friends, partners and children, it is impacting the culture in ways that can only benefit the next generation.

At a time when traditional patriarchy and masculinity are being examined with a goal of transforming them and their destructive effects on men as well as women, support groups whose purpose is to shine a light on those effects can only serve to enhance our capacities to both undo the damage and go forward with more compassion for ourselves, our relationships and our planet.

CHAPTER 17
MISCELLANEOUS GEMS

Not all the questions on my interview sheet, which is in the Appendix, became chapter topics for this book, not all the responses were able to be included in the chapters, and some of the interviews produced impromptu questions leading to spontaneous reflections that didn't easily fit into any category. So, what to do with these incredibly perceptive, deeply thoughtful, original and articulate gems? How about giving them their own chapter?

So many of my interview subjects found unique ways to respond to the questions I put to them, both planned and unplanned, and I did not want these to be lost. Once again, I must express my appreciation for the level of commitment that each person I spoke with brought to the conversation.

I will set the stage for each "gem" with a question, followed by the individual's answer, starting with the group that has been around the longest:

Older Men's Group

What was a time when you had a lot of fun with the group?

> **Alan Surprenant:** There are a lot of times in the past where I would just be laughing 'til I hurt. That was a really nice release. I haven't actually felt that in a while, and it could be lots of things. It could just be our age now, but I do remember that happening a number of times over the years in the group. I think there are lots of different times of great fun. Some of them happened in the circle of the group in one room in a very focused way and some of them happened with us out in the world, but all together – mountain climbing, sailing. Sailing was a lot of fun, because we were just out, free. Everybody had different experiences the few times we went. I want people to remember all the good parts, too. So trips are nice.
>
> I really value our time going up to the St. Lawrence

238

River. I like how that bloomed, and that we all created a space in our lives to do that. That's really unheard of. Ten men taking off five days – especially since we don't all work for the same person. Somehow everybody just made time for that in their lives and we were all desirous of it.

How do others in your life see the group?

Stephen Bannasch: I think Dina (Stephen's wife) sees it similarly to how I've been expressing it in this interview. If we've been having a tough time she will say, "I think you should check that out with the men's group." That would be one of the ways she might talk about it. If she and I were having a conversation we could actually go pretty far in talking about the men's group as part of the fabric of my life – the fact that it's just woven in – and how that supports other parts of my life. That would make a lot of sense to her.

For my kids, it's part of who I am, so I don't know that they think about it a whole lot. I'd be really curious to ask them. It's interesting, because my daughters (14, 17, and 20 at the time of the interview) haven't had, as far as I can tell, boyfriends. I'm not exactly sure why. I don't think they have had girlfriends either. There's one thing I feel really confident about and it may be related to this larger fabric idea and, of course, the men's group supports this. I can't imagine them putting up with someone who they were involved with who treated them badly. But it's even more than that. I can't even imagine them getting mad. I'd more imagine them laughing at somebody who thought that it was O.K. to mistreat them. That it is just so ludicrous. What planet are you living on that you would think or act like that? I don't know all the contributions to that way of being in the world or how exactly real it is. I suspect it's quite real. They seem very, very self-assured.

How do friends and family see your participation in the group?

> **Dick McLeester:** I noticed something while watching the biography of the singer-songwriter Donovan, and how he was described as having this very close friendship with this much younger guy, Gypsy Dave. He said, "We weren't gay. We just enjoyed being together." For the longest time I was thinking theirs was just a relationship like our men's group. It could be really close with deep sharing and real importance. I think my friends and family get that. What it ends up with is sometimes other friends being jealous of it or joking around about it. I felt a little frustration, because at a certain point our group had an all-family gathering – everyone's partner and children getting together for a day and a potluck meal. I miss that, but it's long past. I wish we could have done that more, but I understand with the various changes that it became more difficult than earlier points in time.

How has the men's group impacted your three sons and your relationships with them?

> **Gary Phillips:** I think Giles and Jesse, my two younger sons, consider the men's group an amazing mystery. Their relationship with the men's group is at a little bit of a distance, but they feel an affirmation that is really strong and they know how important it is to me. My oldest, Adam, is connected to the group. He is good friends with Paul and Tom. Adam spent a lot of time with Llan and Llan's been a part of my whole family, so all the boys know Llan really well because he's been in and out of our lives.
>
> Adam came to a men's group session. He spent the weekend with us. He wrote a lovely note on Facebook about me and Paul creeping up on his Facebook, because we were making comments about the lovely woman he had in his arms in the photograph he'd

posted of them dancing. It was both an admonition and an expression of love. "You know you boys can't come creepin' up on my Facebook. Not everybody in the world will understand how much we love each other."

I've tried with my boys to bring a lot of lessons from the group to them. All three of them express that in their lives. They're all three emotionally dependable in ways that people in their lives are really glad for, and I consider that a legacy of the group as much as anything else. I consider the group as giving me ground to act like a man who doesn't have to act like a man. All three of my sons have that as part of their characters, part of their lives, and as one of the reasons they're loved by the people they love. I think there is a direct connection back to the group in that.

What is one of your earliest memories of the group?

Steve Trudel: One significant thing that occurred early on is that, at least for me, I thought that it was O.K. for us as men to just want to be together and know each other, instead of being driven by a political agenda, which seemed a little cold compared to spending the time together around our own lives. It seemed almost like the thing that I had been worried about – that we would just be concerned with ourselves and we wouldn't be interested in taking political action – was what needed to change. That's what the women's movement had done! It just seemed to me like – this is a pretty radical agenda. For men to get together for the right reasons, not to entrench our privilege and control over women, but instead to really get to know each other and see where that leads. Time has proven that that has been one of the more radical things that could have been done in this period of time.

Have you ever felt the group has come close to ending?

Tony Clarke: I've never had a sense of that at all. I know, in my own personal space, there have been times when I've been so frantic with work and juggling work and family and everything that Sunday men's group will come and I'll be like, "Oh, God, I can't. I just don't have the energy." The thought is going through my head, "You know, maybe this is just too much. Maybe I need to step back from it." Whenever I really look at that, it's like, "No, I don't think so," because there's a depth of bond with the men in this group that goes back so far. It's another marriage. I was married in '86. The group's another seven years on top of that. That's 40 years of relationship. It's really meaningful to me in a very deep way. It's a funny relationship, because I don't feel like everybody in the group is my closest friend. I don't hang out with everybody in the group in a social way outside the group. As a matter of fact, I don't see most people socially outside of the group. But when we're in our group together there's just this space and an understanding that we share from so many years of being together and sharing our highs and our lows – our sense of commitment, what's important to us.

What was it like answering all these questions about your group?

Robbie Leppzer: It's been good, because the men's group is an incredibly valuable experience in my life and I want to share it with more people. I'm really glad that you're writing this book and putting it out there in the world. I feel it's something that's been a personal experience that I can share and be a mentor for other people – to show both men and women that there is another way that men can be. That gives hope not only to men but to women as well who can often feel frustrated with men being in limited roles. Our group can show that not all men are like that and we're proof of it and my life is a proof of it. I'm happy to share that. I'm eager to share that whenever I have the chance. You providing this opportunity got me a little anxious in the beginning, but I welcome it and I appreciate it

Is there something you wanted to say and didn't get to express in this interview?

Paul Richmond: One thing I would try to convey is that McDonald's is always there with their product. They almost always put out the same exact kind of hamburger. Life isn't like that. So if someone thought, "O.K. I'm going to try a men's group," they might have to go through a bunch of different groups, because some groups don't work and some people are not the right people to do it with. Even if you said, "I'm taking your formula for meeting once a month," and people think that this is a format that will produce the kind of group they're hoping for, I'd say, "I don't know if that's going to happen."

Even with me saying, "This has been a great group," there are still disappointments and things that didn't happen or things in myself that I sometimes wish, "Geez, I wish I had been pressed more." Or maybe you guys were pressing me more and I wasn't ready to make that change. Why didn't that happen? I don't know why it didn't happen. I don't know why I'm just having this realization now. It can be too much that any of us puts on what you hope for the group, be-cause the group is only what everyone else agrees to. If the group doesn't know that I wanted them to pres-sure me more, because I didn't ask for it or if I asked for it and they don't want to do it, then that's my thing to think about how to respond.

I think that was asked of the group that you and I were in (from 1979 to 1989), because both you and I wanted something out of that group, of a depth that we realized and pointed to, but it wasn't going to go farther. We got to a place where we could actually articulate that. For a while we didn't do anything about it. Then I got the option to be in the group we've been in since '89 and our other group was going down. That gave me the opportunity to ask you if you wanted to be in this one, because what we both wanted wasn't happening in the other and it was ending. The rest, of course, is history.

Older Women's Group

What role does ritual play in your group?

Sara Elinoff Acker: We really like to bring ritual and ceremony into our groups. Our opening ritual is an essential part of creating depth and spirit in our time together. The woman hosting the group that month sets up sacred space and invokes a process that invites us to go inside and get in touch with what lies below our outer personalities. We'll use a singing bowl or chanting, meditation or movement. We love to begin the circle this way, where we get connected to our own souls first. The hostess is in charge of the ritual, but we all add our wisdom. Each of us knows how to create sacred space and ritual.

We create our own rituals, drawing from different traditions, particularly earth-based traditions, Judaism and Buddhism. We've done many rituals over the years: healing rituals, divorce rituals, miscarriage rituals, the death of a parent — all kinds of losses, births and transitions. Our rituals really span the spectrum.

But we also show up for each other in fundamentally practical ways. A couple summers ago, one of the women in the group was selling her house and needed to pack up her belongings and she was feeling really overwhelmed. We said, "O.K., we're dedicating the whole day of group to you." It felt great. We got so much done in just a few hours and helped to lessen her stress.

I love how we can move between so many different worlds: emotional, spiritual, playful, practical.

How has the group responded to an individual in crisis?

Nancy Knudsen: This past year I went through a health crisis. Both of my women's groups rallied around me. It was an amazing process. I would say the level of support in my women's circle was just unbelievable. I had an ovarian cancer diagnosis and I went through a surgery in November. Then in February we had our retreat and one of the activities that we did was that we body-painted around my scar. It was part of a transformation of that event into art work. Diane did a series of photographs of it that reflect the poignancy of the group experience.

My two groups actually came together. They had met each other at social events at my house, but not as part of a healing circle. There were various healing circles dealing with the diagnosis and then leading up to the surgery. I really felt so blessed with the love being directed towards me.

Is there anything you think is missing in your group?

Morning Star Chenven: I would love if in some way our partners were able to tap in more to the kinds of things that we offer each other. We do have social gatherings that include partners. For a while some of us had a New Year's Eve circle, where the men of the couples would also share. My husband, Moonlight, and I are usually playing music on New Year's Eve, so we come at the end of it and we don't get all that. It's like the other half of my life is left out of this amazing thing I'm doing. Our women's group is meeting once a month, so we're getting a lot of this support, this lovely energy, and I miss that not happening with and for Moonlight.

How has the group impacted you as parent and partner?

Annette Cycon: Being with my group for an entire day once a month gets me out of the weeds of my life so I'm in a more magnanimous place with greater perspective. Whether it comes from talking deeply, listening, eating together or biking together, it fills my soul with a bucket of jewels and I come home and I share them. I'm more loving, affectionate, patient and grounded. I'm simply more present. There's just more of me – more of the good part of me available to my husband and my girls. If I'm in a hard or stagnant place with my husband, I come home to him with an open heart, able to give more, listen and resolve whatever is difficult together.

Sometimes it's hard for my daughters that I am gone all day, but I know it's worth it to them. They know how important my women's circle is to me, and the women have become like aunties to them. This means a lot to me, since I don't have sisters.

I have also brought circle-type experiences home, which gives us the opportunity to share deeply, listen to each other and share appreciation of each other. I believe it's really important to take a pause in the busyness of our lives to remember what's most important and express that love and gratitude to the ones we love. It has brought my family closer and made it possible to process feelings and transitions in our lives. Just last week, my youngest daughter said, "Let's go around the table and say one thing we're grateful for and one thing we're looking forward to."

How does the group impact you as a partner?

Diane Norman: There's a certain kind of vocabulary that I've learned over the years that we share in our group that I bring to my partnership. I think that some of the women in the group have really modeled well what it is to reflect – not just using reflective listening in the group, but to put themselves in the shoes of the other person. I think this is one of my strengths and one I continue to cultivate. I'm reminded when I feel oppositional with Robert, my partner, that I have the capacity to hear him and to put aside my own agenda and really go to what he might be experiencing. Keep in mind that he was my friend for 30 years before he became my life partner. There are times now when I literally say, "I'm taking off the hat of your girlfriend and I'm putting on the hat of your friend." We can then explore what might be best for him as an individual, even if the result may mean less time, for instance, spent as a couple. This level of inquiry was something I learned from my time spent with my circle. He may not make the connection, but I do.

How has the group affected your parenting?

Sara Schley: All the rest of the women had already had their children, so they're my mentors. My mother was not very physically affectionate, was not there so much emotionally and was not there spiritually. I am by nature all of those things. I am by nature someone who wants to wrap my kids in my arms and say, "I love you, I love you," and show lots of affection. I had models in Ruth, Annette, Morning Star, Diane and Susan. All of them are just awesome moms in the ways in which they showed what was possible.

Plus, we've mothered each other, because people are allowed to show up small and feel the need to be nourished and loved. There are a couple women in the group who had unconditionally loving mothers,

247

but most of us were like, "That's not the mom we grew up with. We grew up with the one that disowned her whole emotional self." We don't blame them now, because we understand their wounds, but we didn't get that, so we're re-mothering each other in ways, and that's one of the draws of the group. We go to a place that's nurturing and nourishing that we didn't have.

What did the group offer, and what didn't it offer, in the early days?

Ruth Olsen: It gave me life. It taught me about what a friend is – what a true friend is, what true devoted, committed friendship is, and it still does. I feel like I entered with a lack of self-love. It took me a long time to understand how much Sara (Elinoff Acker) loved me. "Why would you love me so much? You have all these other friends." I just didn't value myself in the way she valued me, because of my family history. To get that reflection of love and "This is why I love you," and "This is who I see you as," and "This is why you mean so much to me," and "Nobody else gives me what you give me" was huge. There was a way in which I just didn't believe that. I didn't understand. I always valued others, so the group helped me to love myself, to see my worth, to see my value, to gain confidence in myself.

Yes, it gave me life in that way. The group parented me, mothered me in ways I never received. I never had a nurturing mother. I never had a warm mother. It gave me my life in that way – to learn how to love myself, to value myself and see my worth in the world and the universe and that I have something to offer that is unique. It taught me about how to love, how to be a friend and to receive love. I'm a giver. My life is of service, so for me to receive was very hard. Hard to believe, hard to receive, hard to let in, hard to ask. It has taught me how to do that – to give and receive and to find a place of balance with that.

What life events do you see the group assisting one another to go through?

> **Susan Loring-Wells:** Divorce. Loss of parents. Illness. I can share my experience of helping someone who was struggling with illness. I felt so grateful that I had space in my life that I could just go over and help out outside of group time. When these things happen, I know that there is time in the circle if someone wants more time, because they are in crisis and they need to process longer than is allotted.
>
> Sometimes I have tried to process things with my partner, but it's just sticky and I get stuck in that rut rather than finding clarity and strength. You sort of regress and you don't get the essence of what your heart wants to say at that moment. I need language to go back to him with. Let's say I had an issue with my husband and I brought it up in an angry place and I just – he would say attacked – just dumped whatever came out at that moment, which I do without consciously planning. I'm not a planner of how I'm going to say things – they just come out. So I would go process this with the circle and get some idea of how to talk about it from them or how to create a safe space to process it with my husband. That's very powerful.

Younger Men's Group

What life events do you see the group assisting one another to go through?

> **Josh LaTour:** So far most of us have been pretty healthy and there haven't been any serious crises yet. One member has from time to time struggled with mental health issues. I wish we were more informed to be a support for him
>
> We've also talked a lot about pornography. We're not a group that is anti-pornography. There was one

person who visited us who had strong views against it. Being someone who was celibate for 15 years and not even masturbating, it's kind of funny for me to turn around and not be dogmatic about watching porn. My biggest problem with pornography is the way in which it is used. It can turn into a very unhealthy habit and affect one's sex life when you're with the real person. I've heard a lot of stories. Even some women think that sex should be done like in the porn videos. There are a lot of problems with the way pornography shows that. I definitely have felt that porn has affected my sexuality. I stopped watching it. Fortunately, I have a partner who turns me on a lot and I don't need to watch it. I still wonder if watching it a lot would affect my erections – like just what gets me off because a lot of it is psychological.

What do you receive from the group?

Ben Blackshear: I think it's the satisfaction that we're doing this together – that we've created this container where we can do this work and we continue to do that and it continues to be powerful. Even if we go in without a plan for the night. If we were basically just going to check in and process whatever is going on in our lives. We don't really talk a lot beforehand, so we don't always know what it's going to be. Everyone shares what's going on and then we focus on what things deserve a deeper dive-in – someone being called out, someone needing to process how they're feeling about their relationship.

It's been really nice to hear your little interjections here and there during this interview, how your group that has been going for so long has been doing it. I definitely am curious to hear deeper answers on all these when we get the two groups together. Thinking about these questions has felt like productive reflection, but also revealing that I should sit with these questions in a much more intentional way over a longer period – the idea of what the group has meant to me, what we all take from it – and I think it would be good for all of us to do that. It's important to keep doing what we're doing, but it's also important to check in and acknowledge what it's meant to us and what we've meant to each other. I feel like we've been together long enough that it would be a productive space to do that.

How did your father respond to the *Voice Male* article?

Ben Foster-Googins: We talked about the part that referred to communication with fathers. He asked me why I thought it was so difficult to communicate with him. It was a very interesting moment, because the way he asked the question was as though he was not part of the dynamic at all – as though it was all on me. Upon reflection, that's kind of consistent with our conversations around race and gender. I don't think he sees himself as part of it. I didn't want to respond by saying, "Well, actually, Dad, it's really about you."

I talked to him about how a lot of the conversations in the men's group, and part of the article, were about the struggle in general with communicating with fathers. I tried to see if we could talk about why is it that there seems to be this consistent struggle with communicating with our fathers. He shared some stuff about his time in the Jesuits, which was interesting. He told me about one time –though maybe it was a recurring thing, and maybe it's a really telling thing – there were all these men who got together and were opening up emotionally. He said that was a really powerful experience for him. Overall it didn't really touch on our relationship, but it was a small step for him and me.

What keeps you coming back to the group?

Dave Ratzlow: I like everybody. My problem with New York is everybody is really busy and I'm not. I could spearhead something and I'm doing that by leading our group tomorrow about Re-evaluation Counseling. I think we should do other things. This is such an interesting moment, with the Harvey Weinstein scandal and everything that has come out of that. I want us to try to figure out a way that we can respond to that.

All men carry sexism. It's part of the culture and some men are more afflicted than others. We're a group of guys that are pretty good. We either hide our sexism really well or we never really adopted that much. We still have some. It's good to work on that and we'll continue to figure out ways to do that. The guys that need help are not the guys in the group. The guys that really need help are not in any group. They'd say, "It's faggy." I don't know what we have to do to change that dynamic. We need to think about it. Are we helping guys who would never join a group or are we just collecting more people like us who have low levels of sexism and want to have even lower levels of sexism? The #MeToo movement offers great opportunity because it is so much a part of the discourse for us to do something. I'm not sure what it is, but I hope we'll talk about it soon

Younger Women's Group

How has the group impacted you as a partner?

Charlie Evans: With my husband, I give him the highlights of the calls – "This is what's going on with so and so, so next time we see them, know that this is going on." It keeps him in the loop, which is great. The complaint that we get from our husbands is that they don't get to participate. We love to see them, but they're not really part of the call. They'll pop on and say Hi and just go away. That's just how it's evolved. There is something to be said about the way the conversation goes when it is all women. It's not dramatically different than when one or more of the partners come on. I don't think there's anything I wouldn't say to any of the husbands that I wouldn't say to the girls. Sometimes we talk about health stuff, and that can get more personal as we've gotten old enough to procreate. Some of us have struggled with getting pregnant or staying pregnant and/or starting a family and what that means. That's the only thing that I would think we would probably limit, although I don't even know if that's true. It would be women's issues, but our guys are pretty evolved.

What issues, crises or life events do you see the group assisting members in going through?

Michelle Chanson: Having and raising children. Navigating relationships. Amelia was the pioneer in terms of having kids and I think it's been really helpful for Heather who just had her first. When Heather was pregnant, Amelia helped her through what was normal to be feeling, sharing what to expect and being a sounding board. Is this a stupid question or should I know this or am I out of touch with my own body? Amelia has a really nurturing, motherly way about her. Should that ever be something that I need to worry about, I have a couple of people now who can answer all of the good, bad and ugly questions around it.

How has your group impacted you as a partner?

Heather Price: It's that feeling of being grounded and loved. I carry it through all of the efforts of my life, including my marriage. I think it's a general feeling. When you are loved and supported there is a security that comes with that. It makes you feel more secure in other aspects of your life. These women have encouraged me to be myself and I have always felt that I could be who I am around them. Having that confidence going into other relationships in my life, whether it's in my marriage or work, is incredibly beneficial. You bring your authentic self when you are confident. You feel good about who you are. It has a positive impact on other parts of my life.

How does your participation in your group affect other friendships?

Liz Sharp: I think it has made me a little bit more aware in my other friendships of ways to be more involved. I have a lot of friends who are not a part of this group and a lot of friends who are part of some group, but not in any formalized way and keeping in touch with everybody is hard. I struggle with it. Now that I have this kind of model of one way that it can work, while I don't want to rush out and start a bunch of other groups, I think it's made me more able to figure out how to invest in other friendships past the once a year check-in, the once every six months drink in the city kind of thing. I think it has changed who I am as a friend.

It has also given me more insight into how to grow with people – to embrace change in relationships, because there has been so much growing up in our relationships with each other and the ways we relate to each other and the things we do and teach each other. It's been really instructive to me in how to evolve a relationship. Also these women are role models for me in many ways. Everybody has such unique skills and passions in this group. I admire every one of them so much. Sometimes when I am really struggling with something, I'll just think, "What would Amelia do right now?" or "How would Michelle handle this?" I hold them up as my spirit guides almost. I'm actually reaching out to them for advice and they're there for me, because they are so consistently there.

Amelia's mother is the Ruth from the older women's group, so I could not resist asking Amelia if she was inspired by her mother's circle to be part of such a group:

> **Amelia Olsen:** Completely. It was a direct correlation of Mom saying, "Well, why don't you create it? Why don't you create a women's group?" A lot of things come from that kind of recommendation from my mom. We made a book for Charlie when she got married. I was pregnant, so I couldn't be at her bachelorette. The book was everybody's marriage wisdom from all the people in her life that had been married. A blessing for her in book form. A lot of little things come from Mom.
>
> The way she explained her circle of women to me was, "I need to go do this to be a good mom for you. This group takes care of me, so I can take care of you." Then there were her meditation retreats, and I knew all of the women to varying degrees, so I would hear through my lifetime the things that they said to her or the support they gave to her. It is very desirable to see that support system.
>
> There's something about structure or habit that makes the commitment. You only have so much time and we have so many other things we could spend our time on. Creating a time for this is what makes it powerful. I got that from my mom.

Is there anything else you'd like to share about being in your group?

> **Naomi Lutra:** I had a really cool moment that happened recently, where I was going through something and somebody else was starting to go through the same thing, encountering some of the same stuff. I was really trying to be a support and offer my experi-

ence and talk about what I had gone through with that person. Then I was hitting a point on my path where I was coming to a big next step that felt very tricky, and I was expressing that on one of our group phone calls. Somebody else on the phone call said, "I haven't really shared this with the group, but I actually have encountered something very similar."

So where I had been feeling that a lot of my recent energy had been to support this other person, and happily doing so, by me finally breaking down a little bit and saying, "Here's this thing I'm feeling really scared about and having a hard time with..." it opened this stage where somebody else said, "Hey, I'd like to offer you some support with that. I didn't know you needed it." It was this beautiful moment. There are these moments where you actually ask for the support you need and it can really open the space up. I hadn't really seen that before.

It's really fun to think about the group this way. It's a little bit like the fish in the fishbowl – they don't really know they are in water. When you're just immersed in something and it feels like it's the norm, it's nice to step back and appreciate that this is actually outside of the norm for most people and to feel that gratitude for this group of women. It's also enjoyable to think about how we're each holding each other's histories. It's fun to think about even sharing it with our children some day. Having our collective history told this way is very cool.

I have chosen to give the final "gem" to Kevin, of the younger men's group, because I see his words as summarizing many of the challenges of support groups in general, and of groups for younger men and women in particular. His thoughts regarding the purpose of a group like his offer insight into the ways in which groups evolve. He talks about the need for group accountability and the ways in which men are so enculturated that it is a major task to become conscious of the ways in which too many of us continue to not even be aware of the impact of our actions on others. Privilege and patriarchy are the culprits, and Kevin speaks to them both in his response. I also value his understanding of the need to forge closeness and intimacy before you can even begin to call people on their words and actions. The bottom line, as he sees it, is that individuals have to both stay true to themselves and also detach from a preconceived vision that may not be either realistic or, ultimately, the only – or even the best – way to get there.

> **Kevin Quirolo:** The purpose that it serves is men doing the work of dealing with emotions and feelings and insecurities – of living in the world. We've unfortunately been held to this masculine standard and often we actually achieve the standard and then say, "Oh, wait, I'm actually hurting people because I'm dating someone and doing this terrible thing to them without thinking it through all the way." Someone who is the victim of that doesn't want to help that person deal with that – victim or survivor, pick your terms.
>
> The purpose the group is fulfilling now, for the men who are in it, is that we're dealing with all of these feelings and emotions together, and that's relieving the pressure on other people in our lives to fill that role. We have been challenging each other more recently, but it has to be even more honest.
>
> This leads into my concern that I don't think we're as candid as we could be. I feel like we could be much more open. Part of it is when you're doing something unconsciously that's damaging to other people, it doesn't get flagged in your brain as "Oh, I need to talk about this. This is wrong." It's another privilege. It's the number one privilege. You're invisible to yourself and everyone else. I don't think we've learned as a group how to acknowledge things we need to talk about to ourselves and to each other. If it doesn't

come up, you can't get challenged.

I also feel that until recently, when things have come up, I've been focusing on establishing relationships with people in the group more than on challenging them on things. There's a kind of tension between being supportive and needing to make people feel uncomfortable – making them question themselves and do the work of dealing with the consequences of their behavior. But in order to do that effectively, they need to feel somewhat attached to you and be interested in what each other think. If you're just some dude and you say, "You know what? When you used that word or you did that thing to that person, you shouldn't do that," the response is, "You're a wet blanket. See you later," or "I'll never see you again."

I've seen small challenges with focusing on building relationships. One thing that bothers me about our generation of organizers is that we're very focused on intersectionality and social construction. These are undoubtedly good things that have come out of all the theory of the last two decades. The good thing is that they have become very well-known and people have thought through them a lot. The bad thing is that a lot of the theorists – people who think about this stuff professionally – are really focused on language, and so a lot of people our age focus on language in organizing groups and focus groups.

A lot of the things in college that I was organizing were all about policing our use of pronouns and gendered terms. I'm just able to let that slide for now, because there's more fundamental stuff that needs to happen first, like relationship building. When we began, it wasn't my plan to work on building relationships first. It was like, "I feel uncomfortable. I don't know what to do," and a year later it was, "That's why I felt uncomfortable, because I didn't know that person at all."

CONCLUSIONS

It is my hope that reading this work has gone a long way towards convincing you of several ideas:

• Support groups can be fulfilling experiences on many levels, including personally, interpersonally, socially and developmentally, enhancing one's repertoire of skills as a partner, parent, friend and family member.

• Participation in a support group can enhance your life by providing opportunities to receive and offer perspective, support, challenge, laughter, tears, understanding and compassion.

• The longer a group stays together the more likely its members are to truly know, embrace, show up for and encourage one another.

• There will most assuredly be bumps on the road to deep sharing and intimacy and to successfully weather these bumps requires commitment to the group on the part of each member as well as a willingness to plunge into the conflict with eyes wide open.

• Our culture could benefit greatly on the individual and "village" levels if more people were able to be part of a support group, regardless of its focus, that encourages meaningful and enduring connection in a world where technology and increasing demands on our time are causing increasing stress and disconnection.

• Support groups can enable members to gain confidence from feeling well-known, safe, able to be vulnerable and resilient in the family, the workplace, social settings and even the political arena.

Now for a disclaimer that I feel is necessary, given the absence of people of color and the very few people of different gender identities and sexual orientations in this study. I am a strong advocate for incorporating these categories and having groups be more diverse. For a whole host of reasons – the groups' geographical locations and their members' origins, along with cultural factors, including the absence of pre-existing friendships across lines of race, gender identity and sexual orientation, leading to risks of tokenism – that does not pertain to these four groups, and that is a loss for all group members.

I am actively involved in a cross-race dialogue group that began in the aftermath of the 2016 presidential election. I have benefited from the experience of developing trust, speaking from the heart and having authentic conversations with upwards of 20 African-American, Hispanic and white men each month in East Hartford, Connecticut. I know I speak for virtually all of those I interviewed when I say that each of the groups would have been enriched in innumerable ways – both gratifying and challenging – if there were more diversity. That will remain a goal to strive for in creating groups or enhancing already existing men's and women's support groups.

In the months since I wrote the above paragraph - in between the completion of the manuscript and the imminent publication of the book - I have had the opportunity to participate in a dialogue group of 18 men and women of different races. Its express purpose is to enable its participants to speak about race with openness, honesty and trust so it is not a support group as the ones in this book define the concept. Nevertheless we meet every month and the sessions are strenuous and intense. I have benefited greatly from the challenges as well as the compassion that the group elicits from each of us and having the group include both men and women has added enormously to its possibilities and its power.

In addition we convened a larger 4-day long dialogue on St. Helena Island in South Carolina where we met with groups from both South Carolina and Kentucky, once again to discuss race and our varied experiences of it based on our upbringing, our age, our gender and our social class. We are bringing the effects of these extraordinary encounters back to our various communities in the form of presentations and brief opportunities to enter into dialogues with attendees at the gatherings. These anti-racism "support groups" across so many social "lines" have provided unique benefits that have been chronicled in various news outlets including this extensive story in the Valley Advocate March 13, 2019 issue entitled, *Anti-Racism Now: Chipping Away at Racism by Talking Face to Face.*

Before I get to a consideration of whether there will come a time when single-sex groups are supplemented by men and women meeting together, I would like to offer a few additional reflections from a couple of men who were not in this study, but who have their own take on what makes such groups not only worthwhile, but vital to men's growth and development.

The first is Rob Okun, whose words have previously been quoted in Chapter 2. Rob dedicated the entire Fall 2018 issue of "Voice Male" magazine, of which he is the founder and editor, to the topic "What #MeToo Asks of Men." In his editorial, he wrote about the need "for many men to take stock, to conduct an internal inventory, to look back over the decades, asking ourselves if we did anything when we were younger – or even more recently – for which we need to make amends." He conveyed his "speculation" that although "some men may have spoken about this with a partner or a friend, such vitally important inner work primarily has been done in isolation, if at all."

I was very pleased to read what Rob wrote next, as an affirmation of this book project. "I've concluded – as someone who has chronicled the pro-feminist men's movement – that a key action for me to consider taking comes from our history, from the early days of what we used to call the 'men's liberation movement': men's groups." Rob doesn't stop there. He references "a man I've known for nearly a quarter century" who told him, "The groups I joined changed my life, and quite possibly saved it from being something far more negative and limited – saved me from being far less self-aware, and thoughtful, intentional, about my own assumptions, behaviors, choices. I'm sure they did the same for many others; in fact, I know they did."

Rob next accentuates the need to do this critical work of essentially dismantling patriarchy with other men when he writes, "It is through unflinchingly investigating our discomfort that we will find the trail markers leading to a portal of honest reflection. We can't do that work alone. ... It's time for straight talk with one another, for deep sharing and for compassionate confrontation." I couldn't agree with Rob more, nor could he have chosen a more synchronous time to express his conviction.

Next is Bram Moreinis, who belongs to a different men's group from mine, who responded to my suggestion that he put words to his feelings about his own experience. His words feel even more essential during this time when toxic masculinity is being seriously questioned and hopefully being greatly diminished by being challenged in all arenas. Here's what he wrote:

> Fundamentally, to me, a men's group is about increasing integrity – personal, group and societal. As men we help each other take whatever personal responsibility we can for healing the world. Women take that same responsibility, but in different ways.
>
> Consider the existential call that brought my group together ("Now what do we do?") and the urgency of that call. We may not have been ready to use our male energy well in those first months – we may have run around in circles – but we are helping each other learn how to conserve and channel our energy to manifest constructive power. We meet because we believe that we can learn more about ourselves, about each other, and about the dynamics of standing up in this world, in a men's group.

That mission, and its urgency, should remain our sustaining drumbeat. Each of us may be attracted to the group for different reasons – maybe even on different days – the theme, the experience, the growth. At base I want to commit to a group constituted around that existential call, to be men working together to heal ourselves and heal the world. A men's group without that context would be less compelling to me.

And yet, it is also therapy for me. I work at the interpersonal level – opening my heart, directing my attention, controlling my expression, and allowing the resonance that effort creates to cultivate personal and interpersonal integrity. Big words but true ones. I have a long way to go, but that's what I'm up to. A group of men who just want to hear ourselves talk would not compel my commitment.

Bram's words certainly resonate for me, especially these additional ones: "As men we help each other take whatever personal responsibility we can for healing the world. Women take that same responsibility, but in different ways."

The work of healing ourselves and one another was at the center of a conference I recently attended, entitled Gender Equity and Reconciliation. About 50 of us, almost equally divided between men and women, spent three days working on the task contained in the conference title's challenge.

The first day was devoted to becoming familiar with one another, creating a safe space and working on building the necessary trust to share our experiences. It culminated in an exercise in which the men and women were separated on either side of a large room and asked a series of questions about the ways in which individuals are treated and how we treat others, especially with regard to sexuality and relationships. It was clear that many of the women had past traumatic experiences based on their gender, from street harassment to date rape. Only a few men could identify experiences of mistreatment based on gender. This highlighted how the men have been safeguarded from traumatizing experiences by our male privilege.

That evening, to lighten the mood following this exercise, we all were put into groups to perform skits depicting harassment and mistreatment in workplaces. It was not difficult to come up with situations, from a pregnant worker being fired to a woman not being given credit for her ideas. Amusing to be role playing, yes, but with a dark side to be sure.

The next day the group work intensified dramatically, as we were split into four groups, once again divided by gender. The work was considerably more personal, as we were asked to share stories of our lives in response to an "emotional mandala" consisting of a five-section circular space containing symbols representing shame, anger, loss, fear and disappointment. The stories in my group were moving – from a father feeling great distance from his son to a younger man dealing with the fallout from an addiction to pornography. When it was time to regroup, the men's and women's groups alternated telling their stories "fishbowl" style, so what occurred on both sides was a silent, attentive, engaged listening – a true witnessing of one another's struggles.

This is when the reconciliation could begin to really take place, as men were challenged to be compassionate, to own some of the behaviors that were being described by the women, and to commit to working to undo the damage that's been done by instead being trustworthy, speaking out, being vigilant for wives, daughters, mothers, women friends – indeed, all women. The women, in turn, were able to witness the men's pain from being victimized by toxic masculinity in the form of the "man box," which so severely limits one's options, one's emotional toolbox.

Was it healing in the ways that Bram was describing a men's group can provide? I think it very much was. It allowed and encouraged all participants to be vulnerable, to acknowledge the sources and experience of one another's pain and to express understanding, acceptance, empathy and compassion.

Such a vision is where a third man, Steven Botkin, sees the work of healing going as well. Steven holds an Ed.D in Social Justice Education from the University of Massachusetts at Amherst. He co-founded the Men's Resource Center of Western Massachusetts (MRC) in 1982, and Men's Resources International (MRI) in 2004. In April 2016, the organizations joined, and are now known as MERGE for Equality, Inc. The acronym MERGE stands for Men Embracing their Role in Gender Equality. Steven now serves as a senior consultant and trainer for MERGE.

From the early days of the MRC, Steven was committed to pro-feminist men's groups as a central means to change the culture. His work was to promote such groups in order to address "the problem of disconnection and dehumanization of men, and the ripple effect that that problem has on us, all of us – men, women, children, society. What the men's movement is trying to do is connection and humanization. And then the question is, what's the best methodology for doing that. And the group format is one of the best methodologies for doing that."*

But Steven does not stop with men's groups alone on the path to healthy masculinity.

> He believes that "the cutting-edge" will be seen in partnerships between men's and women's organizations. For the support group itself, he sees a merging of gender-segregated support groups on the horizon. He "feels like where we are in the movement itself, in the movement of gender justice and gender liberation, is in mixed gender work" and he anticipates a point where women's crisis centers will develop into human wellness community centers that will include men's C-R/support groups, women's groups, and mixed gender groups. The practical up-and-coming work will

* This quote and the one following are excerpted from Amanda Pickett's Master's thesis, *Subversive Masculinity: Cultivating Men's Engagement in Gender Equity*, 2016, University of Massachusetts at Amherst.

be, in his opinion, in exploring the methodology, challenges, and shape of mixed gender groups.

I endorse and embrace Steven's vision for mixed-gender groups, along with women's groups and men's groups, in the future of gender equity work. The #MeToo movement has made it crystal clear that toxic masculinity has comprehensively outlived its past and its shameful legacy. Women and men still need to do some of their healing separately, in women's groups and men's groups, to establish deep trust based on shared experiences. Men's groups like the ones in this book are committed to honestly, forthrightly and devotedly addressing the ways toxic masculinity negatively impacts girls and women as well as its negative impact on themselves.

One more example of how far we still need to travel presented itself in an article by John Engel entitled "Babysitter Training: Where Are the Boys?"* John, who is executive director of MERGE, writes a monthly column called The Fatherhood Journey, which I have been enjoying for the past few years, not infrequently writing to John to thank him for the stances he's taken or quoting him in articles I've written for the newspaper. This time he tells of enrolling his soon-to-be 12-year-old daughter in a babysitting class run by the local branch of the Red Cross. After describing the ways in which he was impressed by the course, including that one of the two instructors was male, he goes on to observe that there were no boys among the 19 trainees. John asked if boys ever took the class. He learned that for every 100 trainees there might be one or two boys. Yes, this echoes the preface of this book, where I described the same phenomenon in my class of student teachers.

John then observes:

> To me, encouraging boys to receive training in childcare and to work as babysitters, when young, could-promote a host of positive outcomes, including more

* *Daily Hampshire Gazette,* August 29, 2018.

men working in caregiving fields, such as early education, nursing, and elder care, to name a few. In turn, more children would observe and experience the inherent caregiving and nurturing capacities of men – qualities that are generally dismissed, devalued or displaced by conventional and outdated ideas that men can only be strong, tough and assertive.

I would add the benefit to the boy participants of feeling good about themselves as nurturers. Assuming they would be protected from any potential teasing or mistreatment by peers, the joy of being with younger children would be an additional reward, along with learning the skills that will benefit them as fathers if they choose to be. John addresses this when he goes on to say:

> Such a skill might also result in more men feeling comfortable and competent as nurturing and engaged fathers, something I struggled with when I became a father at age 40, having had very little experience with child care and caregiver roles. And when more fathers equally share caregiving roles and responsibilities with women, tasks that are traditionally more heavily shouldered by women, children might come to experience a new normal – boys having equal interest in babysitting.

John is addressing the ongoing need, despite the presence of a men's group like ours challenging traditional masculinity within our group and in the rest of our lives for 40 years, for cultural shifts like the one he is strongly promoting. Going forward, it can only benefit both sexes for additional work to occur with men and women speaking the truth of their experiences to one another. Such work has the best chance of enabling the true healing and gender equity our society so desperately needs, if we are to remain a viable place to raise children, to provide for equality of opportunity for boys and girls, and men and women, and to nurture the full potential of all of us.

Yet another development has occurred since I wrote the above paragraph. Steven Botkin made it possible for me to become part of MERGE's consultant team that is committed to the training of early childhood educators in "HOW TO RAISE HEALTHY BOYS" through day-long workshops throughout New England (and hopefully someday, beyond!). The workshop includes devoting time to understanding everything from the Man Box that limits men's potential, to the impact of enculturation on boys and girls from birth. It is just such work with care providers and educators that I am hopeful will contribute to imbuing boys with a fuller range of emotional responses to their lives, so they can grow into men who are living to their potential to be deeply engaged with other men, to support and encourage the women in their lives and to be nurturers for children. Of course, it is particularly gratifying for this man – as I presented in the introduction – when there are men in attendance at the workshops. As a society we are still not there, but the three men of the 24 attendees who came to our last training were fully engaged and I felt encouraged by their presence.

Each of the groups in this book represents ways in which women are empowered to face life's challenges, and men are encouraged to access the broad range of their emotional lives. Needless to say, our work is far from done.

ACKNOWLEDGEMENTS

As with my first book, *Called to Serve*, it is the interview subjects who made the writing of this one a labor of love. I was consistently moved by the honesty and the dedication I was gifted with by each person with whom I had the honor to speak. I would have wanted to find a way to share all of the interviews in their entirety, in order to give the full sense of what I got to experience. I am grateful beyond words to each person who opened their hearts and their minds to me in this process.

I also want to acknowledge the pioneering work of Steven Botkin, whom I admired from a distance as he developed the MRC and Men's Resources International while I taught at the Smith College Campus School during those same years. Since my retirement Steven and I have at last gotten to really know one another in our own mini-men's group. It is a most satisfying friendship and an enhancement of my vision for men through his work and his life.

I have had some dedicated editorial assistance from several people who deserve mention. First and foremost is Chris Rohmann, editor extraordinaire (as well as drama critic and theater director), whose expert advice has made this book much more effective, providing the objective view I needed. I am enormously grateful to him. Michael Dover, who encouraged me to join his once-a-year bike adventure group as I was preparing to retire, read the manuscript and provided invaluable feedback, much of which was incorporated into subsequent iterations. Steve Trudel, men's group member and beloved brother from another mother, along with Gary Phillips, our North Carolina member, provided insights and suggestions that improved my work, including Steve's recommendation for the book's title (**An Inside Look**) that was chosen over many others. Naomi Yanis, whom I've known since we ran a local Unitarian Jews group together in the early 90s, kindly offered to read the manuscript and offer her reflections. I was particularly interested in feedback for Chapter 11 – What Happens When Conflicts Arise? – and

John Reiff was most helpful in providing both affirmations and challenges. His insights into how to make the chapter more useful as well as more engaging were invaluable.

I want to give special recognition to the men of the three men's groups with which I have been affiliated. Each individual has made a contribution to the man I have become as well as being willing to bring to men's group gatherings as much of themselves as they could gain access to. In particular I want to express my deepest respect, esteem, pride and love to the eight men in the group that will celebrate its 40th anniversary this fall. They welcomed me with wide-open arms 29 years ago and I have never looked back. Through the trust, caring, love, honesty and support they've shown me in good and hard times, I have been able to undo some of the damaging trauma that occurred as a result of some significant mistreatment by my agemates growing up. For all that and so much more, I thank my men.

The cover photograph is one of mine, but it is a result of one of the many gifts given to me by my wilderness brother to whom I've dedicated the book, Michael Sample. It was Michael who made all the arrangements for us to spend 4 days canoeing on the Missouri River in 2004. He wanted us to honor the 200th anniversary of the Lewis and Clark Expedition that had journeyed along the same route. The calm river provided endless opportunities for reflective photographs. Arising with the sun each morning enabled us to capture both the setting and the "sweet light" Michael sought for his outdoor/nature photography. His renown in Montana and beyond is richly deserved and having the great privilege of watching him in action and assisting him over the course of my nineteen Montana adventures over 44 years are some of the most precious of my treasure trove of memories of our time together. His inspiration is evident in my photos and the one on the cover is an example of his influence.

Finally, my wife, Susan, has once again shown steadfast support of my work and has been a sounding board for many of the excerpts and the ideas contained herein. I am also grateful for the life of equal partnership in all realms that we have co-created – from parenting (and now grandparenting) to household chores, from trip planning to decisions about where to go out for dinner, we have lived out our individual commitments to gender equity. It is my hope that our children will find their way to make similar commitments, and I see strong evidence that is already happening. It certainly was a key part of my mission as a teacher and it remains my hope, even in these dark times, that men and women will be able to go forward as partners dedicated to bringing out the best in one another.

APPENDIX

INTERVIEW QUESTIONS

The following are all of the questions asked in each of the 27 interviews I conducted. Needless to say, not all of the questions ended up as chapter topics, but this will give you the full range of what each person was asked to reflect upon.

1. Begin by telling about yourself – age, relationship or not, children, work, years in current group, and anything else about yourself that feels relevant to your sharing about your support group.

2. Why did you choose to help create or join your group? What were you seeking?

3. What are your previous experiences, if any, with support groups? In particular, why did your involvement and/or the group end?

4. What were your hopes in becoming part of such a group?

5. Describe the process by which you joined the group.

6. What were your concerns or fears, if any?

7. How has the group changed over time? Focus on either its purpose or functioning, but include any other changes as well – membership, routines, etc.

8. Has the group ever come close to ending? Why? What enabled it to continue.

9. What do you feel you contribute to the group?

10. What do you take from the group?

11. How do you think you and the other members of the group have changed over time?

12. What experiences or feelings have you been able to share and process with the group that have made a difference in your life?

13. How does your participation in your group, and what you've taken from it, affect who you are and how you act in the world?

14. How has being in your group impacted your life? What might be different without your participation in the group?

15. Describe a time when you had a great deal of fun with the group.

16. Is there anything about the group that you wish were different? Why or why not?

17. How has participation in the group affected your relationships with friends and/or family?

18. Has the group affected how you see men/masculinity, women/femininity, and how you see yourself as a man or woman?

19. How has the group impacted you as a partner and/or a parent?

20. How do others in your life see the group – partners, parents, friends, associates?

21. Do you want to stay a part of the group going forward? Why?

22. What do you think has sustained your group for as long as it has been in existence?

23. What issues/crises/life events do you see the group trying to assist its members to go through? How might that occur?

24. What does the inner processes of your group look like? Do you have written or unwritten rules for interaction and process?

25. What kind of conflicts arise, and how are they resolved?

26. What happens if the group decides to expel or separate themselves from a member?

27. If applicable, where are your favorite group field trips?

28. How do you interact with each other outside the group? Are there collaborations, deep friendships, feuds, etc.?

29. How would life be different without the group?

30. How does the group impact your community?

31. How do you see the role of support groups in society?

32. Do you do purposeful actions together that have a larger import: demonstrations, support for social and economic justice, publishing, organizing, direct action, performance art, etc.?

33. Is there anything you would like to have been asked?

34. What has it been like answering all these questions and thinking long and hard about your group?

35. Has this interview given you any new insights about the group or yourself?

THE FLYER THAT LAUNCHED THE 40 YEARS OF THE OLDER MEN'S GROUP

MEN TO MEN

We are looking for anti-sexist men who are interested in forming a group that would concern itself actively with radical social change in the valley area. We want to focus our energies on confronting patriarchy, sexism, heterosexism, mysogyny/womon hating, and homophobia. these institutions of male privilege are internalized in us and need to be confronted simultaneously on personal and political levels. In addition to these major focuses we want to be constantly aware of the direct interrelationships with exploitative economic structures, racism, classism, and ageism.

We would like to gather to get to know each other and develop a common analysis and strategy. We have a commitment to taking direct action against sexism. Possible projects include men's community nites, men's childcare collective, organizing workshops and discussions, men's caucuses within existing political organizations, working against violence against womon, networking, initiating support groups, etc...

We would like to work in a collectively run group of 5-12 men, who are able to consider a long term commitment. If you are interested and/or have any further ideas you'd like to share with us please call or write:

GARY SELDON   ALAN SURPRENANT   BOB KADAR
137 FARVIEW WAY   P.O. BOX 387   323-7778
AMHERST, MA 01002   EASTHAMPTON, MA 01027
549-1685   527-7220(1)

in love and struggle Alan, Gary, & Bob

275

MEN'S GROUP FILM, CIRCA 1981
ORDER FORM AND FLYER

These words from the order form below are quoted from the film and capture some of the essence of the group in its early years – an essence we have maintained:

> Discussions have led us to realize that our group has developed a positive kind of relationship not easily achieved by men... Intimacy is a political choice we make.

> We challenge homophobia with physical affection and commitment...

This intimate, touching, at times zany film is a unique celebration of men's lives. Produced by the members of a five year old feminist men's collective (heterosexual, bi and gay), this film presents a provocative look at ways men can be together and share their lives. Through a series of vignettes, the group is portrayed together and as individuals, clothed and unclothed, serious and unserious, at work and at play, on the ground and in the air.

"Discussions have led us to realize that our group has developed a positive kind of relationship not easily achieved by men. Initially, we focused more externally on political action, but now our support for each other nurtures our activism. Intimacy is a political choice we make. We challenge homophobia with physical affection and commitment." From the film

ORDER NOW

Running time: 25 minutes. Color ¾" , VHS or Beta Video Cassetten Rental: $35   Sale: $100. Allow 3-4 weeks delivery. Make checks payable to: Positively Men Films, 151 Montague City Road, Greenfield, MA 01301. Members of the collective are available are available to give presentations and workshop with the film. For arrangements, call Robbie Leppzer at (413) – 774-5983

"positively MEN(to)"

APRIL 24th
HORACE'S
(7 EATON)

SATURDAY EVENING

7:30 ··· SHARE DESSERTS

8:15 ··· SHOW TIME

9:00 ··· IT'S UP TO YOU

a donation to help the work will be requested

"really cute" "disgusting homo film" "zany" "do you really live like that?"

"Positively Men" Film's Written Accompaniment

What follows is the write-up that functioned as a press release following the initial screening of the film, which was referred to during a number of interview excerpts. It sought to explain the history of the men's group from 1978 to 1981 when the film, "Positively Men" premiered. Other sections of the written material were entitled, "Who We Are" and "Additional Message". Having been given a copy of the original statemen from the premiere at the NOMAS (National Organization of Men Against Sexism) Conference that took place at Tufts University in 1981, I am able to offer it here as a reflection of how the group saw itself, how individuals were living their lives and how much both the group and its original members have evolved... or not.

HISTORY

In the 3 years we have been meeting, the focus of our group has changed from one which nurtured specific activist community, anti-sexist involvement to one of providing a supportive base for us to pursue lives that challenge established values across a broad spectrum. We see ourselves now more as a group of men endeavoring to live their politics.

This film and its distribution grew organically out of the way our members express themselves and the June 1981 proximity of the 7th National Conference on Men and Masculinity

WHO WE ARE

We have resistance to labels in helping you toward an understanding of who we are and what our individual personal politics encompass. As the film points out, we called ourselves in successive years: "Men Against Patriarchy," "Men on Mushrooms" and "The Mind Adjestesrs." But at the 7th National, where we showed the film, shared in discussions groups and staffed an

"Unraveling Center," (the often messy and difficult work of acknowledging how cultural conditioning unconsciously keeps us bound up in cycles of suffering) we could not find a name we felt comfortable with, which was a bit inconvenient.

We can affirm some values all 11 of our members share. We seek to shed conditioned roles so that real intimacy and trust can develop. We endeavor to merge the concepts of work and play through "right livelihood." All of us work at alternative jobs. Seven of us work in collectives. Sources of income include:

- Video media activism

- Political/spiritual publications clearinghouse

- Solar/geothermal energy construction

- Wind energy harnessing

- Regional wholesale food cooperative buying

- Quilting and auctioneering

- Care of children

- Cotton goods sale/distribution

- Computer/solar student

We are additionally active in:

- Community organizing

- Reevaluation counseling

- Movement for a New Society

- Non-violent training collective

- Natural foods cooperative

Most of our ages are mid to late 20's with one member in each of the next decades. Seven live "in community" (collectively) including 2 of the 3 married members and one formerly married. We are college educated, white anglos. Our "deviation" from the heterosexual standard is +.227 (around 2 of us are gay).

ADDITIONAL MESSAGE

With our film we want to pass along what worked for us in developing a reality of long-term commitment in the group. An initial commitment of three months of weekly evening meetings using meeting facilitation concepts that have come out of the Movement for a New Society, moved us securely into a leaderless consensus-developing organism where it became apparent to each of us that no one else could be held responsible for seeing that our individual needs were being met. This personal empowerment, coupled with a weekend retreat specifically planned to afford each of Us up to two hours for sharing our personal history, led to a group state with its own momentum and nurturance. The weekly format did not meet the ends of so variously involved and individually committed a group of men; meeting once a month all day (usually Sunday), with the dates set two months in advance, does work in our active lives. Seldom is anyone missing. The full day allows closer connection through the cycle of both work and play with each other.

The possibilities or our relationships with each other are so varied that we came to realize that "the group" was meeting whenever two or more so intended. The first two hours of each meeting are "gathering time", when what is supposed to happen always does, because no one person can "hold up" the group. We share two meals and rotate home locations – choice dependent upon season, agenda and arrangements with housemates. It is not in our contract with each to leave the group without its consensus.

MEN'S GROUP INVITATION
TO START ADDITIONAL GROUPS

This flyer of guidelines was created during the fourth year of the older men's group – 1982 – to encourage other men to form groups. Notice the reference to "consciousness-raising" in the section on "Commitments around ways of being together."

Suggested Contractual Concepts and Format

We would like to share with you some of the things about group commitments or group contracts that have been helpful to us in maintaining a meaningful group, a group that, thru the yeaers, has become an organic part of our lives.

We have found that focused attention on the quality and ways of being together, on the influence of time decision, and on the understanding around structure, all facilitate commitment to the group.

Commitments to time

Most groups start with the usual 2 ½ hour weekly meetings. Extended time improves quality. Consider, instead or in addition, one all day monthly meeting. Dates set 1-2 months ahead almost assure everyone's attendance. Have an occasional overnite retreat, especially with the first few months.

Agree upon continuance and discontinuance. Make an initial contract to stay together for (3-9) months and for everyone to be at each meeting. As well, agree to process leaving the group in the whole group, with the intention to get clear on reasons (everything 'up front').

Commitment to STRUCTURE

Decision making and leadership need to be clear. We suggest conscious acceptance of self-leadership as the basis for group direction – a cooperatively led group with shared leadership (no one else 'responsible' – no one 'to blame'). This is an agreement to operate by consensus – to clarify for yourself and express your needs, to consider each other's needs. Everyone agrees to the agenda/plan: Movement for a New Society models, for facilitation, agenda making, prioritizing, time-keeping, and evaluation are helpful.. A group size suggestion is 8 to 12.

Commitment to QUALITY OF TIME TOGETHER

This can be a time to explore ways of being amongst men that are not 'altogether common' in the society in general and keeping that as a focus. It is a time to nurture and be nurtured, to offer and receive intimacy, to be playful, open, honest, direct, caring...

By a Valley Men's Collective celebrating its 4th year.
Sometimes called Men Against Patriarchy - Men on Mushrooms (MOM) or The Mind Adjesters. Contact thru Gary Seldon 586-2454

WHEN TWO GENERATIONS OF MEN'S GROUPS MEET

Voice Male Magazine, Oct 12, 2017 | Fall 2017

BY TOM WEINER

For three decades, Tom Weiner has been part of a western Massachusetts men's group (that's been meeting for even longer). He is currently writing a book about men's and women's support groups, emphasizing the purposes they serve for their members and their role in society. When his son Stefan told a friend about his father's book idea, Ben Blackshear shared that he, too, is in a men's group that has been together for two years. Intrigued, Tom began a relationship with the Brooklyn, N.Y.–based group, interviewing two members and attending one of their groups. The older man and younger men peppered each other with so many questions that Tom suggested the younger men come north to meet with his group, formed in 1978. Its nine members spend one Sunday a month together, from brunch through supper. They also hold a five-day annual retreat on an island in the St. Lawrence River's Thousand Island region. The younger men's group, ranging in age from 26 to 40, has six members, and includes Ben Blackshear, Kevin Quirolo, Joshua Latour, and Ben Fuller- Googins. (Two new members have joined their group since the weekend.) Members participating from the older men's group, who are 58 to 67, include the author, Steve Trudel, Paul Richmond, Alan Surprenant, Steve Bannasch, Robbie Leppzer, and Dick McLeester. (Two of its members were unable to attend the weekend.) What follows is an edited conversation among members of the younger and older men's groups.

WHAT PURPOSES DOES YOUR MEN'S GROUP SERVE IN YOUR LIFE?

Josh (Younger Men's Group): I see the group helping me with my own needs as a man and with being a better ally as well as with managing my relationships with women by being emotionally more aware. The group encourages me to be more emotionally available, to be a better listener, and to be more informed about how to be with other men.

Ben B. (YMG): Our group offers the opportunity for structured reflection. We also come for the camaraderie. There are times when we offer one another advice. I have also received—and offered—emotional support.

Kevin (YMG): I see our group as a space to develop emotional intimacy with other men based on a shared commitment to anti-oppression politics. It also offers me opportunities to practice patience with myself and others.

Ben F-G (YMG): The practice of sharing has been critical. One of the features of patriarchy and toxic masculinity is the feeling that a lot of the traits and habits are my own—thoughts about sex or about women or the inability to be in relationship. Then I pathologize my own issues, so coming together and sharing in group lets me know there are others who have similar feelings and tensions, which is very healing.

Steve T. (Older Men's Group): The group reduces my

individuality. It has created a collective identity as a result of the maturation of our men, which is a joy, because it is so different from what I usually experience in relationships with men. I see the group as having expanded our sense of being human. The area where it has been the most important has been to be able to feel trust in other men—the trust to be challenged and to challenge each other's limitations within a context of the ocean of trust we've co-created.

Robbie Leppzer, left, and Josh Latour talk about men's groups then and now while hiking along the banks of the Quabbin Reservoir in western Massachusetts.

Paul (OMG): Making a commitment and being able to have much deeper relationships—the group has fostered that in my life. I learn that a lot of similar things go on for all of us. Whatever ways in which I might have thought I was unique I find out I'm not so unique.

Dick (OMG): Being in the group means I'm thinking on an ongoing basis, "This is something I could bring to group—something to put out to the group as a whole." Or, it's something I want to ask. A lot of other times it's just about hearing what other people are wrestling with that will be an occasion for me to think about that aspect in my own life. I've learned ways to share, to listen and to challenge other people and particularly other men.

Robbie (OMG): Having this support group going through life has been priceless. I feel very grateful. I was 20 when I joined; the youngest member of the group. As a teenager, I had long considered myself not macho, having grown up and witnessed the ravages of patriarchy, domestic abuse and violence in my own family. This group gave me validation and support to continue on my path as a pro-feminist man. As the men's group became my chosen family over time, it has provided a continual grounding and support for me on my evolving journey as a man.

HOW DO YOU SEE MEN'S GROUPS BEING BENEFICIAL TO MEN?

Ben B. (YMG): Our group has encouraged me to feel more vulnerable. We have been getting better at helping each other look at our lives and our pasts through different and more critical lenses, such as reflecting on the balance of emotional labor in our relationships.

Ben F-G (YMG): I see in white men, in the older generations of my family, that patriarchy is still the prevailing frame of masculinity and it is individualized. So the concept of being in connection with other men is in direct contradiction to how we're conditioned to be in this world—alone. Having a group structure invites the possibility that there are other ways of being that are rooted in sharing and being visible.

Josh (YMG): I need to issue a disclaimer. I wrestle with the idea that our men's group isn't challenging enough or isn't inclusive enough or whether it's really needed since women's voices are not heard enough already. People can criticize us for being together with only men and not being open to women, but I feel our group is just getting its toes wet in terms of what to do to be more effective.

Steve T. (OMG): All the female partners I've talked to like the idea that their men are having other ways to explore their needs—not just in their marriage/partnership—because men tend to not do that. They traditionally do that kind of exploration with their wives and then think that's the only place they have to do it. In my work with men who are abusive and controlling, it's pretty characteristic that men are isolated without networks of support. Men's groups like ours work to undo the isolation.

Tom (OMG): Men's groups can greatly help men to experience a much wider range of emotions and cultivate nurturing and intimacy understandings and skills that serve in other arenas, including romantic relationships, friendships and child rearing, a topic our men's group has discussed regularly as some of us have become fathers.

DESCRIBE HOW YOUR MEN'S GROUP FILLS YOUR NEED FOR CONNECTION WITH OTHER MEN.

Ben B. (YMG): I think it demonstrates to us the truth that we need each other. It clearly shows that peer support and realizing our interconnectedness are important in a culture that is so built on individualism.

Ben F-G (YMG): It fills the need for connection because it's explicitly rooted in wanting to both outwardly confront and challenge patriarchal violence and inwardly deal with how patriarchy shapes our relationship to ourselves. Since it was the intention of our group from the start it changes how I show up for it compared to how I am with other men. Right from the start we were talking about pornography or violence or how we objectify women or how we can't cultivate a relationship with our fathers. It's been a consistent invitation for me to reveal more, and there's nowhere else in my life where that happens.

Josh (YMG): It's about being more intentional and talking about different things—like what it was like growing up as a boy and all the pressures society sets to be tough or being talked down to if you showed emotion; talking about sexuality and how to be a better lover. Many of us have been affected by the phallocentric view and it was all about penetration and not how to pleasure a woman. We grew up hearing phrases like, "Did you get your dick wet?" No, we don't want to be that way. Also being in group allows us to talk about our sexual identity preferences. We don't have to identify as male or female. Seeing the group through a queer lens—we want the group to be more inclusive for people of all sexual identities and orientations—the group is very open to that and it helps us inform our language.

Alan (OMG): I would add the size of the group—not one-on-one or a threesome. There's a certain energy that comes from seven, eight, or nine of us being together. It's unique. I don't experience that any other place in my life.

Paul (OMG): It's about being in a safe place to explore and be challenged to help me grow. It's people who know you for a long period of time that can reflect along with you about what's happening, what you've gone through. Are you still telling us the same story that you were when we met you? Now we're all tied up in it, too, so what do you want to change? Plus there's the commitment we share to really show up and to go deeper, to ask those questions.

WHAT ARE SOME SPECIFIC THINGS YOU'VE LEARNED ABOUT YOURSELF FROM BEING IN A MEN'S GROUP?

Ben B. (YMG): It's helped me learn how to be more vulnerable with people in my life who are not my romantic partner. I've learned that sharing ways I am working on improving myself or things that I am struggling with helps me do the work I need to do to make the changes I want and need to make. Being in the group makes me more accountable to myself—and the group.

Kevin (YMG): I tend to avoid connecting with men outside our group because having to confront the sexism I encounter is stressful. By facing and dealing with our own sexism in a controlled environment it's made me more confident I can deal with it outside the group.

Ben F-G (YMG): I want to touch on sex. I think I have a

lot of shame around sex and my body—particularly about male violence in sexual dynamics. It's hard for me to bring my full self in sexual romantic partnerships because I censor and police myself so I don't express violence. One hundred percent of my female partners have experienced this and it impacts our relationship, because if I'm putting a lot of energy into policing and censoring my behavior, partners can't experience my whole self. So I'm seeking a balance between feeling my full self, but not replicating patterns of violence and dominance that is still the norm. Even as I hear myself talk about this it's such a release to have a space to talk about with other guys saying it's hard for them, too.

Steve T. (OMG): In our group, I'm more interested in finding out where everyone is at with a bigger discussion, not one where one person talks and the rest of us listen. The group gives me a place to explore things I know about myself and get feedback. I like being able to feel safe and trusting, to challenge the other men in the group, but I feel a certain amount of judgment and a sense of an accompanying irritability when we don't change.

Alan (OMG): Any time I take time out from the hubbub of my life to do something and I'm conscious of what's going on, I'm learning something. The act of taking that space is what's central. I'm still learning...

Tom (OMG): I've learned to be more trusting of men having had numerous experiences of being bullied or rejected. I learned I could trust an entire group of men and I found out how satisfying— rather than scary and disappointing—that could be.

IF YOU HAVE ENCOURAGED OTHER MEN TO TRY A MEN'S GROUP, WHAT HAPPENED?

Ben B. (YMG): I encouraged a student at the college I attended to start one. He had told me he wanted to be more aware of his position in social justice organizing spaces on campus and he seemed interested in starting a group that would give him support and feedback about that work.

Kevin (YMG): A friend of mine, who I thought would be interested because he is a feminist, isn't interested. I think there arc two points here. First there's a suspicion of a group of men focused on themselves, and second there's a sense of urgency to organize outwardly. The first point, the suspicion, is crucial to this work because sexism is so insidious it can (and often does) corrupt seemingly earnest efforts by men to support feminism. Any men's group of this kind has to directly address how patriarchy shapes who we are and how we relate to other men. The second point, the urgency, is understandable, but could be counterproductive. Getting out in the world and working against oppression can be transformative. But urgency could be an excuse to ignore your own sexism.

Ben F-G (YMG): I invited someone I knew and he's now an awesome part of our group. There are a lot of men in my world that are politicized and have a lot of awareness. But I notice hesitancy—"Do I deserve, as a man, to spend time in a group setting like this rather than an outward organizing project?"

"It's possible to have deep friendships." From the left, Steve Trudel, Keith Quirolo, Ben Fuller-Googins, Ben Blackshear.

Josh (YMG): It's been hard to follow through with people. Our group is still in its infancy so it's hard to know what we're inviting people to. I'll say, "Come to our men's group," and someone will ask, "What are you doing?" I'll say: "We're talking," but they want concrete examples. This kind of organizing takes time. Two new people have joined since our weekend together. New York is a rough city to be doing this kind of work, because everyone is so busy earning a living and negotiating their lives.

Alan (OMG): I had the experience of helping a men's group form. They're 68 or older and there are seven in the group. I met with two of them—the conveners—over breakfast to describe what we did and they've started with how we did, meeting weekly.

Paul (OMG): Any time the idea of men's group comes up, the person I'm talking to thinks I'm talking about drumming and walking on coals. Sometimes I get a reaction just because of the years we've been a group. You have a group of people you've known for 38 years? Do you still actually meet with them? That is actually a source of amazement—that we even get together.

HOW HAS BEING IN A MEN'S GROUP RESULTED IN YOU BEING MORE VULNERABLE AND TALKING HONESTLY WITH OTHER MEN ABOUT YOUR LIFE?

Ben F-G (YMG): With my dad there's been a major shift in our relationship. I've noticed in the past couple of years being able to talk more than we have historically, particularly around family issues and relationship stuff. I don't think that would have been possible without the practice and support around being vulnerable that I've taken from our men's group. I've just seen the joy of that. It's totally deepened our relationship.

Josh (YMG): I've been finding more ways to be vulnerable and communicating that vulnerability. A specific example would be with my sexual partner where I've been communicating my needs and wants and intentions. We talk about it together and it helps me be more aware of what's going on. I have a better understanding of consent culture—not just having an idea about it but practicing it.

Steve T. (OMG): Our group has enabled us to develop a sense of confidence in intimately exploring one another's paths. It allows and encourages me to see through men's defensiveness in the world at large and seek out and invite men to experience their own exploration of vulnerability. It also enables me to be in the moment with another person as they are rather than trying to change them or make something different happen, which is probably the best way to experience mutual vulnerability.

Steve B. (OMG): Many years ago I was walking with one of my daughters. She was about three years old so I was holding her hand. We were about to cross the road at a crosswalk when somebody drove past really fast. I yelled loudly. The car, which had passed us by then, slammed on its brakes, screeched to a stop, and backed up really fast. A much younger, muscular guy said, "What the fuck is your problem?" I said, "I made that loud sound, because I was afraid. I'm walking with my daughter." That completely disrupted his narrative, because he wasn't expecting that. It was so out of the narrative that he gruffly responded, "I'm sorry..." and then drove off more slowly. I think that is something that came from my life experience, and my life and men's group are totally linked up.

Steve T. (OMG): The only feeling that can commonly be shared between men is anger. We can share being pissed off. That guy in Steve's story expected to be met at the level of anger and so anger is up here (gestures with his hand) and beneath it is often some other kind of feeling, like confusion or another feeling that's related to anger. Then, beneath that level of being confused is sadness and grief. You could notice that's also in there when you initially feel anger—if you have the opportunity to be able to pay attention and if you're

291

listened to. We're a group that is committed to nonviolence, so anger isn't going to be the currency that we use, but still it is possible it could show up. We've added more complexity to the story.

Paul (OMG): I appreciate our willingness to let each of us experience the pain that we might be having in our lives and to realize that there's nothing else anybody can do besides letting us have a safe space to experience that pain and witness it. If you need to be held that's available. Nobody is putting you down, telling you to suck it up. That vulnerability makes it possible to get through some really difficult stuff.

Tom (OMG): I think of my vulnerability numerous times when something really difficult has happened in my life and my first thought is I can't wait until I can talk about that in group. I'm thinking of my friend's tragic death, of my son's innumerable brain operations—of lying on the bed at Steve's house and having the whole group give me a loving back rub so I could just cry out my fear and my sadness.

WHAT DO YOU SEE AS A TAKEAWAY FROM BEING WITH AN OLDER AND YOUNGER MEN'S GROUP?

Ben F-G (YMG): I went into the weekend having some skepticism based on not having very positive relationships with older white men. It was such a joy to see your group's friendships with each other. On one level, "Wow, it's possible to have these friendships that are expanding, challenging and deepening over decades." The level of curiosity I experienced you showing about us—that was fantastic. I so appreciated that because it is not what I experience a lot in relationships with older men. I left very joyful and hopeful having seen that if you commit to such a group it can be rich in lasting joy and transformation.

Ben B. (YMG): The biggest takeaway for me was an affirmation that this work is valuable and the "project" of men's groups is worthwhile. Seeing the deep bonds the older men have, their happiness, their political astuteness, their willingness to challenge each other, and the shared memories they've built over the years was powerful. It made me feel that the benefits of this work are ongoing and get even richer with continued time and emotional investment.

Steve T. (OMG): I felt like I got to experience my wisdom and our collective wisdom from having been part of our group for so many years. I also felt a great sense of relief knowing that there are young men who are finding value in being with each other, supporting each other in the same way that we've had the opportunity to experience—that sense that, "Oh, good, our men's group wasn't just a blip on the radar screen that went away."

Paul (OMG): It felt like they are a younger version of ourselves. In this time and place they are political guys who are questioning and working on issues that they think are important— whether it be about issues of race or climate change or the environment. They are being confronted with how they are being men in the various organizations to which they belong. They are being supportive of each other and trying to be different from traditional masculinity in what they're doing.

Robbie (OMG): I was so delighted and amazed that men's groups like ours are still forming in the 2010s because it's a very different era than when we started our group. To know that there's a lifeline of consciousness about men's groups and that young men are aware and feel the need and see the importance of forming a men's group is heartening because I'm generally somewhat disheartened that the consciousness we helped to develop has experienced a backlash against it.

Tom (OMG): I found the younger men to be incredibly open and honest with men they don't know. They sought that in their group and you could tell that we welcomed and invited intimate interactions. I was gratified that it happened so quickly.

THE WHEEL OF CONSENT

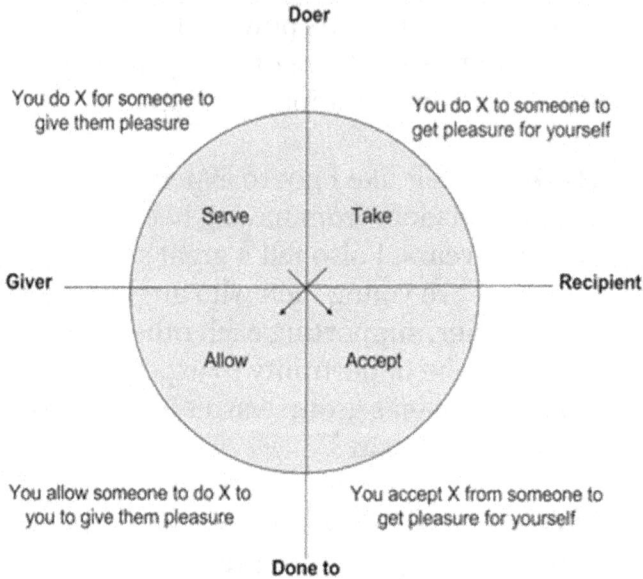

Doer

You do X for someone to
give them pleasure

You do X to someone to
get pleasure for yourself

Serve   Take

Giver ———————————————— **Recipient**

Allow   Accept

You allow someone to do X to
you to give them pleasure

You accept X from someone to
get pleasure for yourself

Done to

Developed by sexologist and intimacy coach Betty Martin

The Wheel of Consent is a model of consent based on, but not requiring, exchanges of touch. The Wheel notes the distinction between the 'doing' aspect of the touch dynamic –who is doing – and the 'gift' aspect – who it is for.

Once the distinction between those two aspects is clear, the entire touch dynamic becomes clear, which brings ease, sensuality, confidence, self-responsibility and freedom to the interaction.

When the dynamics are clear, it becomes apparent how they apply to both touch and non-touch dynamics. Indeed, the application to non-touch dynamics may be of greater import.*

*http://schoolofconsent.org

CALLED to SERVE

Stories of Men and Women Confronted by the Vietnam War Draft

Tom Weiner

Preface by Charlie Clements
Afterword by Victoria Safford

CALLED TO SERVE: Stories of Men and Women Confronted by the Vietnam War Draft (adapted into the play entitled "The Draft" by Peter Snoad)

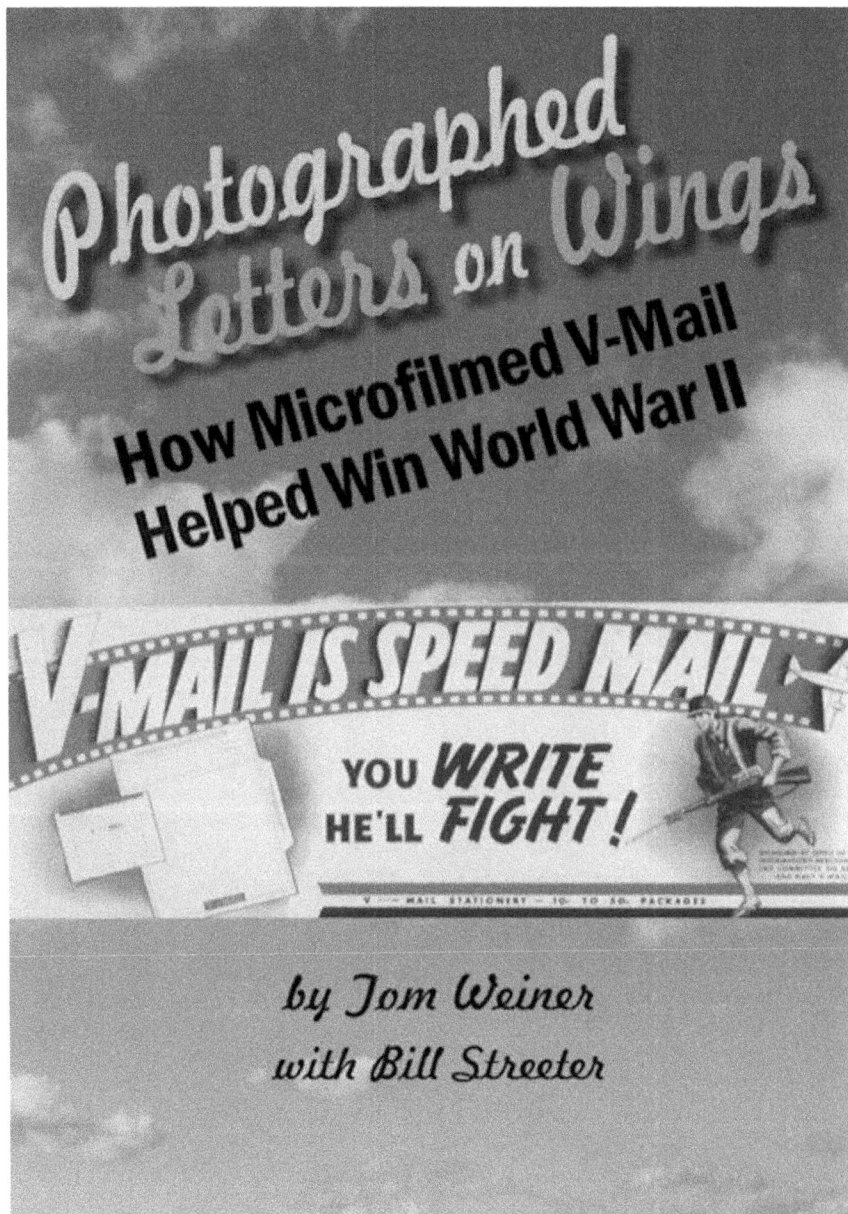

PHOTOGRAPHED LETTERS ON WINGS: How Microfilmed V-Mail Helped Win World War II.

Tom retired 3 years ago from teaching after 40 years at the Smith College Campus School in Northampton, MA. He has written 2 other books.

He is the father of 4 and the grandfather of 4. He is a supervisor of student teachers and a consultant training early educators in "How to Raise Healthy Boys."